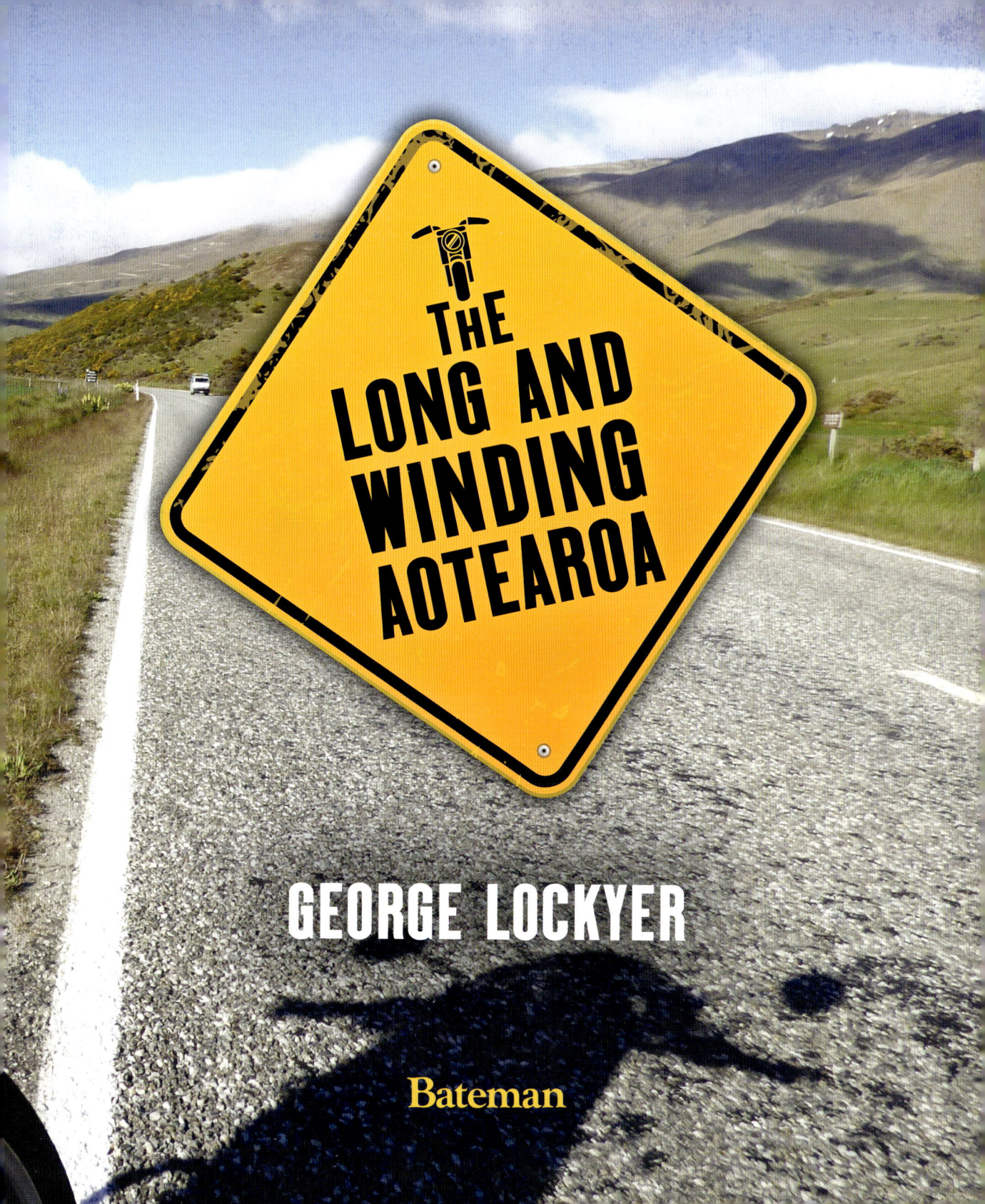

Text © George Lockyer, 2017

Published in 2017 by David Bateman Ltd
30 Tarndale Grove, Albany, Auckland,
New Zealand

www.batemanpublishing.co.nz

A catalogue record for this book is available from the National Library of New Zealand.

ISBN 978-1-86953-977-1

This book is copyright. Except for the purpose of fair review, no part may be stored or transmitted in any form or by any means, electronic or mechanical, including recording or storage in any information retrieval systems, without permission in writing from the publisher. No reproduction may be made, whether by photocopying or by any other means, unless a licence has been obtained from the publisher or its agent.

Publisher: Bill Honeybone
Book design: Cheryl Smith

Cover photographs: Terry Marshall

All internal photographs are taken by the author, with the following exceptions: Judy Bosworth — pages 274, 275, 276(B); Albie Burgers — page 159; Kerry Chapman — pages 129, 131, 132; Doug Cornes Photography — pages 223, 224; Mike Cron — pages 115, 116, 117, 118; Debbie Curle — pages 232, 236; Kate Du Plooy — page 256; Defence Public Affairs — pages 287, 291; Ron Hebberd — page 167; Gary Husband — pages 174, 176, 177; Mike Little — pages 207, 208; Ginger Molloy — pages 226, 227; Jo Morgan — pages 192, 193; Donald Pannett — pages 79, 80, 81; Annika Naschitzki — page 187; Ray Shoebridge — pages 22, 24; Jim Sykes — pages 60, 63(B); Rob Tinning — pages 96, 99; Shirley Whyte — page 91

Printed in China through Asia Pacific Offset Ltd

CONTENTS

Introduction 8
Acknowledgements 10

PART ONE: TE WAIPOUNAMU/SOUTH ISLAND 12
My own backyard 15
Yachtie — Ray Shoebridge 20
Renaissance man — Ralph Woodward 28
Extinguished mayor — Garry Moore 39
Architect — Sir Miles Warren 46
Riding south 53
Ex-cop — Jim Sykes 58
Planet Earth guide — Gavin Wills 69
'Dusty Don' — Donald Pannett 77
The deep south 83
Tuatapere resident — Ngarita Dixon 88
Moonshiner — Rob Tinning 95
Restaurateur — Fleur Sullivan 106
All Blacks assistant coach — Mike Cron 114

Go west, young man! **121**
Goldminer — Kerry Chapman 128
Barrytown knifemaker — Steven Martin 136
Environmental entrepreneur — Paul Murray 145
The top end **151**
Quaker — Albie Burgers 156
Collector — Ron Hebberd 166
Biker — Gary Husband 172

PART TWO: TE IKA A MAUI/NORTH ISLAND **178**
Across the water **181**
Craft brewer — Annika Naschitzki 186
Naughty Nana — Jo Morgan 191
The Wairarapa and Hawke's Bay **197**
Veteran biker — Mike Little 204
Poverty Bay and westward **211**
The middle bit **217**
Red Devil — Graeme Cole 220
Racing legend — Ginger Molloy 225
'Buelligan' — Debbie Curle 232
Craftsman — Paul Downie 237
The Far North **243**
Russell artist — Helen Pick 247
Artist/jeweller — Kate Du Plooy 254
Firefighter — Colin 'Toss' Kitchen 261
Heading south **267**
The Coffee Lady — Judy Bosworth 272
'Matchy' — Robert Bullot 280
Training Commander — Colonel Karyn Thompson 287

INTRODUCTION

I travelled much of the world in the 1980s when I was in my twenties before the word 'backpacker' became part of the lexicon. And though I had an incredible time, I often look back wistfully on those days and wish I'd possessed the maturity that only age bestows. (The only good thing it brings actually!) And I must confess that some of the travelling was done simply for bragging rights back down the local pub. Taj Mahal — tick; Himalayas — tick; Blue Mosque — tick; Uluru — tick ... I realise now that what makes travelling so rewarding is meeting people. People from all walks of life with a story to tell.

Sir John Hunt, leader of the successful 1953 Everest expedition, had it right when he said 'life is meeting', which incidentally is the title of his autobiography. In my last book, *Living the Dream — Kiwi Bikers*, I interviewed 50 fascinating motorcyclists from around New Zealand. In *The Long and Winding Aotearoa*, I rode around this wonderful country on my Triumph motorcycle, dropping in to talk to more fascinating people willing to share their stories, only this time I threw my net wider, interviewing not only motorcyclists but a huge variety of colourful characters.

It was a pleasure to make the acquaintance of people for whom the acquisition of wealth was not their sole driver. From a famous architect, craftsman, restaurateur and craft brewer to a rugby coach, artist, firefighter and Quaker. They all had tales to tell of lives well lived, and it was very gratifying and often enlightening to make their acquaintance and share their passions.

When at home, working, paying bills, going to the supermarket, the pub, watching tele, the days blur into one another. New places intensify the simplest things; making every day an adventure. Which is why riding the 'long and winding' around *my own* country, discovering new places, was such a pleasure, And I can say that now — for during the writing of this book I became a Kiwi citizen! In fact, I'm proud to say that I'm now a citizen of the United Kingdom, Australia and New Zealand.

Many of the roads I travelled were familiar to me, and I'd written about them previously in issues of *Bike Rider Magazine*. So if the prose looks familiar to some readers, then I offer my apologies but I did try my best not to plagiarise myself!

LONG MAY YOU RIDE

ACKNOWLEDGEMENTS

First, I'd like to thank my wife, Karen, for helping me out when I came to her, almost in tears, thinking I'd deleted everything by mistake! She showed a lot of patience as my sounding board, especially as she was up to her ears in her own writing, finishing up her PhD thesis.

Thanks to my mate and fellow writer/motorcyclist Des Molloy for proofreading and giving helpful suggestions.

Thanks to Bill Honeybone at Bateman for sticking with me.

I must thank the weather gods, who certainly smiled upon me during my ride. To hardly get wet at all on such a long trip is remarkable. Soon after arriving home, the remnants of Australia's Cyclone Debbie, followed by Cyclone Cook, pummelled the North Island and I breathed a huge sigh of relief.

A huge thank-you goes to the 30 people who invited me into their homes and agreed to share their stories for this book.

And finally, thanks to Mr Spock (the Leonard Nimoy version), who accompanied me on my trip, cable-tied to my mirror. 'Live long and prosper!'

Takaka Hill  60 Open

 Southern Scenic Route

The Buller Gorge Highway

The Heritage Highways

PART ONE: TE WAIPOUNAMU/ SOUTH ISLAND

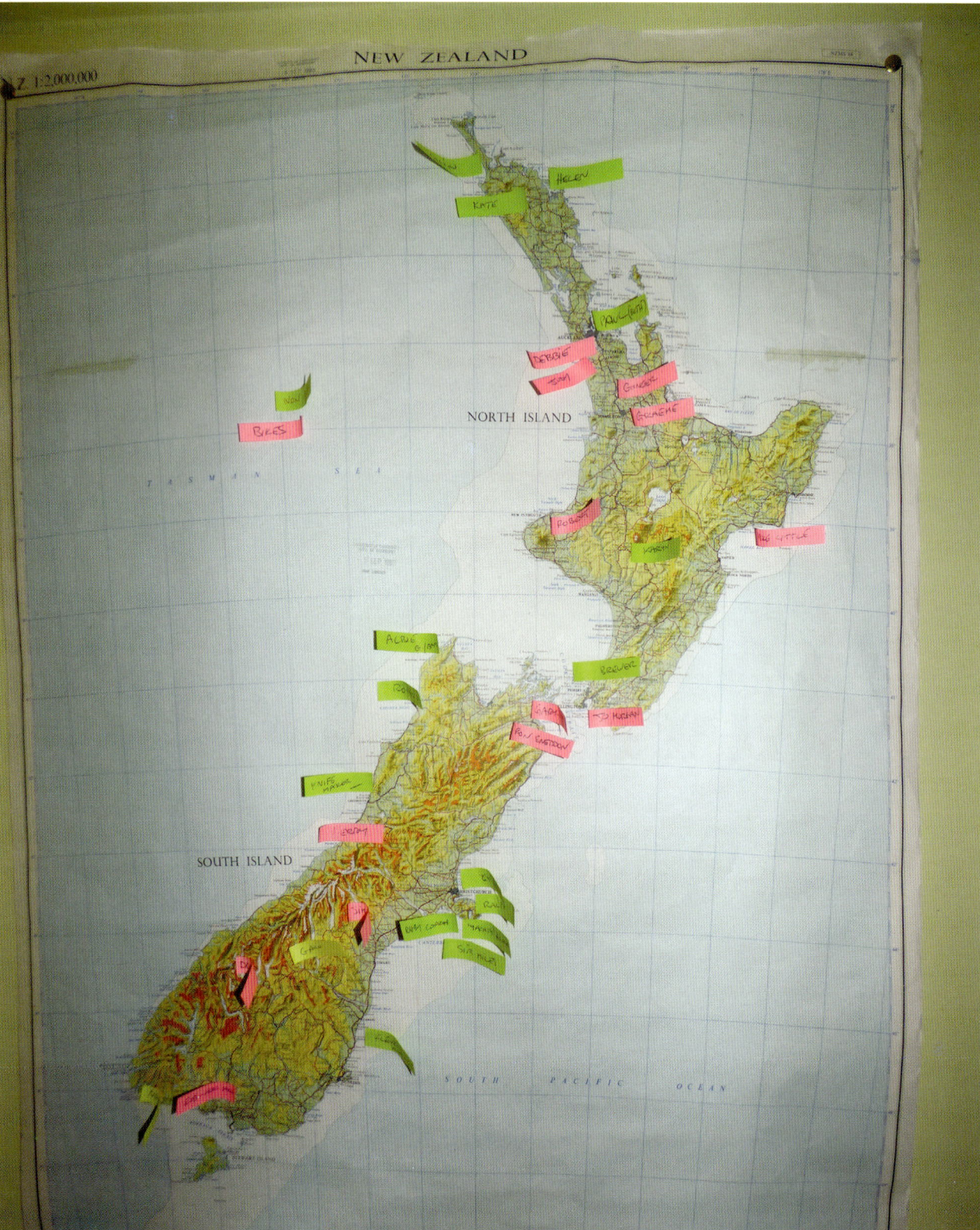

MY OWN BACKYARD: A YACHTIE, A RENAISSANCE MAN, AN EX-MAYOR AND AN ARCHITECT

'The long and winding road, that leads to your door.'
— Lennon and McCartney

Like a fighter pilot, I unconsciously go through my routine. Riding pants, boots and jacket are first, before turning the ignition key and seeing that reassuring green light of neutral. Then little foam earplugs, helmet, sunnies and, lastly, gloves, before swinging a leg over the bike, pulling in the clutch, pressing the starter button, kicking up the side-stand, clunking her into first gear and heading off. With that familiar flutter of excitement, I twist the throttle and accelerate up my lane on a sunny spring morning to begin the first leg of my ride of exploration around this wonderful country of ours. Banks Peninsula, a 1150-square-kilometre chunk of steep and broken land, jutting out into the vast Pacific Ocean, is right on my doorstep and is today's destination.

Named after Sir Joseph Banks, the botanist on Captain Cook's first exploration of the South Pacific, in 1769–70, the peninsula was once two offshore volcanoes. When these volcanoes erupted, about 12 million years ago, they formed two craters, which are now occupied by Lyttelton Harbour to the north and Akaroa Harbour to the south. Akaroa means 'long harbour' ('Hakaroa' in southern Maori dialect). As recently as 1839 it was known as Banks Island (as so it appeared to Captain Cook from 10 miles off), until it was discovered that it was in fact connected to the mainland. The solidified lava flows created the tentacles of land which shelter numerous bays and inlets, and, what's more, it's a motorcyclist's heaven.

I wind my way up and over Gebbies Pass and turn left onto State Highway (SH) 75, which winds lazily around the east coast of Te Waihora/Lake Ellesmere, New Zealand's largest coastal lake. The lake is only 5000 years old, which in geological terms is an infant. Interestingly, the lake has at one time in its short life formed the mouth of both the Rakaia and Waimakariri rivers! The magnificent snow-covered Southern Alps are too distant to be reflected in the lake's brackish, green waters.

At any one time, some 100,000 wetland birds call Te Waihora ('the spreading water') home. The quality of the water flowing into the lake is gradually improving, thanks to Environment Canterbury's Living Rivers programmes.

Clouds roll briskly across the sun as a breeze springs up. An easterly maybe, I'm not sure. I love the way Kiwis always seem to know the wind direction, as though they have an inbuilt compass. ('Oh, yes,' I remember a builder say to me once, 'that's a southerly with an easterly on top.') State Highway 75 is very popular with motorcyclists, with it sweeping high-speed bends and beautiful views, and on sunny Sunday mornings it can resemble a peg-scraping, mini grand-prix circuit as leather-clad bikers on sports bikes jostle for position as they disdainfully overtake Sunday drivers (including me).

Past Lake Forsyth I stop to stretch my legs in Little River, a quaint little 'historical' town and popular coffee spot. Here, I discover some cast-iron tri-pots in front of the old railway station, used, I am told, for boiling whale oil, which at the time was the best lubricant known to man. Whaling was carried out in the 1830s all around the peninsula, and was partly responsible for the drastic reduction in the numbers of the Humpback and Southern Right (so-called because they were the 'right' ones to hunt).

The road now begins to climb. My Triumph has plenty of power for the hills and good handling on the curvy bits. It also has enough grunt to get me out of trouble (or into trouble if a radar gun happens to be pointing at me).

The blessedly dry and gravel-free tarmac twists me through gently folded, sheep-dotted hills, as I interrupt a seagull feeding on what looks like a hare and it takes to the air with a shriek. I pull over to take a photo at the Hilltop Tavern (476 metres), a popular watering hole with bikers and tourists alike.

I now concentrate on the tight, descending bends. T. E. Lawrence (Lawrence of Arabia) knew a thing or two about motorcycling. He reckoned that to ride a bike properly it had to become a 'logical extension of our faculties'. I'm trying my best to will this to happen! Bikes are more easily lost on downhill than uphill bends, as gravity becomes your enemy and not your friend. I recently dropped the Bonneville while doing a U-turn on a very steep section of road at the top of Richmond Hill in Christchurch. Gravity proved to be the dominant force over my forward motion, and down I went. Nobody was around to witness my blushes and I picked her up easily (adrenalin), and was glad of the dresser bars, which protected everything. Dropping your bike is certainly a thing to avoid.

I lose speed; change down and brake before the bend, accelerate smoothly until I am halfway through it, then increase the roll on the throttle, keeping my eye

glued to my 'vanishing point'. I'm not a fast rider. Far from it. I like to ride at my own pace. I did 'the ton' once. It was on a straight stretch of road in Holland one sunny morning in 1982, on my trusty Honda CB400N, and to be honest I haven't felt the need to do it again. I've seen the results of peer pressure while riding in groups, trying to keep up with a rider who is far more skilful than yourself. I've always admired the rider on the sports bike, though: knee down, hanging off the bike in full leathers, but that's simply not me. I'm more of a smelling-the-roses kind of rider. In fact, the only time I get my knee down is when I lubricate my chain.

The French attempted to colonise Akaroa until the gallant crew of HMS *Britannia* got wind of their imminent arrival and hoisted the Union Jack, it is said, just as the French entered the harbour. The area then became the centre of the first planned settlement in the South Island. The first-ever cattle to be run in the South Island were run just outside the site of present-day Akaroa.

The French still landed, however, and stamped their Frenchness on the area. I'm not saying that swarthy, Gauloises-puffing blokes wearing berets and de-mobbed suits and riding old black bicycles with strings of garlic draped over their handlebars are on every corner, but Akaroa and its surrounds still bear an obvious French influence, and this old-world charm is maintained nowadays in the interests of the tourist dollar. It's hard to believe, but back in the 1830s French politicians even suggested that if Britain took the North Island, there was no reason why France shouldn't colonise the South. That would have put a new slant on inter-island rivalry!

Akaroa is absurdly charming. I feel as though I'm inside a picture postcard as I wander around the historic cottages, draped in wisteria and roses, and the trendy shops along the waterfront. Handsome couples who belong in a glossy magazine are breakfasting *al fresco*, while on the waterfront, a group of Asian tourists are clicking away madly with their cameras. I ride to the end of the Akaroa Wharf and find a tanned and smiling Captain Ray who invites me onto his beautiful boat. This is his story.

YACHTIE — RAY SHOEBRIDGE

Ray Shoebridge is a handsome and cultured 61-year-old who has been sailing for over 40 years. 'I had a kayak when I was five years old, and boating sort of runs in my family,' he begins. Aside from his association with the water, Ray has enjoyed a lifetime of entrepreneurship, making and losing millions in the cut-throat world of business, and often starting over again. He has worked in the fields of glass and acoustic insulation, computers, real estate, charter boats and even farming. He has been business owner, general manager and even had a two-month stint on the DPB, which he describes as a real eye-opener!

'Luckily I paid all my debts,' he continues, 'so that's cool, but one thing led to another, and one wife led to another, and in 2005 my then wife and I were working in a business we had started from scratch in Auckland. I had just turned 50, and I decided it was time to do something completely different, so we decided to sail around the world.' I raise my eyebrows.

'I had read many accounts of people who had done it, and the freedom they had enjoyed, especially the exploits a Kiwi chap who had done it by the name of Johnny Wray. He had built his own boat, *Ngataki*, out of kauri. It's still around — in fact, a trust in Auckland has restored it, and it features in the Auckland Regatta.'

Ray had been inspired after reading Johnny Wray's book, *South Sea Vagabonds*. 'He was no literary giant,' says Ray, 'but it made me think about coconut palms wafting in the South Pacific breeze, with a bevy of Polynesian beauties surrounding you. It was inspirational stuff.'

So when Ray turned 50, he and his wife sold their house and business, bought the boat we're sitting on, and in April 2006, along with the cat, they set sail and left Auckland for good. They gave themselves 10 years to sail around New Zealand to get the hang of the boat, before heading off around the world to find a new place to live. 'Six months later,' continues Ray, 'we landed here in Akaroa, fell in love with it and didn't go any further!' I laugh, and looking out at the wonderful view I can see why he stayed. 'I always imagined living on a lake in Switzerland or Austria, or somewhere exotic, but at least here there's an entrance so I can escape if I get sick of the place!'

Eventually they bought a house in Akaroa, started a bed-and-breakfast business ashore, and a sailing business afloat. But a few years ago the cat emigrated and Ray parted company with his wife. He now lives on board and runs Akaroa Sailing Cruises. 'To be honest,' he says, 'in the last seven or eight years it's like I haven't worked a single day, because I'm doing something I absolutely love.'

The boat we are sitting on, and being very gently rocked, is a living slice of Australasian maritime history. Built in 1946, *Manutara* is a rare 47-foot classic ocean-sailing yacht, and one of the last of the A-Class Keelers to be built. Ray's love and enthusiasm for *Manutara* is obvious. 'The 20-tonne hull was designed by Tasmanian Jock Muir to win the Sydney-to-Hobart race,' explains Ray, 'and was handcrafted from a single 850-year-old kauri tree! In fact, three of her sister ships won the race in 1947, 1948, 1949 and 1953.' Ray is getting into his stride now. 'Kiwi craftsmen John Salthouse and Jack Logan hand-built her,' he says, and raps his knuckles on the hull. Even I, a real land-lubber — let's just say, I can get motion sickness sitting on a park swing — can see what a beauty she is.

'Even though I'm never going to become wealthy doing this,' says Ray, 'I'm having just the most wonderful time. I get to see the rare Hector dolphins, seals, penguins and sea birds, and I love to sail. Akaroa Harbour is simply a delightful sailing area, and the locals are lovely people.'

Despite the wonderful harbour, Ray's is the only commercial sailing boat here. I ask him why that is. 'Well, George, Christchurch people, it seems, just don't get sailing. They're power-boaters and jet-skiers and petrol-heads, as opposed to Auckland people who *do* get it. But then they have the Hauraki Gulf, which is probably the best sailing area in the South Pacific.'

Ray looks pretty fit for his age, and puts it down to being active, always busy on the boat. 'You've really got to love your paintbrush and sandpaper,' he says. 'As any boat owner will tell you, maintenance on a boat never ends. When a shop puts the "marine" tag on an item, it's usually followed by a string of zeros on the price. Did you know that the word "boat" is in fact an acronym which stands for "bring out another thousand"?'

But it hasn't always been plain sailing for Ray (if you'll excuse the pun). 'They say that if you can sail around New Zealand, you can sail anywhere, because we have some of the loveliest waters to sail, but also some of the roughest. I remember we got caught in a storm on the east coast just south of Castle Point, which sticks out of the Wairarapa coastline. There's nowhere to run to down there, nobody lives there; there are no roads, streetlights — nothing! So on leaving Castle Point at midnight, heading for Wellington, we got caught in a southerly storm. It was forecast to blow 30 knots, but it blew 75. Things were pretty rugged. My mainsail shredded itself; I had to put that away along with the headsail. So we had to motor most of the way through waves that were as tall as my mast, which is 65 feet above the deck! Even the cat was seasick. But nothing broke on the boat, and 12½ hours later we crawled into Wellington. But I never imagined I'd see seas like that *anywhere*, let along nine miles off the coast of the Wairarapa. Luckily, Steve, the former owner of *Manutara*, had joined us for the Napier-to-Wellington leg, and was a big help. We managed to do an hour on at a time before the hailstones, sleet and hypothermia drove us below. But we toughed it out, and thank God for radar is all I can say. It's a fabulous tool.'

So eventually Ray made it to Akaroa, where he now takes customers out on two cruises per day around the harbour. 'It seems to appeal to all sorts,' he says. 'They can steer the boat if they want to, or sit in the Royal Seat at the stern and relax and watch the action. Some, particularly my Asian clients, like to go up the front and do the *Titanic* pose for a photo.'

Ray's clientele are from all over the place. Mainly Aussies and Brits, with Europeans and 'dribblings from all round the world'. A few Kiwi customers make the trip to Akaroa, but not many apparently from Christchurch.

'I have seen a huge upswing in Chinese tourists recently,' he points out. 'Clearly the language barrier is an issue, especially when I'm giving my safety briefing.' The image of the Chinese tourist is usually a horde of 30 or so disgorged from a coach, travelling in a pack, but recently there has been a rise in the number of FITs, or Free Independent Travellers, from China, which has benefited small businesses like Ray's. 'Not one of my Chinese customers has sailed before, so good on them for being a bit adventurous. They all seem to have a great time, and there must be some Chinese kind of TripAdvisor, because their numbers are growing all the time.'

'So do you think you'll ever pull up anchor and continue your trip around the world?' I ask Ray, as two paddle-boarders glide by.

'Well, I've just met a new lady who's very keen on sailing. She arrives next week, so we'll see what happens,' he replies with a glint in his eye. 'I'm thinking that the business and this classic boat kind of go together. So if I left it would make sense to monetise the effort I've put into the business over the past eight years and sell it as a going concern, which means of course that if I want to carry on sailing I'll have to buy a new boat. I have a hankering to at least sail to Tahiti, so we'll just see how things pan out.'

I leave Ray, who is clearly living the dream, with a firm handshake and a cheery wave, as he prepares for the arrival of his next clients and I head for my bike.

I gaze out at the mirror-flat water, trying to imagine what it looked like in 1791 when the first (English) vessel dropped anchor, inviting inquisitive Ngai Tahu Maori on board, and bestowing axes and nails on them.

I'm in no hurry, so a few k's out of Akaroa, reminding myself to smell the roses, I turn right, twist my way up to the Summit Road, and then dive down towards the sea again at Okains Bay. Some of the bends are quite sharp (most would be 25-ers if posted), and coasting around a left-hander (which should be a 15-er) I almost come a cropper, narrowly avoiding one of Nature's speed bumps in the form of a dead possum.

Okains Bay is the largest of the eastern bays, and once supported a sizeable Maori population, judging from the large number of artefacts discovered here. No evidence of the origin of the bay's name exists, but it's thought to be a European corruption of 'Okein Stream', which I sometimes follow as I wind my way down. The first Europeans to purchase land from the Canterbury Association in 1850 were timber-cutters and were attracted by the dense bush, featuring some of the best

MY OWN BACKYARD

stands of totara on the Banks Peninsula. When the timber was felled, the settlers turned to dairying, and even had their own cheese factory up until 1967.

There is usually a huge crowd in Okains Bay on Waitangi Day, and I once had the pleasure of being among the Maori and Pakeha paddlers of a war canoe as part of the celebrations. The speeches inside the museum grounds, to mark the partnership between our two cultures, were all rather stirring stuff!

The beach has a distinct 'Aussie' feel to it, and features a lagoon which is safe for kids to play in and easy to launch boats into. I stretch my legs and wander around the rocky footpath, past the remains of the old wharf, where ships would ply their loads of meat, livestock, wool, timber and dairy products the 21 miles to Lyttelton. The last wharf was built in 1912 and dismantled in 1964, providing timber to repair road bridges on the peninsula.

Back in the saddle, I notice my fuel warning light is on, and I'm relieved to discover the fuel pumps open beside the ancient workshop and general store which has stood on this spot since 1873. The smiling blonde lady kindly unlocks the pump and takes my photo, and I wonder if she's a relation to the grey-bearded Mr Thacker, a direct descendant of the original settlers, who I was told sometimes manned the pump.

On the Summit Road now, I admire the rugged, volcanic landscape, and pass sheep grazing with spring lambs amongst the sad old stumps of the ancient totara forest. I look around me and try to imagine what the area would have looked like to the first European settlers in the 1850s, when around two-thirds of Banks Peninsula was forested. In my mind's eye I see the majestic forests of totara, kahikatea and matai, which took the settlers only a few decades to decimate, and not just with logging. The European animal species introduced by the settlers in their innocence, such as possums, did terrible damage. One of the biggest environmental disasters of them all was the ravenous feral goat, which soon reproduced in plague proportions, and is still a serious problem today despite the best efforts of the Department of Conservation (DOC). Small forest reserves have been established, which are home to bellbird, native pigeon, tomtit and brown creeper.

I head for home, enjoying SH75's fast sweepers once more.

TOURIST
DRIVE
Eastern Bays
VIA Summit Road
Wainui
Akaroa
75

RENAISSANCE MAN — RALPH WOODWARD

Ralph is a neighbour of mine, so I really don't have far to go for a chat. I could take the dog for a walk, but for form's sake I fire up the bike and complete what will be the shortest ride of this book.

Ralph, who is a debonair 91 but looks and acts 20 years younger, can be found most Friday nights down the local Governors Bay Hotel, glass of red in hand, entertaining locals, me included, with his rapier wit and spontaneous outbursts of

either song or poetry. Before we begin our little chat, we enjoy a spot of lunch made by Ralph's lovely wife, Adrianne (who wouldn't be short of a story or two herself). Ralph has been weeding his vegetable garden all morning, and is happy to have a break. He warns me that he's not that good remembering dates.

'Yoga is probably the biggest thing that's happened in my life,' begins Ralph, 'apart from marriage and kids. I started doing it when I was 17, but it was called Surya Namaskara. Only much later did I discover that it was an ancient form of Hatha Yoga or obeisance to the Sun God.' He shows me some old sepia-tinted photos of him from the 1960s in various impossible-looking positions. 'It's one of the main reasons I still enjoy good health,' he says. 'Well, I've been doing it for going on 75 years.'

Ralph still starts his day with his yoga routine, but not, he points out, to the extent he would have done years ago with headstands. He concentrates more on the balancing and abdominal aspects of the workout. For years, Ralph ran yoga classes all over Christchurch, where he was born in September 1925, as well as running workshops in places like Pigeon Bay and Darfield. 'Dr Johnny Moffit started a class at Mount Pleasant Community Centre, which I attended, and a couple of years later he said he couldn't continue, so when several of the people in the class

approached me to carry it on, I obliged. Johnny was all for it, and allowed me to use his library. He was something of a mentor to me.' Ralph also received many invitations to talk about yoga at various clubs and service groups around the traps.

Ralph was a keen sportsman in his youth, enjoying swimming, climbing, boxing, cricket and rugby, as well as running. Although 'youth', it must be said, is a relative term, as he participated in many sports until quite recently. 'John Drew got me into running,' he says. 'It was he who coached me through my first marathon. I did two or three with him. That man could run huge distances. I probably started around the late 1940s, when a workmate, Jack Austen, encouraged me to start running with his club, the Rover Harriers. I'm still with them today, though I don't run with them anymore.'

I ask Ralph what it was like in Christchurch during the war. 'Well, I was put in charge of the household as a 15-year-old when my father joined the Army,' he says. Ralph has a great speaking voice; very easy on the ear. 'It sounds a bit melodramatic now, but I kept a rifle alongside my bed, as the threat [of invasion by the Japanese] was very real. Sydney had been attacked by submarines, Darwin bombed, and the approaches to Auckland, Wellington and Lyttelton had been mined by a German raider. The Home Guard was unrolling the barbed wire along New Brighton Beach, while the bulk of our troops were in far-flung theatres of war.'

He adds that, although many may be in disagreement with American military adventures today, we should all be eternally grateful to American marines at Guadalcanal and to their fleet at Midway for putting a stop to almost certain invasion and Japanese occupation.

In 1943, at the age of 18, Ralph, like many other Kiwis, was conscripted into the Army, and was immediately put to work harvesting, which he loved. When I look at him quizzically, he explains that you had to be 21 to be sent overseas. Ralph had had his heart set on a tank regiment, but instead found himself driving a tractor around the potato fields of Halswell, Springfield and Darfield. 'We wore our uniforms, and every day, after a breakfast of liver and bacon, the officers would run us out to work. Our camp was in Addington.'

After a few months of this, young Ralph (who fancied he was due for promotion as he was driving tractors!) was called up and told, 'Son, back to barracks, collect your gear: you're out of this man's army.' His old employer, Victoria Insurance, dragged him kicking and screaming back to his desk, where he was required for 'semi-essential' work as a war-damage insurance clerk.

'I was bloody ropeable!' says Ralph. 'So back at my desk I thought "bugger this", and immediately went around to the RNZN office to apply for the Navy.' After many frustrating weekly visits, Ralph was finally accepted to be trained at HMNZS *Tasman* in Lyttelton as an ordinary signalman. 'Semaphore, or the use of flags, was used a lot for sending messages between ships,' says Ralph. 'In a flash you could send a message. And reading a message from the front would be quite different to reading it from the back.' Ralph leafs through his photo album and digs up a photo of himself as a fresh-faced youth in naval uniform.

Eventually, the keen young signalman shipped out, but it was to prove frustrating. After many delays due to snowstorms, Ralph finally arrived in Auckland, eager to move on to Sydney, only to discover that all of the ratings required for the proposed assault on Japan had been culled from the minesweepers. 'So they all went and we were shoved onto the minesweepers to replace them. And we served on those until the end of the war at £2 10s a week, all around the shipping lanes in the Hauraki Gulf.' I tell him I had no idea that mines were laid in New Zealand waters. 'Oh, yes,' he says, 'there were some 300 mines laid by a German raider.' Ralph rubs his chin, thoughtfully, dredging up memories. 'So we were out sweeping, and news came over that the Yanks had dropped the bombs [on Hiroshima and Nagasaki], and that was that: the war was over. We were kept on for a few more months, and then they were pleased to see the back of us.'

After tramping and adventuring down south for a while with a backpack, Ralph started back in the insurance office. 'But I'd outlived it, George. I needed an outdoor job, so after about a month I applied to an advertisement in the *Star* to be a wool roller.' 'I don't know what that is,' I interrupt him. 'Well, that makes two of us, George.' And we laugh. So, keen as mustard, Ralph rushed down to the address in Woolston that very night, hammered on the door, only to be told by his prospective boss's wife that he was drinking with his brothers at the Woolston Hotel and really wouldn't want to be disturbed. Undeterred, Ralph cycled around to the hotel and approached the publican, who asked him what his poison was. 'No, I'm not drinking,' said Ralph. 'I'm here to ask Mr Beaumont for a job as a wool roller.'

'And what does a wool roller do exactly?' the publican enquired. 'I've no idea,' replied Ralph, 'but I'm keen to find out!' After finding the Beaumont brothers in the snuggery, known as 'Beaumont Corner', Ralph asked the man in question for a job. 'He wasn't at all pleased to see me. He told me he was busy, and to report to him on Saturday morning with the other aspirants and he'd look me over. But I was nothing if not determined, so I said, "The publican told me to tell you that if you don't employ me, your credit here will be cut."' When Mr Beaumont asked if Ralph knew the publican, he replied, 'Yes, he's my uncle, Charles Watkins Stafford!' And the job was his.

That started Ralph out on a career in the wool trade that would last into his ninetieth year. A wool roller (Ralph explains) works on the table in the shearing shed with the wool classer, and skirts the wool, rolls it up, then carries it away to its respective bins. After six weeks away, an old-timer told him that the clever thing would now be to get himself into a wool store. He helped Ralph get a start with Pyne Gould Guinness, where he worked for a season doing menial jobs, before being taken to the Kaputone Wool Scour, which employed a lot of wool sorters. 'Wool sorting,' he explains, 'is what I aspired to do, with the hope of becoming a wool classer. Then I could travel about under my own name, get into the wool sheds, and if you played it well you could get into a buying company, travelling to the wool sales and maybe even get into buying and manufacturing or whatever. And that,' reflects Ralph, 'is what I did.'

One day Ralph, still only in his early twenties, came home from some wool sorting in Kaputone and his dad said, 'Ralph, you've just missed the opportunity

of a lifetime. A fellow was just here, wanting to employ you to class his station and others in North Canterbury, offering £2 10s a day.' A tradesman at the time was earning around £6 a week, so this was big money. 'He knows where I am,' replied Ralph. 'If he comes again, tell him my price is £2 15s.' His dad almost fell off his chair! He could not believe his son's arrogance. But it worked, and Ralph steadily made his way up the wool ladder from roller to sorter, to classer, to skin grader ('We used to be smothered in DDT powder!'), to supervisor, to general manager, wool buyer and eventually with two partners running their own company. 'We had a shop in Colombo Street. People must have thought we had a call-girls service going or something,' he says. 'We never sold anything, but there we were inside, beavering away, with people coming and going at all hours.'

Ralph's stories from a lifetime in the wool trade and his subsequent world travels pour forth and would fill a book, and I have to leave out so much. As well as the above, he also dabbled in growing and selling lettuces ('my partner suffered from spondylitis of the spine and couldn't bend, so who do you think had to plant the 20,000 lettuces?'). Ralph was also the secretary of the Fendalton Branch of the Labour Party back in the 1980s, arguing in the arbitration courts for workers' rights. I imagine he was quite formidable.

As well as sketching and painting (he shows me his cosy studio later), Ralph is a poet, and a good one, with two poetry books to his name, as well as a memoir (interspersed with poems) on the way. 'When I was a young lad, I'd toy with writing rhyming couplets and it just grew from there,' says Ralph. 'I like the brevity of poetry,' he says, 'the way you can paint a picture with words, be it a sunrise or something ridiculous happening in the world.'

He is often called upon to talk at ANZAC Day remembrance ceremonies. 'I have been privileged to visit Gallipoli, and particularly Chunuk Bair, where a small group of New Zealanders captured the heights and could have changed the course of the war had they been supported,' he says.

Below is one of Ralph's poems.

> ANZAC Day as often is
> Was bitter cold
> His poppy shook with stress it took
> To push the tired old blood along
> That might well have stained
> Gallipoli.
> At attention far too long
> He stooped, buckled, fell
> Tribute stain mid the poppies
> Last of the regiment
> Conditioned for
> That far-off war
> That all but he had long forgot.

For the past 20 years or so, Ralph has been a serial attender of adult education courses. 'Every bloody subject you could think of, George — astronomy, cosmology, theology, logic, economics, the lot.'

I tell Ralph that it's hard to get my head around someone telling me stories from

40 years ago when they were in their fifties. 'Well,' he says with a chuckle, 'when I get up every morning, *I'm in my fifties*. But I don't really think about being old. Boredom is the killer. You have to have projects, you see. Without a project, people can just give up. The best things in life, I think, are for one to just sit back and enjoy company, as we are now. But, looking back, I don't think there are too many unpleasant thoughts there.'

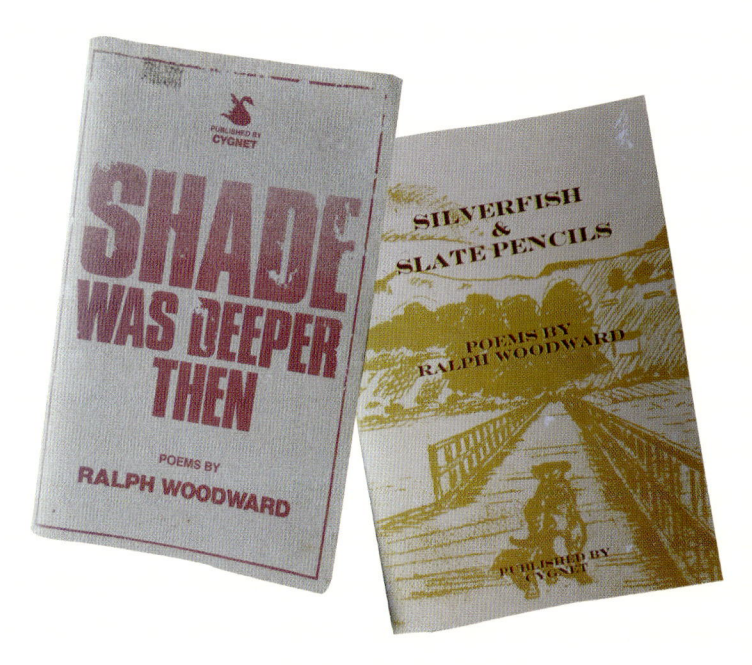

Governors Bay originally had the name of Dyer's Bay, after one of the early farmers in the area, John Dyer. When a pass was forged through the Port Hills, Dyer provided the provincial government's surveyors with valuable advice. Later, he was awarded the contract to feed the road builders and, as a reward, the road and pass, as well as the beaches and bays below, were named after him. Before this, in the 1850s when the Governor Sir George Grey would visit the burgeoning Canterbury settlement at Lyttelton, he would anchor his brig in the upper reaches of the bay. The Governor had an 'avowed dislike' for 'Church' settlements, and so as a politeness would anchor here rather than between Quail Island and Lyttelton, which was the usual anchorage. At the time, the name of Governors Bay was given to what is today Allandale and Teddington. As time went on, the name Dyer's Bay disappeared and was renamed Governors Bay, while the old Governors Bay became Allandale and Teddington.

In the saddle once more, I clunk her into first and head off for my next interview, another local one. I think the high-viz vest I wear over my leather jacket is probably superfluous in Christchurch these days, as every man and his dog seems to wear one.

Much of the original road passing beneath my tyres was constructed 150 years ago, with the use of chain gangs, some under armed guard from Lyttelton Gaol. James McKenzie, the infamous sheep rustler — the Mackenzie Country in South Canterbury bears his name, albeit with a different spelling, and is another slice of motorcycling heaven — was apparently one of the convicts who reluctantly contributed his labour to the project.

The bike has warmed up now, and the big motor (although 'big' is a relative term these days) spins merrily away, hundreds of components meshing together to propel me onwards. There's a spot where the exhaust note can echo off the steep hillside if you give it a handful at the right time, and today I get it just right — music to my ears.

I wind down to Rapaki, named by the Ngai Tahu chief Te Rangi Whakapatu. Rapaki means 'waist mat', which the chief symbolically took off and laid on the shore, thereby claiming the land. Te Rangi then proceeded to drive the then-resident Maori tribe out of Lyttelton Harbour, beheading some, so it is said, for good measure, and placing their heads in a basket overlooking the harbour.

Before European influence, Lyttelton Harbour (or Whakaraupo) was a rich source of shellfish, but today bilge water from ships and sewage have taken their inevitable toll. Lyttelton was proposed as the capital for the Canterbury area, but when the 'Canterbury pilgrims' arrived in 1850 they trekked over the Port Hills and decided on Christchurch instead. These 800 settlers were so-named by the Canterbury Association back in the 'Old Dart' (England), with the intention of forming an Anglican settlement in New Zealand.

Lyttelton tunnel, which I now enter, links the harbour to the Garden City. The road tunnel resembles nothing less than a tunnel from the London Underground, with its white ceramic-tiled walls and Victorian-like subdued lighting. The rail tunnel was engineered in 1867, while the road link was not built until 1964 at the equivalent cost of $6.6 million.

I meander about the town centre for a bit, checking out the new artworks that have sprung up on the sides of damaged buildings and have become a familiar sight. It's a shame that most will be obscured when the new buildings are completed. Parts of the centre are still unrecognisable; acres of desolation, surrounded by a million road cones. But almost six years on from the February 2011 earthquake, and after years of seemingly no progress, the much-vaunted rebuild is really gathering pace, and every time I come into town a new building seems to have sprung up. I pause by the site of the CTV building, and have a flashback to the night of 22 February and into the following morning. I remember digging away on the pile of rubble, with my crewmates from the Governors Bay Volunteer Fire Brigade and many other emergency workers. It all seemed quite surreal at the time, as though I were looking down on the scene from a great height.

I park my bike outside Smash Palace in High Street, wander in and get myself a beer, maudlin thoughts soon replaced by a fierce optimism for Christchurch's future.

EXTINGUISHED MAYOR — GARRY MOORE

After listening, along with 30 or so others, to the very interesting anecdotes and stories of Tom McBrearty in the Tuesday Club, I sit down with former Christchurch mayor Garry Moore for a chat over beer and chips. Behind us is the funky old bus which serves as the bar. There are outdoor tables, and some undercover and coloured lights strung about. Music blares from scattered speakers, giving Smash Palace a very cool vibe.

It soon becomes apparent that Garry is one smart cookie, an eagle-eyed free-thinker who rails against conformity. That annoyingly over-used phrase 'thinking outside the square' fits this bloke like a glove.

I kick off by asking how the Tuesday Club, which has been going for over a year now, came about. 'Well, we used to have a bar, over there where that sign is,' he waves a chip, 'called Goodbye Blue Monday, which collapsed in the earthquake. Part of it fell on my son Johnny. He left the bar with an unregistered, unwarranted bike, no crash helmet or licence, and rode it home, and a policeman waved him through, so we've kept that bike as part of our family's history.' People are gradually leaving the talk, and stop to chat with Garry on their way out. He continues: 'Anyway, in that bar we used to have an occasional gathering called "Drinking Liberally", which was about liberal debate and discussion. Also, every month we had "Theology on Tap" discussions. We had a fantastic line-up of guest speakers, like Sir Paul Reeves; speakers from all walks of life.'

Garry is a polished talker, and has obviously had a bit of practice. 'See that bald guy in the corner?' he says. 'That's John, he's a Geordie. Well, he and I were involved in economic development when we worked for government departments in the 1980s. We ran an organisation called Te Mahi Tangata. It had no rules, no constitution and no subscription, and it was brilliant. An example of how we worked was in 1986, when we had 17 computers all linked up to each other, pre-email. Some were on maraes, some in government departments, some in community groups. Whale Watch came out of our work there; we worked with Ngai Tahu, and the Women's Division of Federated Farmers, unemployed rights centres and all sorts of community agencies, assisting displaced workers throughout the South Island. We were all in it together.'

So, Garry and John, along with the former Dean of ChristChurch Cathedral Peter Beck, decided to start the Tuesday Club. They had been told that it would take five years before something like what they had in mind would be acceptable. John was insistent that there be no rules, no subs, no legal structure — just like Te Mahi Tangata — and any interesting personality could be invited along to speak. 'It's turned out to be a very successful enterprise, with over 230 people on its mailing list.'

Those on that emailing list, incidentally, get to read some pretty thought-provoking stuff. 'I had two journalists contact me last week talking about the topics I'd covered in those emails, and neither of them were on my mailing list,' says Garry.

'"Motorbike Night" actually started at Blue Monday,' he points out. 'It began when my son Johnny had an old Matchless 500 single, which wasn't going. Thursday night was a quiet night, so Johnny and my son-in-law, Greg May, decided they'd fix the bike up, and Thursday nights became "Matchless Night".'

When the February earthquake hit, Goodbye Blue Monday was debt-free and very well insured. So Johnny Moore and architect and urban designer Jim Lunday came up with the concept of Smash Palace, a bar that reflected the state of Christchurch, post-earthquake, complete with scaffolding on the outside. Greg was the constructor, and both bars are his creation. With the purchase of the old school bus off TradeMe (painted by artist Tony Delatour in exchange for a bar tab), they were in business, and were one of the first bars to open in town. 'Soon,' Garry says, 'a sort of *avant-garde* atmosphere developed, bikers got wind of it and it just kind of snowballed.'

As Thursday nights gained in popularity, Greg and Johnny realised that bikers simply loved to gather and chat. They initially had some trouble with the police, who objected to all the bikes parked on the footpath. As their customer base grew, they started hosting master classes in such things as rebuilding wheels and frames, and exhausts, etc. The motorcycle part of the bar was a levelling point. It didn't matter if you were rich or poor. Whether you had an expensive bike or a heap of shit, you stood with everybody else and shared your passion.

'There's a great little film called *Art of Recovery* by Peter Young, which shows us shifting to here last year,' says Garry. 'I was in charge of health and safety and traffic management. I did absolutely nothing on either of them. Just shows what crap a lot of that stuff is. We told people to look after themselves, and there were no problems. We had about 100 people join us in the shift. We called it the bar's hikoi. When the neighbours came over to say goodbye, we said "Come with us", so they all hopped on the bus, which had no registration or warrant.'

Garry Moore is obviously a passionate man. His conversation is like a stream of consciousness, and at times I struggle to keep up. 'Our family's philosophy is all about hospitality,' he muses. 'If you want to drink your beer lying down on a couch, then you can. If you want to stand around and argue and scrap with people, then you can do that here, too.' He nods towards the bar, where a group of young people have gathered. 'See? The tourists have started to arrive.'

Garry's passion isn't motorcycles, but cars. In fact, as a 22-year-old he shifted to Christchurch from Palmerston North simply because the Vintage Car Club was founded here! 'I don't like pure cars, and am only one step away from being a hot-rodder! I am a complete petrol-head. I own a Vintage Special,' he says as he pulls up photos on his phone. 'It's a Chrysler. The Vintage Sports Car Club in the UK call cars like mine "Anglo-American Sports Bastards". It has American running gear with an English body. I built it with the help of a lot of mates. There's no other like it in the world. I wanted something which was uniquely mine. I went around my mates' workshops and picked up bits and pieces for years until I had what I wanted. In my mind, I had the wheel-base, the attributes of the motor, the gear ratio and the body style I wanted. It's just full of idiosyncratic ideas. The car is a pleasure to drive, is very good-looking — and it absolutely offends the purists. I find purists an easy target for fun, and when they rise to your bait I enjoy their unease hugely.'

I now move Garry (reluctantly, I'm guessing) away from cars and on to politics. 'Well, I've always been interested in politics,' he begins. 'I joined a political party at school as a 15-year-old, then I became the second National President of the Polytechnic Students Association. I joined the Labour Party because I was so pathologically angry at Rob Muldoon.'

I ask why.

'Superannuation,' comes the reply. 'The arsehole got rid of it! We had an excellent superannuation plan in the 1970s that was far better than KiwiSaver. The bastard canned it in 1975!' He shakes his head, obviously still angry. 'We could have had billions of dollars in savings by now. So I joined the Labour Party because of that.'

Garry later got involved in stopping a motorway going through his suburb in Christchurch. 'One of the members of our association was put on the Transit New Zealand Board, and she stopped it at that end; then I became a city councillor and did my bit at the other end.'

'So you only became a councillor to stop that motorway?' I ask. I can be a bit slow sometimes. 'Yes; also the council looked like a lot of fun, and I found I quite enjoyed it. Then Vicki Buck, the mayor at the time, decided to step down, and I looked around, wondering who was going to stand, and thought, "God, I could do as good a job as any of them." And I did.'

He became mayor in 1998 and finished in 2007, and says he's very proud of the fact that there were no changes in personnel in his office during those nine years. It proved to be an exhausting job, and Garry was knackered at the end. In one three-month period (he discovered only after he'd left) his work hours had been recorded, and he'd been booked in at between 90 and 120 hours per week! I ask him what he's most proud of in his tenure as mayor.

'I think the fact that I kept my feet on the ground, and I did it all with my wife, Pam,' he replies. 'The institution didn't take my head off me, and I stayed a constant questioner of many things that came in front of me. I've always been a rebel, and so had to balance that with the expectations of the office. I'm incredibly sceptical of bureaucracy, and I think I'm getting worse. People say you mellow as you age, but I'd say I'm getting more radical as I get older.'

Garry has a pathological loathing of the Chicago School of Economics. When I ask him to elaborate, he explains, 'Thatcherism, Rogernomics and all that. We've individualised our society, and I'm a great believer in community. We must have room for each other. But I'm proud of the fact that at CCC we did a whole lot of innovative things. When I left the mayoralty, the council was debt-free and we had the lowest rates in New Zealand.'

'That would have made you popular,' I venture.

'Look, if you want to be popular, then don't go into public life. It's hard to say what you did individually. The mayor is first amongst equals at the council table. All you have is the power of moral persuasion. But some things stand out. I started the Mayor's Task Force for Jobs, which spread throughout New Zealand, fought hard for the protection of Hagley Park and many other things. I can't remember them all. I just was the advocate for whatever seemed to be needed at the time. One thing I'm proud of is that I was determined to show that publicly-owned trading companies could thrive. That was Christchurch City Holding Ltd. The Business Roundtable hated us. One thing I really pushed for was the need for CCHL to invest in a fibre-optic company here in Christchurch. That business, Enable Ltd, is projected to be worth $750 million by 2022, and it is still publicly owned. This city now owns the sea port, the airport and the data port. Through these companies, combined with the lines company also owned by CCC, is how our city trades with the world and the world with us.'

Garry fell in love with Christchurch when, as a 20-year-old, he attended the Irishman Creek Vintage Car Rally. He drove off the ferry at Lyttelton and through Hagley Park on a cold, smoggy day, telling himself he'd be coming back here to live. Two years later, he did.

'A couple of years later,' he says, 'I met my wife, Pam, in the polytech café, and we will have been married for 40 years in 2017. We have had four children, two boys and two girls. We still have three living in Christchurch, we are in business with two of them, and we also have three grandchildren in the city. They will scatter my ashes here. Hopefully, this practice will be banned by then, and my family will undertake my last act of rebellion and ignore the rule.'

ARCHITECT — SIR MILES WARREN

I am chatting to this distinguished gentleman in the comfortable library of his beautiful stone house, Ohinetahi, now fully restored after the 2010/11 earthquakes. My first question is an obvious one. 'It's always been a puzzlement,' he replies in cultured tones, seemingly from another era, 'how I got into architecture, as there was certainly no art or architecture at school. When I decided to become an architect during my last year, the headmaster shook his head and said, "Oh, and we had such high hopes for you, Warren minor!"

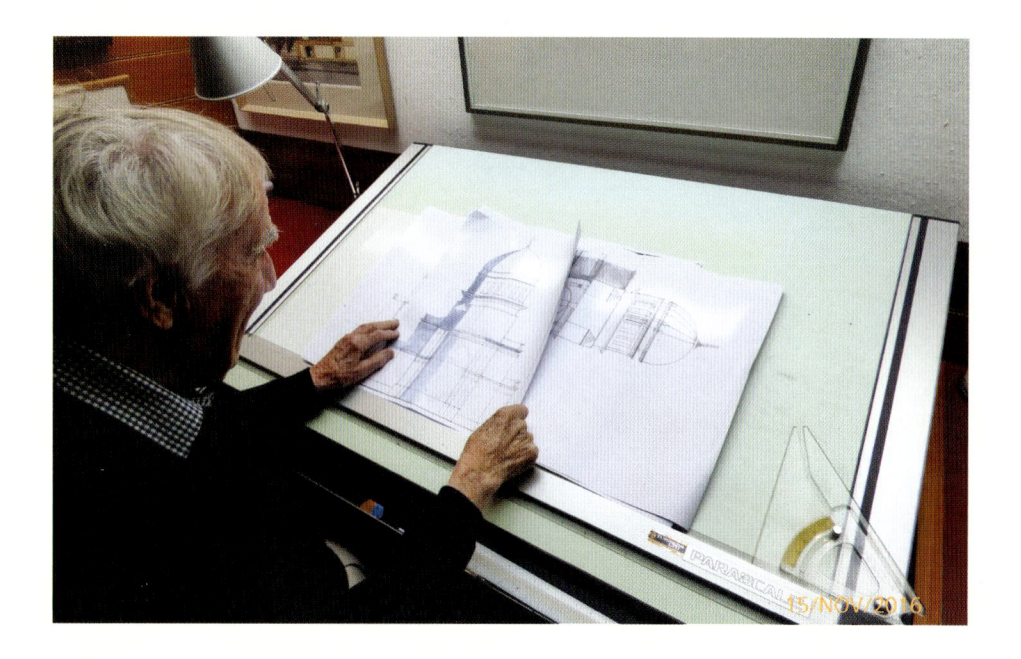

'In those days (the 1940s) at Christ's College, the pecking order was: law, medicine and accountancy. The Church was rather low down, and if you didn't have any brains you went farming.'

Miles was born in 1929, living his childhood during the Great Depression, followed by a world war, so consequently architecture and construction were at their lowest ebb. His father ('a philistine as far as art was concerned') visited three of the top architects when Miles left school, and the advice he received and passed on to his son was a resounding 'NO', as they were all broke.

Says Miles, 'Gordon Lucas, with whom I was briefly in partnership, told me that when he was in practice around that time, nobody had crossed the threshold of his office for over a year. In fact, just before the war, the total value of building work in New Zealand was a paltry £9 million.'

Despite this advice, his father said he should work for Manson of Manson, Seward and Stanton over the summer holidays. This Miles did ('Manson was a taciturn, non-communicative and rather grumpy fellow'), until taking up a more permanent position with Cecil Wood in the new year as a junior draughtsman on 30 shillings a week. 'It was great good fortune for me, as I was now being paid 5 shillings over the going rate, and due to receive training from one of the country's foremost architects who was working at the time on the Wellington Cathedral,' says Miles, as his old black dog snores loudly at our feet. 'And I was more convinced than ever that this was what I wanted to do. The only university that taught architecture was in Auckland, so in Christchurch we studied what was known as the Professional Course, which meant producing testimonies of study.' I give Miles a questioning look, and he explains: 'We had to produce certain defined drawings, the first and most important one was to select one of the great classic buildings. I chose, of all absurd things, the Parthenon. Three drawings were sent up to Auckland, and it was a hard slog because I had to do them after-hours. Back then draughtsmanship and lettering were vital, but of course today, with computers, that is completely gone. At Cecil Wood's, one would practise lettering for hours in the morning. If you were drawing a "C", the pen would rise and the "C" would become a bit wider coming up than going down — it's a skill that today has been completely supplanted.'

Miles stuck at it for three years, sitting the same exams as the Auckland students, before moving up to Auckland for the last two years to complete his studies. As an 18-year-old, away from home for the first time, he describes the experience as 'a great delight'.

He initially boarded at the grandly named Royal Court, which were three crumbling buildings filled with an extraordinary mixture of tenants. 'The boarding house was run by Miss Farquhar, who was affectionately called "Aunt Dolly",' says Miles. 'The financial arrangements were that you paid when you felt like it, and Dolly would stuff the money into her handbag, which she then took to the races and blew. She was a very able woman, and the tax department simply couldn't get at her.'

Returning to Christchurch as a qualified architect in 1950, having won the Auckland University College prize for excellence in architecture, Miles went to work in the 'cheerful' offices of W. H. Trengrove. 'He was the only architect at the time with any substantial practice,' says Miles. 'He wasn't a great designer, but was very practical, and in those days controlled pretty much all of the factory building in the postwar boom. So there was plenty of work for the eight of us in his office.'

When Bill Trengrove's son John, also an architectural student in Auckland, came down to Christchurch for the holidays, he got to know Miles, and in the process was introduced to and duly married Miles's sister Pauline. 'Architecture was very much in the family at that stage,' says Miles.

It was John and Pauline Trengrove, along with Miles, who purchased the run-down Ohinetahi in Governors Bay in 1977, and restored the house and gardens to its present high standard.

ARCHITECT — SIR MILES WARREN

Miles worked and saved for three years before boarding the *Mataroa* for the five-week passage to England, where, after the usual escapades around Europe that you'd expect a young Kiwi full of beans to get up to, he started work for the London County Council. 'During the interview process,' says Miles, 'I had to present some drawings to be assessed in this huge, grand space with a dais at one end. When I presented plans from the first house I'd designed, the comment from the assessors was "There seems to be a lot of timber in this, young man!" When I explained that that was the predominant building material in New Zealand, they said it could be useful with the Roehampton Group. And it was the greatest good luck to join a team that produced some of the very best council work being done at the time. It was a great opportunity for me in a period of expansion and hope.'

Back in New Zealand, Miles was soon busy with his own practice, but at that stage didn't drive. 'There I was, a practising architect with staff and a lot of work and I still bicycled everywhere. Until my father said, "There you are, boy: there's a car, now get on with it." It was a little Ford Anglia.'

Miles thinks he was very fortunate to start up business in a period after the war, when things were coming alive. Most of the pre-war architects were in their sixties and seventies, and either were on their way out or had given up, so Miles was among only a handful of practising architects.

'I was extremely lucky to go into partnership with an older architect, Gordon Lucas, who after a year said he was retiring and asked would I take over the business?'

Gordon's main clients were Ballantynes, Whitcombe and Tombs, and Pyne Gould Guinness. Amazed at Gordon's largesse, Miles, along with his new partner, Maurice Mahoney, appointed accountants and eventually paid Lucas a fair price for a lifetime of valuable contacts. 'Not long after, Ballantynes had their fire, so one of our first commissions was the rebuilding of Ballantynes. Our builder was the roughest, toughest builder you could ever imagine! We got there in the end, but he'd try every trick in the book, and it was a splendid fight from the word "go". But again, it was extraordinarily fortunate for two young architects to be chucked in at the deep end, as it were. After that project, everything seemed much easier.'

Warren and Mahoney went from strength to strength, and prestigious projects rolled in. 'In the late 1960s, the bursar of Christ's College telephoned,' Miles says. '"Dobson here, Miles. Would you like to work for the college?" And I replied, "I'd be delighted, sir. What's the project?" "Day-boy bogs," came the reply. "Oh," I said, rather disappointed. "It's a start, lad, it's a start!" he said.' And it truly was just the start. That project led to a whole succession of buildings, and Christ's College remained a client up until Miles's retirement in 1994.

Sir Miles's travels, accomplishments, awards, achievements and anecdotes could (and have in fact) filled many books, and would take up far too much room to be included here. So I ask him which buildings he is most proud to be associated with. He ponders for a while as we flick through his autobiography, which includes illustrations of many of his buildings.

'That's a difficult question,' he says. 'Well, we were very lucky to be appointed as architects to the Dental Nurses Training School. It cost £60,000 when the average house cost £3000.' Miles is a bit vague on dates, but has a great memory for figures!

'But my most ambitious project was the town hall, which was an architectural competition with about 40 entrants,' he continues.

'Which of your buildings gives you the most pleasure to look at?' I ask; another difficult question which results in much pondering.

'The restored Christchurch Town Hall and of course the Wellington Town Hall, and then there's the TVNZ building in Auckland and the New Zealand Embassy in Washington.'

Finally, I ask about the process of being knighted. How does it work?

'Well, one simply gets a letter from Government House asking would one accept a knighthood,' he answers. 'And the answer was "Yes, one would be delighted to accept it." But it was a complete surprise.'

Nowadays, Miles can often be found weeding somewhere in his magnificent gardens or guiding a tour party around. He is also one of the team rebuilding St Cuthbert's Church just around the corner in Governors Bay.

Inland Scenic Route 72

West Coast 73 ↑

Ashley Gorge
Lees Valley →

RIDING SOUTH: AN EX-COP, A PLANET EARTH GUIDE AND 'DUSTY DON'

'But you'll never see the end of the road while you're travelling with me.'

— Crowded House

The great Johnny Cash used to say 'the best part of a journey is the last mile before home'. But for me the opposite has always held true. The first few miles of a journey are always the best: almost a re-birth. Whatever your view, each stretch of tar-seal is a mini-adventure all its own. With optimism pulsing through me, I cruise out of Christchurch on empty roads and head north to Amberley early on an overcast Saturday morning. My cunning plan is to pick up the Inland Scenic Route and head south rather than endure the tedious sameness which is SH1 for the first 100 or so kilometres south of Christchurch. Also known as SH72, this 'themed' route stretches in a gentle sweep across the Canterbury Plains, the largest in the country.

Amberley in North Canterbury is an important service centre for the wealthy agricultural Hurunui district, and, interestingly, has one of the lowest concentrations of non-Pakeha in the country. It came into being in 1864 when a Mrs Carter subdivided her pastoral run and sold off quarter-acre lots at eight quid a piece. The town remained quiet until the railway arrived in 1876.

A couple of years ago, I suggested in *Bike Rider Magazine* that the route should perhaps be re-named the 'Canterbury Plains Highway' or the 'Foothills Freeway', or perhaps the 'Giant Moa Highway'. I'm still waiting to hear from Tourism New Zealand.

After passing over the Ashley River and winding through Rangiora, I enter the tiny village of Cust, formerly known as Moeraki Downs (nicer, I think). Cust was named after Sir Edward Cust, who, among other members of the Canterbury Association, organised the European settlement of the region in the mid-1800s. Between 1936 and 1963, with a break during the war, this sleepy little town played host to New Zealand's first motorcycle grand prix. This unique annual event took place on Easter Monday, with riders practising on the Saturday. A crowd of 6000 — with not a bare head among them, if the black-and-white photos are anything to go by — turned up at Easter 1936 to watch the 24 starters shoot away in clouds of dust. W. Nelson won that first race, roaring around the 152.5 miles (25 laps) of gravel road in 2 hours and 41 minutes. In 1950, 20,000 spectators witnessed riders reach 100 miles per hour on the front straight. That year, 3000 gallons of waste oil was sprayed onto the track in an effort to keep the dust down! The legendary Burt Munro came second in 1938, riding his Velocette, and competed here a total of six times.

I enjoy a hearty breakfast and the first coffee of the day, a palatable flat white in the Route 72 Café, while chatting to owner Annette, who along with partner Steve has owned the café and shop for 24 years. I can't find the grand prix memorial plaque, and the museum up the road is closed, so I must be content with the smell of cigarette smoke, hot pies and Castrol racing oil of yesteryear that my imagination supplies.

Back on the road with a full belly, it's not long before I hit Oxford. Advertised as the 'Best little town in New Zealand', Oxford is connected to Christchurch by Tram Road, which has the longest section of straight road in the country.

The Maori population has probably never been great on these plains. Land was purchased from them by well-to-do Englishmen under a scheme masterminded by Edward Wakefield in the mid-1800s. After the original First Four Ships colonised Lyttelton Harbour and then began the building of Christchurch on swampland, settlers started to spread west across the wild, featureless 'flats' to build their cob houses and plough up the tussocks. Apparently, these settlers were known as 'cockatoos', because they scratched around in the dirt for a while before moving on.

Patchworks of paddocks, sheep, cows and the ever-present, huge agricultural irrigators flash past. The land looks verdant and prosperous. At the evocatively named Windwhistle, which is only a small cluster of buildings, I have to smile as I feel Canterbury's famous nor'wester vibrate my visor. Next stop, Patagonia.

The approach to the picturesque Rakaia Gorge provides some welcome bends in the road. I pull over to admire the bridge, completed in 1882. Then enjoy the magic views up and down the mighty braided river as I sweep over the bridge and continue through Alford Forest and on to tiny Staveley. Early settlers in this area made their living as timber merchants, sawyers and mill workers, but by 1913 (before the notion of sustainability) the business was no longer viable, as most of the millable trees had been chopped down. This once-thriving community also had a coal mine and lime quarry, operated by the Christchurch Lime Company, which shut its doors in 1910.

As I pass through Mayfield, the 'long and winding' is just 'long'; straight as a ruler, like a miniature Meridian for the next 10 kilometres or so towards the Rangitata River. The spectacular upper reaches of this river were used as locations by Peter Jackson's *The Lord of the Rings*. It's just one of the many braided rivers I've ridden over today that make their way from the mighty Southern Alps to the sea, across the Canterbury Plains, which was created eons ago by the sedimentation from these shifting river systems. I now join SH77, which soon takes me over the much smaller Orari River and into Geraldine.

Geraldine is one of countless New Zealand rural towns that I could imagine living in. It looks like it should be in Surrey or Kent. It fits right into my 'Goldilocks Zone' theory of small towns: not too big and not too small. With a population of around 3500, it's home to an increasing number of artists and artisans, whose wares are on display in the main street, as well as several good eateries. There's a movie theatre, good coffee and a general 'feel good' vibe, which I soak up as I wander about with gaggles of Asian tourists to stretch my legs, finally fetching up at the farmers' market in the grounds of St Mary's Church.

A final short section of SH72 and the end of the Inland Scenic Route (Great Moa Highway?) takes me to Winchester and the dreaded SH1 (although, to be fair to New Zealand's 'mother road', it does improve as you head south from here).

I turn right onto SH8 just after Temuka, and 15 minutes of easy riding takes me to the very aptly named Pleasant Point and my destination. I've not time to ride the world-famous Ford Model T railway, nor visit the excellent Railway Museum. Instead, I pull up outside one of a collection of those fantastically iconic Kiwi baches to have a yarn with a real character.

NELLIGAN'S RAILWAY HOTEL.

MEALS & ACCOMMODATION

EX-COP — JIM SYKES

Jim ('or James or Jimmy, whichever you like') was exposed to bikes as a schoolboy, and remembers kids riding to St Bede's High School in Christchurch on Matchless 500 singles, while he was squirting around on his mate Steve's 175 Bantam. 'We thought we were kings!' he says with a chuckle. 'I remember once, after drinking sparkling wine, seven of us on a Vespa, riding around the park and hitting a tree. But nobody was hurt.'

His elder brother, Rennie, was a big influence. He took off up to the North Island at 16 or 17 riding an AJS, and when he returned bought himself a 1951 Triumph

Tiger 100 with a GP frame. It was this 500cc twin that Ted Simon famously rode around the world in 1973–77. Around 1971, young Jim bought the bike from Rennie and, he says, lighting up a Pall Mall as we sit on camp chairs in his shed, 'it all started from there, really, and bikes have been filtering through my life, as it were, ever since'.

He rode the now-chopped Tiger for quite a while, then travelled up to Upper Hutt to see a bloke called Sunshine, who rode a Norton Commando, and Rob Nesbit (RIP) aka Fat Chap. 'He was a wonderful bloke, and rode a 1970 Bonnie back then. But you didn't call him Fat Chap unless you knew him,' comes the sage advice. 'Anyway,' says Jim, 'I swapped the Tiger for a 1969 BSA Lightning, which I quickly put together, as it was in bits.'

Always slightly in awe of people who do this, I ask him if he's much of a mechanic. 'Oh, yeah,' he says, 'I don't mind building motors. It's a bit of fun.' When I tell him just how bad a mechanic I am, he says, 'There's nothing to them. It's just like a jigsaw puzzle; they're not complicated.' I look dubious.

At that time, Jim was a window dresser. 'Well, I went for a job as an electrician,' he says, 'but didn't get it, so my dad rang a family friend who was a window dresser and knew of an opening at Haywrights Department Store, so I started there. It was a great way to meet the ladies,' he says with a grin. 'Then I worked down the road at Hamilton Perry's, a subsidiary of Hamilton Jet, repairing stuff like the test boat where it had hit the rocks. It was there that I bought a '67 Tiger 100SS off a bloke, which I rode the absolute shit out of!'

Now 1973, back at Haywrights and flatting in Innes Road, Jim painted his bedroom matt black and had a bike in his room and two in the hall. Jimi Hendrix and Deep Purple blared into the street as his flatmate John worked on bikes in his garage at the front. 'The police would regularly pop round to check the engine numbers on the bikes. Eventually, the phone would ring and the police would say, "We're coming round. Put the kettle on and tie the dog up." But we had nothing to hide. We weren't hoons, we were just motorcycle enthusiasts. It was a mutual respect thing.'

Jim would ride the Tiger to work, sidle up between the cars by the clock tower on Montreal Street and wait for the lights to change. There was always a traffic-bike cop on a Yamaha XS650 waiting there. 'The lights would go green and I'd be gone!' laughs Jim. 'And he'd be furiously trying to start his bike to chase me. When the lights changed on Bealey Ave, I'd nail it, chuck it over and rip it up Springfield Road and disappear. This went on for over three months. He was always waiting for me at the same place.'

Then one afternoon after work the disgruntled traffic-bike cop was standing beside Jim's Tiger in the car park. 'He introduced himself,' says Jim, 'and said, "I really admire you, because you stop at every stop sign and every red light and I still can't bloody catch you!" Then we shook hands and away I went, zip-a-dee-doo-dah.'

Jim then had a stint of working at Ballantynes, riding to work in his greasy jeans and biker jacket and changing into a suit. 'Mark Ballantyne, who died recently, would greet me at the door, look at me and just grin.'

Interestingly, Jim tells me that in 1947 his dad was standing in the window of DIC Beaths, across the road from Ballantynes, when the big fire started. The heat just exploded the windows, and he watched people jumping to their deaths, trying to escape the flames.

In 1977, Jim travelled to Melbourne, where he bought a '73 Bonneville 750 for $900. 'I put high-level crossovers on it with Dunstall megaphones, made a toast-rack for it, put a 21-tooth sprocket on, and rode it across to Perth. I picked up a guy on a Honda 750 Four at a roadhouse somewhere, but he lasted only four hours before he gave up. Because of that 21-tooth sprocket, the Bonnie was hardly revving. It pulled like a young schoolboy! But, shit, it was stinking hot. Birds were literally falling out of the sky. I had a nose like a bloody reindeer.'

Jim sold the Bonnie in Perth, bought a 1977 3CL Laverda 1000 and shipped it back to New Zealand. 'It must have been made on the right day of the week,' Jim says, 'because it never broke down.' His claim to fame was that the Laverda did 100 miles per hour every day that he owned it, including down Barbadoes Street!

On another jaunt over to Melbourne, Jim bought a 1979 Harley Lowrider and shipped that home. Back in New Zealand, the Lowrider would always attract a crowd. As it turned out, it was one of only four 'big-block' Harleys in the South Island. Jim reckons that you couldn't ride behind him for more than 15 minutes because the noise was simply deafening!

One day, Jim and a bunch of mates decided to ride to Ruapuna to watch the races. Out of the blue Lindsay Williamson, who owned Christchurch Motorcycles at the time, said, 'Go on, boys: get out there on the track and have a go. It's OK, I've organised it.' So Jim and his brother Rennie took two big-block Harleys out on the track, did a few laps, had a blast and impressed Lindsay so much that he suggested they start a club and race in earnest.

'The Canterbury Motorcycle Club didn't want anything to do with us, because they said we leaked oil and were too slow, so it was decided that we would all meet at the Governors Bay Hotel the following Thursday night and sort something out,' says Jim. 'There was Lindsay and Jon White and his brother Dennis; about 26 of us at the pub,' continues Jim, as he brings in a chest of motorcycling memorabilia, full of BEARS T-shirts, caps, flags and stickers. 'So, cut a long story short,' he says, 'after a few beers Rennie says, "We need a President", and next thing you know I'm steering this thing.'

The next meeting is at the Corsair Motorcycle Clubhouse, where the lads are deep into their cups, trying to come up with a name. Joe Hannah, who'd had a few, holds up his can and yells 'BEERS!' Someone else yells, 'Yeah — British, European and American Racers.' They weren't sure about the 's', until someone piped up 'Supporters!' and they had 'BEARS'.

Jim was president for six years, and says he enjoyed every minute of it, and insists that it simply wouldn't have happened and been the success it was without their wives' and girlfriends' participation. 'We turned it into this great family-orientated club,' says Jim proudly.

In 1982 Jim met Lesley, the love of his life, and they shifted to Australia, where they set up in the beach suburb of Manly and Jim treated himself to an '83 commemorative Harley Sturgis. He reckons he was very fit in those days as he was always on the go, buying and selling furniture. He's had stints as an auto-wrecker, had a panel and paint business, and worked for a spell for Anglo America doing regional geochemistry and soil sampling in the Western Australia desert.

He also worked for a security specialist company in Sydney, where he did covert cash carry. This involved driving around in a little Barina picking up large amounts of cash in a backpack from places like Harvey Norman, often as much as $500,000, and delivering it to various banks. 'I had a beard down to my waist, and wore a domed shirt (for quick access) with a .357 Magnum underneath it,' he explains. 'I'd work all the bad-ass areas like Auburn, Liverpool, Parramatta and Bankstown.'

Jim was robbed only once. Even then, a sixth sense warned him of trouble as he noticed a dude loitering in the alley. He quickly stashed about $300,000 under the passenger seat, and put a bag of $800 in coins in the rear of the hatchback under a cargo cover. Back in the bank, he told his partner what he'd done. When they returned, the rear window was smashed and the coins were gone.

'So I called the cops, and when they arrived I had my report all written down, ready, with the robber's description, everything. "Oh, you bewdy!" said one of the cops. It was an exact match from another description.'

After a while a young colleague suggested that Jim join the NSW Police. Thinking he was too old at 49, he applied anyway, and 'before you knew it, I was down in Goulburn, training at the Police Academy. There were 1265 of us on the first day, and next morning there were half that number remaining.'

Jim spent 12 years in the police force, working the beat in Manly for five years, before becoming a weapons instructor. 'I had a lot of fun. It was probably the best job I ever had,' says Jim. 'The power's all yours — you have to use it fairly and justly. I could draw and fire two rounds from my Glock 40-cal. in under two seconds.'

'Shit,' I say, 'that's faster than the outlaw Josey Wales!' and we both laugh.

EX-COP — JIM SYKES   63

As I sit here with my coffee in Fairlie with my notebook and pen, in sight of my bike at the kerb, you could say I'm totally sorted, even gruntled (I'm sure that's a word!). I should be working on my last interview, but I can't resist dipping into the book I'm currently enjoying: *M Train* by Patti Smith. (See, Karen? I *can* read female authors.) Much of this quirky book has the author simply sitting at her favourite table in a coffee shop, doodling her musings onto napkins and reminiscing. Strange woman.

I've always been an obsessive devourer of books. But, as with movies, I find I'm getting fussier these days, and if I'm not enjoying it after 10 pages I'll stop. At school I always carried a paperback in my blazer pocket, sci-fi mostly, to dip into like a guilty pleasure. I became quite adept at dodging the blackboard eraser as it whistled by my head: 'Lockyer, put that book away!' In French, kids were not game to sit directly behind me. I recall how my dad would come home drunk as a skunk after an afternoon session down the boozer. My mum would be doing her best to placate his rising temper as he paused in the hallway. He'd demand: 'Where's Georgie? Probably with his 'ead stuck in a book. Bleedin' bookworm!' As though that was the worst insult he could imagine. My dad wasn't a very nice man, but I'm grateful in a way, as he gave me the incentive and desire to leave our west London council estate and see the world. I'm reminded of when the Dalai Lama was asked who his greatest teacher was, and him replying, 'Mao Tse-tong, because he taught me patience.'

I always try to have a book on the go. Without one I feel as though I'm not whole, naked, almost panicky. I also loved (and still do) to read an atlas. As a kid, I could read an atlas like others read novels, plotting my escape, dreaming of adventure. The first little globe I saved up for with my paper-round money was like a treasure to me, like some religious artefact. I feel sorry for people who don't read. They're missing out on so much.

I overtake a couple of coaches along the tree-lined route out of Fairlie, then stop at Burkes Pass for some pictures of touristy automotive stuff. The wind is getting up, and it's quite blustery as I make my way over the actual pass and onto the flat stuff.

As I mentioned earlier, the Mackenzie Country got its name from James (Jock) McKenzie, a Scot who emigrated to Australia, before crossing the ditch and being caught red-handed rustling a flock of 1000 sheep in 1885. His sheepdog Friday was reputed to be able to move the entire flock on his own. There is a plaque telling of his exploits at the pass that also bears his name just south of Burkes Pass.

No attempt was made to take up land in the Mackenzie until 1856, when 10,000 acres were awarded to a Francis Sinclair. After M. J. Burke discovered the pass that now bears his name in 1857, there followed an explosion of settlers, and vast areas of this inland plain were applied for. Mainly from Yorkshiremen, followed on their heels by the canny Scots, with their expertise in all things sheepish.

One of the attractions of long rides is the opportunity to give your imagination a bit of a workout. In our frenetic, First-World, twenty-first-century life, time to reflect is a rare commodity. Nowadays even a spare 10 minutes is to be taken up with furiously tapping away on an iPhone or laptop. What is it we are so afraid of missing out on, I wonder? The other thing I'm wondering is how long I can stand the exquisite torture of the tenacious flying insect that's found its way inside my right ear. Not long, it seems. I pull over, and it's all I can do not to skid to a halt as I rip off gloves and helmet and wriggle my pinky inside my ear ecstatically.

As I press on through this huge landscape, harried by wind gusts and agitated by bad rental-car drivers, more controversy rages. Moves are afoot to transform the brown into green and replace huge areas of tussock with dairy cows. Up to 15,000 cows have been suggested, most of them housed indoors for up to nine months of the year. On the other hand, DOC is proposing the establishment of a 30,000-hectare Mackenzie Basin Drylands Park, which is obviously clashing with the farmers' plans.

I pull over at Lake Tekapo, stretch my legs and get a picture of the bronze statue of a collie that stands sentinel over the lake. Unveiled in 1968, the plaque beneath it sums up the runholders' appreciation of the collie dog, 'without the help of which the grazing of this mountain country would be impossible'.

Just around the lake a tad lies the famous Church of the Good Shepherd, popular with tourists (there must be millions of photos of it in albums around the world) and built from local stone as a monument to the Mackenzie pioneers.

Over eons, advancing and retreating glaciers have carved this tussock grassland into the magnificent and iconic chunk of Kiwiana that we enjoy today. The great Mackenzie Basin contains, among others, the lakes Pukaki, Tekapo and Ohau, which flow into the mighty Waitaki River. In the background is, of course, the Main Divide, featuring Aoraki/Mount Cook.

Surely the emotional power of this Big Sky Country will eventually win out over temporary economic gain of dairy farming, I think to myself as I wend my way across the plain. The wind buffets me, I round a bend — well, a curve really — and a hawk flaps awkwardly into the air with half a road-killed rabbit in its talons. Lupins add a splash of colour to the dun landscape, and are popular with photographers, me included, but also another cause for controversy. Originally from northwest America, lupins are one of DOC's pet hates, and it spends a lot of money trying to eradicate them. Unfortunately, lupins are able to cope with the layer of aluminium that runs through some areas of the Mackenzie, and flourish in this harsh landscape.

I'm now in the World Heritage Starlight Reserve, which protects the clear sky above Tekapo for the astronomers at nearby Mount John Observatory, 300 metres above sea level. The popularity and growth of Tekapo is worrying astronomers, as increasing light from the growing village threatens to ruin its clear-sky reputation. Council ordinances are in place to protect against future light pollution. There is talk of turning this road into another themed highway from Fairlie to Twizel, and calling it the Starlight Highway, which I'm all for.

Back on SH8, under the huge sky I reach Lake Pukaki, and, no matter how many times you ride here, the first glimpse as you come around the bend of the aquamarine blue never ceases to impress. On a clear day, Aoraki/Mount Cook can be seen in all its glory at the top of the lake, but not today. I pull into Twizel to fuel up. Twizel is the closest town to Aoraki/Mount Cook and the adventure capital of the Mackenzie Basin. It started life in 1968 as a hydro town for workers on the Upper Waitaki Power Scheme. The plan was to bulldoze the town once the scheme was completed in 1983, but residents rather liked living here and lobbied the government, and 'The Town of Trees' was born.

Leaving Twizel and heading past Lake Ruataniwha, it's plain that the landscape is rapidly changing. I ride alongside an enormous irrigator, which must be a kilometre long. Behind it, cows graze peacefully on green grass which was brown tussock not long ago. But change is inevitable and, as they say, is the only thing, apart from death and taxes, we can really rely on.

Centuries ago, giant moa would have grazed where these cattle graze today. I imagine them striding along like oversized emu beside my speeding motorcycle. It's believed that the largest species, the 10-foot-tall *Dinornis maximus*, was hunted to extinction way before Pakeha landed on these shores.

Crossing over the canal that runs out of manmade Lake Ruataniwha, I bid farewell to South Canterbury. I'm soon as snug as a bug in my little cabin in Omarama's Top Ten campsite, and, after a quick pint to settle the dust in the strangely named Boots and Jandals Hotel, I hit the hay. As I drift off I wonder, not for the first time, where the day has gone. Another revolution of the Earth, another one of my remaining number ticked off. Mounting chronology. God, I can depress myself.

There are some days when you appreciate waking up and realising you are still alive more than others. And today is such a day. I'm nursing a flat white and watching Omarama wake up. A steady stream of customers enters the café: farmers in gummies and shorts, Asian tourists looking concerned and dressed for the Arctic, and a rep in a suit and a tie. A small Live Jucy camper van, with *Don't play hard to get. Be hard to forget* painted on it, pulls up as I start the Triumph and put my helmet on. I only need to ride a couple of k's down the road to where Gavin is waiting in his beautiful house.

PLANET EARTH GUIDE — GAVIN WILLS

Gavin Wills, a youthful-looking man of almost 70 years, is sitting with a coffee, gazing out at the skyscape. As the owner of the nearby Glide Omarama Soaring School, studying the weather and cloud formations is vital to his business. He tells me that some gliders have already launched this morning, and are attempting to glide to Napier and back! 'My first gliding flight was in 1955, when I was seven,' he begins, 'with my younger brother sitting on my knee.'

Changing tack, I ask him how he got into mountaineering. 'That was a long time ago. Well, my mother was a keen climber and my father had a farm in the Mackenzie Country, so growing up in the area I was exposed to the outdoors from an early age. At school, instead of playing cricket I was into Outward Bound activities, which took me into mountaineering instructing and eventually guiding at Mount Cook.' His father was into flying and gliding, so it was almost inevitable that Gavin followed suit, getting his pilot's licence in 1972. He's basically been a mountaineering, skiing, rafting and gliding guide all his life. 'I suppose you could call me a guide on planet Earth,' he says.

As a guide, he's climbed Mount Cook 13 times (the last time in 1983), but points out that a fellow by the name of Sean Norman in Twizel holds the record with 36 or 37 summits of this very dangerous mountain that has claimed so many lives.

'We lived at The Hermitage for about 12 years, in the old mountain guide's house. It started out with three or four of us in the business, and ended with about 24 mountain guides,' he says. 'And in the winter we did helicopter skiing — the first in New Zealand. We even had a rafting business for a while, floating people down the very cold Tasman River.'

If that wasn't enough, while at Mount Cook Gavin also owned a couple of gliders and formed a small club. 'I have this terrible habit of turning my recreation into my job,' he laughs.

As a heli-skiing pioneer he was constantly discovering new places to ski. 'It's potentially very dangerous, with the risk of avalanches,' he says, which I suspect is something of an understatement. Gavin was the first in New Zealand to use explosives from the air to control avalanches. I try to picture the scene: Gavin flying his small plane 40 feet above the snow, while his mate behind uses a match to light the 18 inches of cordite fuse attached to some TNT, bound together with tape. The cockpit fills with cordite smoke as he opens the window and chucks it out …

While at university in the 1960s, he worked part-time for Alpine Instruction Ltd at Mount Cook. After becoming a geologist, Gavin worked in Indonesia and Western Australia. 'While in WA in 1972,' he says, 'I invested in the mining market, and through good luck made enough money to return to New Zealand and buy an aeroplane.' And he still owns the 180-horsepower, three-seater Piper Cub today, and uses it in the business. That same year he took over the guiding business at Mount Cook, now Alpine Guides (Mount Cook) Ltd, which he ran for 12 years.

'I then went to the US for a six-month trip, and ended up motoring around in a VW Kombi for two and half years with my first wife and two kids,' says Gavin, 'working at ski resorts in the winter, and in the spring we'd run rivers in Utah, and then Alaska in the summer.'

Later he started a heli-skiing business in Colorado, which he sold at the end of the 1980s, only to return home and work as a freelance guide, organising treks in the Himalayas and Europe. And if that wasn't enough for any one lifetime, Gavin then travelled the world for three years in the employ of a Frenchman, sussing out places to take him heli-skiing, and doing Adventure Races in various countries. Oh, and did I mention running the avalanche programme on the Milford Road, which involved throwing *really* big bombs out of helicopters? 'The bureaucracy drove me nuts in the end,' he says, shaking his head.

He has been involved in the gliding school at Omarama since 1998, when he lived on the airfield in a cabin he built. 'It's a difficult business,' he points out. 'You have only one passenger, who needs an instructor and a plane to tow it up, so it needs a lot of equipment. It's much easier to put six people on a helicopter and take them all up at once. We specialise in longer flights. Some outfits take you up for only 10 minutes, but we try to show people what cross-country gliding is all about, taking them up for a couple of hours. Going places in an aeroplane with no engine is really fun!' The two-seater gliders made of carbon fibre and Kevlar have a wing span of 20 metres, and are sophisticated machines. At $250,000, they cost more than a small plane.

    Gavin's wife, Mandy, calls us up to the table for eggs (laid that morning) and bacon, which we eat as we carry on talking. I steer Gavin back onto mountaineering, and ask about any hairy moments he's had. 'God, where do I start?' he says. 'One time I was coming off Mount Dixon with two American astronomers. We were making our way along this narrow ridge with the idea that if someone fell one way, I'd jump the other way. Well, the guy's big, wide hat blew off his head, so I, thinking he'd fallen, jumped the other way. Here, he's hanging over one side, his wife's in the middle, and I'm hanging over the other side with a thousand-foot drop below me …'

    He sips his coffee, thinking, then continues: 'Back in 1973, I was working with Mike Firth, a New Zealand film producer, and a small group of skiers, making a documentary at Mount Cook. On the first day's filming, we were skiing down the Murchison Glacier, and he was filming on very short skis for manoeuvrability. The Murchison head wall is quite a steep slope with fresh snow on it. I went down the slope a little way, and called him to the edge so he could spot me. As he came to the edge, the whole 800-foot slope avalanched in a big slab. I managed to get rid of my skis and slow myself up with my poles, jumped over a couple of ice cliffs and things, and ended up at the bottom at the back of the debris. Mike and the rest of the gang skied down to me and asked if I was OK. "I seem to be," I replied. I was buried up to my waist, one ski was stuck in the snow above me and one below, and I had hold of both my poles. So, I said, "We'll carry on then, shall we?"'

Later Gavin had to rescue Mike, who fell into a 'slot' and was stuck, hanging over a crevasse by his arms and shoulders. That was the first day's filming of the movie *Off the Edge*, which became the most successful New Zealand movie of the 1970s and was nominated for an Academy Award for the Best Documentary Feature of 1976.

Gavin and Mandy are regular visitors to the States, as the gliding season ends here in the winter. They have only recently returned from six weeks of gliding and tramping in the mountains of Idaho and Wyoming. For many years, they have been heading Stateside, running a gliding school, lecturing and teaching. 'But,' Gavin says, 'we're trying to retire, and when I started growing feathers under my arms, it was time to stop.'

'Life is a lot more relaxed than it was 10 years ago,' adds Mandy, 'when I would be in the office doing the accounts, and Gavin would be manager and head pilot, seven days a week.' Today, 12 pilots are employed, who, Gavin reckons, 'are all trying to break my equipment'.

My last question for the planet Earth guide is: 'When are you going to write your memoirs?'

Two hours later I'm strapped into the front of a glider, with Gavin behind me. 'You're in the hands of the master,' says the young man who hooks us up to the plane. Towed along the grass runway, we are soon in the air, and Gavin releases our tether, before expertly riding the atmospheric waves up to calmer altitudes. I have a sick bag tucked behind my parachute strap, but thankfully I don't need it.

'It's like surfing,' Gavin says, as we swoop towards Lake Pukaki and I imagine me on my Triumph down there yesterday about the size of an ant. It's an amazing experience as we rise to cooler air at 22,000 feet and hover over Mount Cook. Entranced, I gaze down on an uncorrupted landscape of rock, snow and ice.

Below us now is the Tasman Glacier Lake, with chunks of dirty ice floating on it. 'That lake wasn't there when I started gliding,' says my pilot. The views are breathtaking. I can see all the way to Christchurch's Port Hills. Two hours disappear in a blink, and before I know it we are back on the ground without a bump. I thank Gavin for my OMG experience, and, still buzzing, mount up and head for Wanaka.

You really wouldn't be dead for quids, I think, as Omarama recedes in my mirrors, for I now have one of my favourite rides ahead on SH8: the gently winding 80 kilometres that is the Lindis Pass. My theory is that whoever engineered this road also rode a motorcycle. The pass links the alpine scenery of the Mackenzie Country to the dramatic landscape of Otago.

I had been warned to expect strong winds, gale force at times, and it's not long before I realise the truth of this, as I am almost blown off the road and must slow down. I read somewhere that the answer to strong wind is more speed, but I think I'll trust my instincts. It doesn't diminish my enjoyment of this fabulous road, though, which follows the Lindis River, and the landscape gradually changes from green to the brown of dry tussock as it climbs to the pass at 965 metres. The Lindis Pass Scenic Reserve was formed 40 years ago, and is one of New Zealand's first tussock reserves. At the risk of sounding like a tourist brochure, it's just a gorgeous, empty landscape.

At the tiny settlement of Tarras, I reluctantly stop for coffee and a bite. Tarras is the self-proclaimed home (so it says outside the shop) of the famous Merino wether, Shrek, from nearby Bendigo Station. He managed to evade the muster and the ignominy of shearing for six years. When he was finally caught in 2004, his fleece weighed 27 kilograms, compared to the Merino average of 4.5 kilograms.

The wind is still howling as I turn right just after Tarras, follow the Clutha River on SH8A, before joining SH6 for the short run into Wanaka. I park the bike on the lake shore and sit on a bench, with the wind roaring down the lake, blowing people's hats off. Nobody is game enough to swim today, as the surf is up and the boats bob about alarmingly.

Wanaka's setting is spectacular. With its sunny climate, proximity to skiing, wineries and Mount Aspiring National Park, and obviously its water sports, it is no surprise that its popularity is growing. Residents enjoy one of the lowest unemployment rates in the country, and are among the best educated. Wanaka really took off with the building of the Haast Pass Road in 1965. The road follows the path to the West Coast that Maori war parties used many years ago.

I retreat from the wind with a good long black, before riding the short distance to where Don is waiting.

'DUSTY DON' — DONALD PANNETT

Like many Kiwis, Don cut his teeth riding a little Mountain Goat dirt bike around the farm in Heriot, West Otago, where he grew up. 'I'd ride up the hill and slide off the seat at the back, because there was nothing to hold you on,' he says as we sit in the kitchen at the new, biker-friendly West Meadows Motel in Wanaka. Don and his wife, Fay, have kindly invited me to share dinner with them. The motel has been open for business for only a couple of months. 'We always had bikes when I was young, but Dad wouldn't allow me on the road with one after he'd seen this bad accident,' begins Don between mouthfuls.

After riding bikes off-road for years doing organised trail rides, Don finally made it onto the road with a green KLR250. 'And it just grew from there,' he says. 'Bikes have been a passion for a long, long time. I used to be glued to all the Superbike races overseas; I was a big fan of Aaron Slight. When I lived in Cromwell, I'd ride the Nevis Valley and Thompson's Track and all those places, but tar-sealed roads never did it for me; I always preferred the gravel.'

When Don shifted to Christchurch, he met the late Mike Hyde (long-distance rider and author of the *Twisting Throttle* series of books). Along with Gavin Sargent and Bill Rodgers, the four of them formed the informal bike club, The Dust Devils, where he picked up the name 'Dusty Don'. As membership grew, the scope of their trips gradually increased, until they were touring around the North Island. Don, first on a Kawasaki KLR650 and then on a KTM 950, spent a lot of time with Mike, and they became close friends.

Don was, like me, inspired by Ted Simon's wonderful 1970s book *Jupiter's Travels*, an account of Ted's four-year odyssey around the world. 'I read that book, and then Mike did his first overseas trip and I wanted to get on my bike and *just go!*' says Don. 'Then a character called Rob West, who rode his bike from the UK to New Zealand and also did the Pan American in the 1990s, joined The Dust Devils, and he was another inspiration. He didn't own a car and would ride his bike come rain or shine.'

Dinner finished, we move to the lounge, and Don continues: 'My ancestors came out here on the first boats, so I suppose there was this thing in me that just wanted to travel and explore.'

Don, I discover, is a shrewd businessman with a wealth of experience. 'I was basically a sheep farmer until I was 40,' Don says. 'I did high-country mustering with 10,000 sheep up near Saint Bathans for a few years, then went back to the family farm. Then the dairy guys moved in, so I moved out and bought motels in Cromwell and then Christchurch. After selling those, I bought a manufacturing business, making chefs' clothes and supplying to the polytechnics.' Don is a very modest chap. I gradually prise out of him the fact that he was the designer and pattern-cutter for the uniforms of famous Kiwi celebrity chef Simon Gault. It also transpires that Don manages Scott Base, a vineyard in Cromwell belonging to famous vintner Allan Scott. And they won Gold in the 2016 Air New Zealand Wine Awards for their Scott Base Pinot Noir.

One day, Don said to himself, 'That's it — I'm doing it!' He sold his business and started planning his big bike trip. Meanwhile, Avon City Suzuki in Christchurch started up, and got in Don and his mate Phil Parish, who was a mechanic, to get things cracking. 'They basically said, "Here's the building, and here are the bikes in crates. Make it happen." I told them I was off overseas in 12 months' time. So, after we got the Suzuki shop up and running in 2009, I took the bull by the horns, bought a KTM 990, put it in a crate, shipped it to Valparaiso in Chile, and flew over there and started living my dream.'

Don rode down to Ushuaia in Tierra del Fuego at the tip of South America, where he says he was so overcome with emotion that he cried beneath the sign. 'Then I turned the bike around and rode up through Argentina, crossed the Andes a couple of times, through Peru, Bolivia, Ecuador and all around Colombia, which was amazing.'

In Bogotá, Don put the KTM on a plane and flew it to Panama City, from where he continued his ride north through Costa Rica, Nicaragua, Honduras, El Salvador, Belize and Guatemala. Into Mexico, he then went around the Yucatan Peninsula, and up Baja into the United States. He reckons he started off with way too much gear, and shipped a lot of it home. There wasn't much need for camping gear, as hotels were pretty cheap. I must take my hat off to Don, because, prior to his big trip, he hadn't travelled overseas at all! 'You certainly threw yourself into the frying pan,' I say. He taught himself a bit of Spanish before heading off, and says he could ask for the essentials like beer, food, petrol and a bed.

'I rode all the west coast and the mid states, then up through Canada, into Alaska and right up to Prudhoe Bay, staying off the tar-seal as much as I could.' I ask if he got emotional again in the Arctic. 'Of course,' he laughs. 'You know, George, I did 65,000 k's, and the only time the KTM let me down was with bad fuel in Peru. I had to pull the tank and fuel pump off on the side of the road and clean them out. I never fell off once. I had issues with corrupt cops and "tourist tax", though. You come to rely on your bike so much that it kind of becomes a part of you. Anyway, I rode it back to LA and shipped it home.'

When Don was in Canada, Avon Suzuki rang him and asked him whether he would manage the dealership upon his return, which he did.

'It was a life-changing experience,' he continues. 'I met some wonderful people who I'll keep in contact with. You come back and it changes you, big time.' I ask, in what way. 'You realise that you live in a pretty good spot and you appreciate it more. You stop worrying about the little stuff that goes on here.'

Fay loves riding pillion, and the couple often fire up the KTM and head off together. But with the new motel, they don't get as much spare time as they'd like, although they recently rode around the North Island for three weeks. Don is a keen photographer, and we share the same problem of always wanting to have our bike in the photo! 'And I was very fortunate to have had that time with Mike [Hyde] when I rode around with him on the North Island leg of *Twisting Throttle New Zealand*, taking photos.'

Donald, much like myself, isn't a big fan of rallies or riding in groups, but prefers to just get out by himself (or with Fay) into the hills and explore new country. In a couple of years' time, he plans to do another big trip, this time with Fay on the back of the KTM. 'I enjoyed Canada so much last time,' says Don, 'that I want to go back there and around Alaska and back to Argentina, which I loved.'

I take my leave of Don and Fay, and retire to the luxuriously-appointed motel room they have generously let me use. I'm busy typing up my notes on the laptop and keeping an eye on the TV, where India are beating England at cricket, when there is a knock on the door and there's Don. He apologises for disturbing me, and then tells me about his most spiritual moment, which Fay told him he hadn't mentioned!

While on a 10-day hunting trip to Stewart Island with his son, he stumbled upon a partly-buried Maori adze. He and his son admired it, and then reverently put it back where they'd found it. Back in civilisation, Don informed DOC, who insisted that they go back with him to find it again. 'I didn't think I'd ever be able to find it again, but it was uncanny; almost like it wanted to be found; like it was calling to me. I led the DOC guy straight back to it, with a Maori representative who performed a small ceremony to lift the tapu. When it was finally dated,' says Don, 'they discovered that it was over 800 years old.' What a great story.

THE HOUSE OF
SHREK
THE WORLD'S MOST FAMOUS SHEEP

THE DEEP SOUTH: A TUATAPERE RESIDENT, A MOONSHINER, A RESTAURATEUR AND AN ALL BLACKS ASSISTANT COACH

'Ride like the one-eyed jack of diamonds with the Devil close behind — we're gonna ride.'

— The Highwaymen

I awake and look out the window. Sun and no wind. Great. The view across to Mount Iron framed by the window is like a giant watercolour. Returning to bed with a coffee (it's instant, but beggars can't be choosers), I watch the *BBC News* for a bit: more bombing in Syria, and President Elect Trump upsetting China and the CIA. It really is luxury accommodation, and I thank Don profusely as I head off on another classic motoring road: over the Crown Range. Despite it being summer, it's cold, and I switch on my heated handlebar grips.

I follow the Cardrona River on an empty road past the turnoff to the Cardrona Ski Field on my right. My wife and kids love skiing and are quite good at it. I, however, am rubbish. And it's not through want of trying. Last time I was dragged up the slopes I had a lesson, and because it was a weekday I had the instructor all to myself. She was a cute-as-a-button, little French student, whose patience was amazing. I came within a whisker of wiping her out a few times, and ended up in a tangle of limbs quite often, with her concerned face peering down at me. At lesson's end, she gave me the most endearingly sympathetic look, and said in her fabulous accent: 'George, I 'ope you don't mind me asking, but 'ave you got — 'ow you say? — an artificial leg?'

I feel compelled to pull over at the iconic Cardrona Hotel for some photos and to stamp around and warm up. The hotel was established in the 1860s as part of the gold-rush town. The area of Cardrona was named by a J. T. Thomson after the Scottish village of the same name. I pull over again just up the road to take a photo of hundreds of bras hanging along a fence — then feel guilty as I don't have a coin to put in the donation box for the New Zealand Breast Cancer Foundation.

The road now passing beneath my Metzelers is in fact the highest tarmac road in the land, and wasn't sealed until 2000. The first Europeans to cross the pass (1076 metres) were W. G. Rees and N. von Tunzelmann in 1860, while they were on the hunt for fresh sheep pasture. Three years later, hundreds of gold-seekers flocked to the Skippers and Arrow diggings via this new route.

I descend, still cold, via some very tight twisties, on to SH6, then at Frankton, with The Remarkables rising up on my left, I forsake the dubious pleasures of Queenstown and open up the Bonneville along the fast road that hugs the side of Lake Wakatipu. I'm having fun now, despite the cold and the threat of rain, for I know that coffee and breakfast await me in the Kingston Corner Café.

The talkative lady inside says she's not surprised I'm cold, because they've just had a fresh dump of snow on the tops. A good plain bacon, eggs and toast hits the

THE DEEP SOUTH 85

spot nicely, but who thought it was a good idea to have moronic commercial radio (my God, those ads!) blaring into customers' ears?

Re-energised, I ride down to see if the Kingston Flyer is in. 'She hasn't been running for a couple of years, mate,' an old bloke walking his dog tells me. The vintage steam train used to operate for tourists on 14 kilometres of preserved track, and was quite a sight with a full head of steam. I've a good distance to cover today and must get a wriggle-on. It still hasn't warmed up as I follow the Mataura River and pass through the small settlements of Garston and Athol before stopping in Lumsden.

Lumsden used to be a major railway junction, with lines radiating to all four points of the compass. The last line, down to Invercargill, closed in 1982. The town has a nice feel to it, nestled as it is amongst tidy, patterned fields and green hills. It would be rude of me not to have a quick flat white in the cool-looking Route 6 Café.

More straight tarmac now, following the Oreti River with the Hokonui Hills on my left. Riding gives you time to think. I read recently that a Kiwi-born philosophy professor in England has been setting up two deck-chairs outside 'stupid places', like the London Stock Exchange or outside a bank, inviting scurrying commuters to sit with him in silence and just think. He calls it 'Pop-up Philosophy', saying, 'People used to have a smoke, look up at the sky and have a think, but nowadays as soon as you get a spare minute you're tapping away on your phone.'

Through Winton and now on the outskirts of Invercargill, I turn right on SH99 and purr through Riverton/Aparima, the 'Riviera of the South' and one of my favourite little spots. Another one of those funky, 'feel good' little towns, it is regarded as the oldest European settlement in Southland, and was a base for whalers and sealers in the early 1800s. It also has an excellent Early Settlers Museum, as well as safe beaches and great fishing in the sheltered estuary. Duck shooting is also popular, as the many maimai that line the estuary shore attest to.

Just past Orepuki, I pass Gemstone Beach, so-named because of the semi-precious gems, such as nephrite, garnet and quartz, that can be found here. The wide Te Waewae Bay is popular with surfers, but you'd have to be a brave soul to be out there today! In Tuatapere I park my Triumph in the driveway of my next Kiwi character, who I hope has the kettle on …

TUATAPERE RESIDENT — NGARITA DIXON

'I haven't exactly moved far in my life,' begins Ngarita. We're sitting in her living room, sipping tea from her best china. 'My parents lived just next door,' she gestures out the window, 'and I was born there back in 1928.'

She went to boarding school in Oamaru, and says it did her the world of good, as it showed her that there was more to life than just a small country town. There were regular air drills, and slit trenches dug in a pine plantation above Oamaru.

Ngarita says that the sense of danger from Japanese invasion was very real. 'When the siren went, we had to race up to the trenches with an old coat to lie on and a peg to put between our teeth for when the bombs fell. Then the war ended, Bill came home, I married him and we went to Dean Forest.' She laughs. 'I was one those young brides, George. Today they just don't do that, and I think they're making a mistake! These days, parents are too old, they leave it too long. I heard of some woman having a baby at 50, which is crazy. My parents had kids in their late thirties, and they were considered elderly. I remember going out and being a partner with my mother at bridge.'

Ngarita's parents grew up with a Depression mentality, which she says she inherited. 'If you can't afford it,' she says, 'then don't buy it. There were people in the Depression who were on their third and fourth mortgage and they lost everything. Even at school, it was drummed into us: "Don't get hire purchase."'

Her husband never wanted to go back overseas after spending five and a half years in the war. 'Bill always said he had a good war,' she says. 'He was sawmilling the whole time, and never shot a bullet in anger, although he did go to Egypt.' Bill always looked at a tree and thought what he could get out of it, yet he told Ngarita that he regretted cutting down those magnificent oaks in Wales, but it was essential to fix up the bombed railways in England.

Bill was a sawmiller, so the newlyweds had to go to Dean Forest for work, where a sawmill had been operating since the early 1920s. There was no power at the mill, as it would have cost £300 to put it on; a small fortune back then. 'My mother had all the mod cons, like an electric range and things like that, so it was a bit of shock moving there,' she says. 'I had to get used to a coal range with a mind of its own. If it didn't want to go, then it wouldn't go, and it would sulk!' There was one telephone in the office and one in Bill Mackenzie's house, with 14 people on the party line. You had to ring your order in to the grocer and the butcher, who would bring your produce out to you. 'It worked out cheaper in the long run than shopping in town,' remembers Ngarita, 'because you only ordered the essentials over the phone.'

The men worked hard at the mill, using huge cross-cut saws. They worked under a state forest licence, seven days a week, with Saturday and Sunday reserved for carrying out repairs on the equipment. Trees to be felled were marked by the state, and the loggers had to take them. Ngarita's husband, along with his two brothers, felled virgin, native forest trees such as totara, rimu and beech. 'The mill ran on a Gardner diesel engine,' says Ngarita, 'with these big flapping belts from pulley to pulley. They used horses in the thick bush to drag out the logs, then onto a locie running on a line they'd built, up to the mill. And when you'd cleared your block out, you had to shift the mill and move on.'

I ask her about the size of these bush mills. 'Well, while they were in Dean Forest, they built a tennis court, a community hall and about 20 houses. It takes a lot of people to run a sawmill: you've got men in the yard stacking the timber, people in the bush sawing it, and men in the bush cutting it down. And, of course, there were the workers' families.' If you went to the site now, you'd find two concrete slabs surrounded by farmland: one where the Gardner sat and one where the mill sat.

So after seven years in the bush (where Ngarita's first child was born), they moved back to Tuatapere. The three Dixon brothers joined forces with the three Evans brothers, who were in financial difficulty building a mill in town, and started milling under the name Lindsay and Dixon.

Tuatapere would have been a real frontier town back in Ngarita's childhood. 'Well, there were no concrete footpaths and no streetlights. It was a two-hour trip to Invercargill, so we used to shop here. There were two picture theatres and five menswear stores. There's a standing joke around here that we didn't go to dances in Orepuki because it was too far at 15 kilometres, but nowadays people go to Christchurch for a pie!'

On Friday nights, everyone would get dressed up and go down the town. Ngarita's father was a baker and owned the tea-rooms with his brother, and people would go there for supper after the pictures or shopping. 'And of course there were the hornybugs,' she says. 'I was terrified of them as a child. They were over two inches long and were attracted to the light. Horrible things.'

Today, the Lindsay and Dixon sawmill, which I rode past on the way in, employs 40 people and mills mainly maple beech from seven blocks in the Longwood and

Rowallan Forests. They are justifiably proud of their sustainable-management principles, with a yield extraction rate of 1.8 per cent, compared to the international average of around 10 per cent.

In its heyday, Tuatapere's population nudged 1000, with 30 mills in the area, but today it's around 550 and is typical of many small towns around the country. 'When the forestry finished, the families left,' says Ngarita. 'And they were the mainstay of the community; the club presidents, secretaries and treasurers, you know.'

It's thirsty work, and Ngarita makes us another cuppa. 'I think my biggest regret,' she talks from the kitchen, 'is that the government never picked up on the idea that we could regenerate beech. They thought that 90 years was too long a period. The Forest Service proved that it could be done, and it would have kept people here. I could have taken you into one of the blocks and you wouldn't have known if you were in a pristine forest or a regrown one. Instead of importing and planting pines and eucalypts, we could have been harvesting native timber down here.' This is a subject that Ngarita is obviously passionate about. 'The beech come up like a paddock of oats when they are seeding,' she continues, 'and when they are thinned out they don't have to compete, and you get a straighter tree and a better tree.'

Ngarita has been involved with work development organisations in getting politicians to come to Tuatapere to listen to these suggestions, 'but when they get back to Wellington, they just ask their taxi driver what he thinks and that's that'. She has also contributed to *The Hole in the Bush*, a history of the area compiled by Des Williams for the local school's centenary in 2009.

Ngarita says the exact date of the book has slipped her memory because she's off out tonight and is a bit distracted. 'I always go out for tea on Wednesday nights with my friend who won't cook. We go to the hotel and have beautiful fish.'

I ask her whether she's got any old photos, and she gets up and beckons me to follow her to another room. 'I haven't got many, because I'm terrible at taking photos — I shake,' she says. 'We had a box Brownie but people didn't take many pictures like they do today, because it was so expensive.'

Ngarita has worked tirelessly for the community for many years in a variety of capacities, and for several organisations, to try to boost the profile of Tuatapere and Western Southland and raise money for local charities.

She is chairperson to several committees: the Amenities Trust, the Dr Eric Elder Bursary Trust, Tuatapere and District Promotions Inc and the Waiau Memorial Library. She is also a member of the Tuatapere Community Medical Trust.

'It seems that the rest of New Zealand ignores this triangle, from Te Anau down to Invercargill,' she sighs. 'They think we've got nothing, but we think we have some of the best views in the world.'

Among a host of other things, she and the promotions group have been involved in the Southern Scenic Route, The Hump Ridge Track and making Tuatapere 'The Sausage Capital of New Zealand'.

In 1998, Ngarita became a justice of the peace, and a year later she was awarded the Queen's Service Order. 'All the family travelled up to Government House in Wellington,' she says. 'It was very well arranged; there was no stepping out of line.'

It's time to go. I leave this charming and modest lady to prune her roses. 'Now don't go making me out to be anything special,' she says as I ride off down her drive.

At Ngarita's suggestion, I take the short-cut across the gentle, productive Southland farmland through Nightcaps to Winton. I'm heading for my final destination of the day, the Hokonui Hills, which encompass a rough triangle with Lumsden at the top and Winton and Gore along the bottom. Areas like this tend to slip under the radar, as they are not the highest or the most spectacular range of hills in the country. However, the area has a rich history and a gentle grandeur all its own.

The late Bruce Banwell, my father-in-law and a famous name in the hunting fraternity, cut his hunting teeth in these hills back in the 1940s. Pour him a whisky and he'd wax lyrical about his young days accompanying his father, Sidney, out of Gore and into the hills.

But it's whisky that the Hokonui area is famous for, and has become part of New Zealand folklore. Illicit whisky-making was always rife in the Southern region, but with the advent of prohibition in 1902 'Hokonui Moonshine' really took off. In 1905 the whole of Southland went 'dry', boosting demand to such an extent that it had to be imported from Otago. I remember Bruce telling me about the time when he was eight or nine (around 1940) and accompanying his father on a pig-hunting trip, when they came across a couple of suspicious-looking old characters in a gully and were told in no uncertain terms to 'Bugger off up the next gully if it's pigs you're after!' As they retraced their steps, they looked back and could see the tell-tale smoke of the distillery hanging in the air.

The most famous of all the whisky-makers, and widely regarded as the founding family of the industry, was the McRae family. When Mary McRae arrived in New Zealand from Scotland in 1872, she was already considered an expert, having been a domestic distiller back in Scotland. Eldest son, Murdoch, took over the reins in the early 1900s. At peak of production, they supplied the hotel and liquor trade at 6 shillings a gallon. Until the arrival of the McRaes, all whisky was imported from Scotland or Australia and was watered down to a large degree. It was said that a wee dram had to be offered a chair as it lacked the strength to stand up!

From the 1870s, the McRaes produced whisky from an original local recipe, and made it available to those in the know (a nod's as good as a wink). The finished product was clandestinely delivered in cans, bottles and even milk billies, and was later coloured to resemble the commercial stuff. The original McRae Hokonui was never labelled, for obvious reasons, but the label on today's whisky is a composite of various moonshiners' labels, along with the legend 'passed all tests except the police', and the skull and crossbones. Nowadays, the whisky is finished in Canterbury for the wider market, while you can purchase bottles from special batches distilled for the museum in Gore. According to Holinshed (1577), whisky was good for all that ailed you. Apparently, among other things a wee dram could 'healeth the strangury' and 'keepeth the weason from stieflying'.

World's Fastest Indian Burt Munro had a fondness for the area, too. He'd famously race in the grass hill-climb at Hokonui, and confound the field by wrapping first rope and then chain around his rear tyre for extra grip. I imagine I can see the ghost of Burt, devil-may-care grin on his face, as he overtakes me on his Indian Scout.

I have been instructed by Rob to wait in Winton for his wife, Sandy, who is on her way home from work in Invercargill, as I'd never be able to find their place on my own. And he is right. I follow Sandy's car at a fair old clip to Browns, before taking various gravel roads into the wooded hills.

MOONSHINER — ROB TINNING

The Tinnings live in a state of comfortable, rural dishevelment, tucked away in the secluded green hills of Southland. 'You'll have to take us as you find us,' warns Sandy. Rob, robust, bearded, bespectacled and dressed in well-used outdoor gear, greets me with a firm handshake as I get off my bike. I'm barely inside before he hands me a jar of moonshine. 'Here, get that inside you,' he says without preamble, and I wonder fleetingly if I'm in Southland or Louisiana. It's quite good, not dissimilar to sake. He also gives me a taste of an experimental one made with juniper berries, which is not so good.

The Tinnings have guests down from Christchurch, so I'm shown a spare bed in the tiny utility room, where Rob keeps his bits and bobs that he can't find a space for anywhere else. Sandy apologises, but it's quite cosy. While Sandy starts dinner, I get a tour of the property with Rob and 18-year-old son Connor, who says he loves the freedom of living here. In the main shed, where the previous owner used to store his microlight, Rob shows me a few of his projects; cylinders, crankcases, spare wheels, old tanks and engineering paraphernalia, some of which is over my head.

We finally settle down in the shed on old couches with beers in hand, surrounded by general flotsam, and Rob's biking story unfolds. 'When I was a little kid in Woolston, it must have been the mid-1960s,' he begins, 'a neighbour of mine, a Dutchman, took me for a spin to Sumner on his bathtub Triumph. I remember him winding it up across the causeway at 90 miles an hour. We never had helmets, and I can remember not being able to see straight, but thinking "This is life!" So, that was that, I was hooked.'

As a lad, Rob had a pushbike with a banana seat, under which he installed a Solex motor, which he covered with a sack so he could ride the bike to school. He hid the bike behind the bike sheds, but was eventually sprung and made to leave it at home. He also acquired a Jawa CZ, which he honed his burgeoning mechanical skills on. 'I learned just by fiddling. And when you didn't have much money, you just learned how to make things go.'

At 14, Rob's education was prematurely terminated and he had to leave school. He walked to every bike shop in Christchurch looking for an apprenticeship, but was laughed at for being too young and having no education. 'Next birthday, George, I'll be 60 and I'm still working on motorcycles, so what does that tell you?' says Rob.

He worked as a wool presser in various scourers, earning top money, and had only just turned 16 when he bought himself a 1970 Bonneville. 'My stepfather was a chief engineer at sea, and one day on leave he saw my pay packet and was ranting because we had both taken home $80 that week. But it was hard work.' Rob regrets not buying a beautiful Comet with sidecar for $1500 at the time. 'I told old Stan Jessop, "I can't buy your bike, I'm off to Australia."' He shakes his head. 'Crazy, eh? I could have bought a Vincent, but I had a holiday in Australia instead. But I can't complain, coz I bought my old Triumph!'

Rob is referring to his 23-horsepower 1939 Triumph 5H, which he'd proudly shown me earlier. He bought it over 40 years ago, from Ernie Brown in Kaikoura, and is only the second owner. 'Ernie Brown made the cams for it, and my friend Norm (who's inside), his father-in-law Bob Bruce made the crank pin for that bike. That old bike will sit on 140 k's all day.' He explains that the bike has a parallel crank pin with a needle roller cage in it.

He hasn't cleaned the old girl for a few years, explaining how disgusted he was after riding it to a Triumph Rally at Lake Okataina in the North Island. 'People had these Hinckley Triumphs that they were trailering up there!' he says. Rallies are a family affair with the Tinnings. Accompanying Rob on this one were Sandy on a Hinckley Triumph, his eldest son on a GSXR Suzuki, with young Connor riding pillion behind Rob.

Earlier, Rob had me in stitches, showing me the homemade calculator on his old Triumph: red beads on a wire, stretched across the handlebars, abacus fashion. 'If a cop pulls me over and asks me if I've been drinking,' he tells me, tongue firmly in cheek, 'I say, "Yes, officer, I've had one … two … three … four jugs,"' as he moves the balls across the wire!

Over the years, Rob has owned every model under the sun, modifying them, pulling them all apart and putting them back together. He's worked as a professional mechanic, and been employed in a multitude of occupations over the years — he's the epitome of the No.8-wire mentality.

I ask Rob how he got into racing. 'Well, years ago I was riding my '70 Bonnie up to Kaikoura, with my mate Mike Provost on the back. There was this tight left-hander and I'd dug it in a wee bit too late, so I had no choice but to keep going over the gutter and up the rockface a bit. I thought, "I'm stuffed now", so I just kept the throttle open, like I'm on the wall of death, you know. I didn't tell Mike, but I just about shit my pants. Anyway, we came down, hit the road again, full throttle and just kept going. When we reached Kaikoura, Mike jokingly said, "Shit, you scared me! We should ride sidecars in Speedway and I'll swing for you."' A few years later, Mike returned from his OE in England, knocked on Rob's door and said, 'Right, are you ready to do it?'

'So, that,' says Rob, 'is how we got into Sidecar Speedway. We had a lot of fun and met some great people. Have you not had a go on one?' I shake my head nervously, hoping that there's not one in the shed, and sip my Speight's. 'That's a shame, coz I could've taken you for a spin.' He tells me about the time he took Norm for a ride in a Kawasaki 1000 sidecar. 'I was in another mate's backyard, doing doughnuts. I spat Norm off to get rid of some weight, then really had some fun doing doughnuts and wheel-stands on the lawn. My mate's missus was a bit pissed coz I'd torn up the lawn a bit, but I told her she'd probably have people ringing up from the nearby Rangiora aerodrome asking about the crop circles! She wasn't happy.'

Sandy comes out with more beer for us. I could get used to the Tinning Hotel! Rob recalls a bad prang at Ruapuna on about his sixth Speedway meeting. 'I rolled it over going into the Prison Bend,' he says with evident relish. 'We rolled six or seven times, and hit a wall at about 80 miles an hour. No broken bones, but we were like bruised pears. Like jellies.'

A week later Rob and Mike, bandaged up like mummies, were at the Speedway Championships in Nelson, and were so immobile that the pit crew had to go out and start their Kawasaki for them and assist them in getting on it. When somebody mentioned to Rob that notorious hardmen Sneaky Meat and Tramp and Trigger from the Lost Breed were racing, he was a bit nervous on the starting grid. 'I've never told anyone this, but I was that shit-scared I could feel myself shaking on the line with these guys beside me. So, when the flag dropped, I had the thing nailed! I popped the clutch, did a wheel-stand and took off like a cut cat. We finished the quarter-mile race half a lap in front of the rest. I don't know how Mike held on. It wasn't until we finished that I realised I'd ridden the whole race in second gear!'

Then, with his old schoolmate Mark Green, he decided to go Sidecar Road Racing. 'We'd only had a ride around the block on this bike with Mark as passenger, but we loaded it up and went to the North Island, not realising that the first one we entered was the Grand Prix. They weren't going to let me ride in the street race until I told them I'd done some Speedway racing on the dirt. Anyway, I hounded this bloke on a real hot Honda 900 Bol d'Or all the way. I hounded him and rode the legs off him on my little Suzuki two-stroke. Every lap on this real tight right-hander I drove straight at him, threw it sideways and scared the living shit out

THE LONG AND WINDING AOTEAROA

of him, until on the last lap he crapped himself and let me through, and so on my first introduction to it, just having a bit of fun, I won.'

Rob was competing against the big, powerful multi-cylinder bikes, but says that his Speedway experience stood him in good stead, for as soon as it rained he'd run rings around them in the slippery stuff. 'I'd just hold the throttle open and go sideways in the mud. Jeez, it was fun!'

Rob then had a go at two-wheeled racing. 'I took a Norton out early on in the BEARS and I blew that to pieces, and went away with my tail between my legs and a pile of scrap iron.' He had realised the potential of BMWs on the road, and gradually tinkered with his old R100 Boxer, finding its weak points, doing some frame modifications, and racing it at Ruapuna and in street races with varying success. 'But it was all good fun,' says Rob.

In between the racing, Rob spent 10 years living in Sydney, and rode a 90S BMW around Australia on a mad caper, the details of which would make your hair stand on end and also make a great book. He's a very practical man, and has turned his hand to many things over the years to make a crust. He's been a mechanic, a wood turner, an aluminium welder, a house painter … you name it, Rob's probably done it.

Rob's now retired, having moved down to this rural idyll from Christchurch a couple of years ago. He's currently working on a revolutionary engine design, the details of which I can't divulge or Rob said he'd kill me.

After a delicious meal of venison, we go through shoeboxes full of old photographs, and I swear there was a motorcycle of some description in every one! Connor kindly offers to take me out in the morning to shoot a deer, but when he tells me we must be up at 5am I decline. Must be getting old.

Perceptive readers will of course read between the lines and realise that there's a wealth of stories here that either there is no room for or are unprintable! I've enjoyed my visit and the Tinnings' hospitality immensely, but after a grand night's sleep, and bacon and eggs prepared by Rob, it's time to fire up my Hinckley, one pannier stuffed with venison, and hit the road again.

As I'm getting my gear on, Rob tells me that over the years he's met literally hundreds of neat and honest people, but there are two who weren't that he'll never forget. 'The bastard who stole my '70 Bonnie, and the bloke who rode off with my old partner. But he's welcome to her, and I thank him because now I've got Sandy.'

I make my way back to Winton and head back down SH6 into Invercargill, for no other reason than the need find a quiet spot to write up my notes. I'm now nicely ensconced in a corner of the excellent Zookeepers Café on Tay Street, with coffee and laptop. Mick Jagger (or was it Keith Richards?), unkindly I think, likened Invercargill to 'the arsehole of the world', and, while I certainly don't agree with him, my thoughts are a tad negative as I prepare to leave, because it's raining; a not uncommon event down here. I think of the old saying that there is no summer south of the Waitaki as I put the sunnies away and enter the breach. Clouds gallop across a sullen sky, and squally showers are about to follow me through the Catlins and north for the rest of the day. Leaving Invercargill, I almost miss the sign for the Southern Scenic Route and the Catlins. There are still some gravel roads in the Catlins, but the main route is good old tar-seal and is now, unfortunately, very popular with campervans.

This wild corner of New Zealand was named after Captain Cattlin — though they dropped the extra 't' somewhere along the way — who purchased a stretch of coast from Maori back in 1840. The region had always been popular with Maori, as they were quite partial to the abundant seafood and to the giant moa that roamed the forests.

Fortrose is named after its Scottish counterpart, and in the drizzle I can see the resemblance. The early settlement of this Fortrose was sited on the hill overlooking the windy Mataura River estuary, and was known as 'the Kaik' (which was derived from the Maori term 'kainga', meaning 'village'). In the cemetery, you can find the grave of the famous whaler Captain James Wybrow, buried here in 1878.

To my right, a 15-kilometre gravel road leads to Slope Point, the most southerly point of the Mainland; it's 7 kilometres further south than Bluff. A bit further along the road I pull over to take a photo of Tautuku Bay, with its perfect, empty, sandy beach. Native forest presses down on my left, part of the Catlins Forest Park. Back in the 1860s as many as 30 timber mills operated in the Catlins, cutting into the huge stands of beech for the Dunedin market.

I clatter over the timber bridge at Papatowai and another spectacular beach is revealed, surrounded by native bush with the Tahakopa River entering a wide bay. Old Maori campsites and middens suggest that this area was popular with moa-hunters, but the Maori population thinned out along with the moa between 1600 and 1800.

The road now heads inland, and I pass the Purakaunui Falls, a much-photographed scenic attraction, but not attractive enough for me to stop, because I'm cold and wet, with a big cartoon thought-bubble containing a flat white hovering

THE DEEP SOUTH

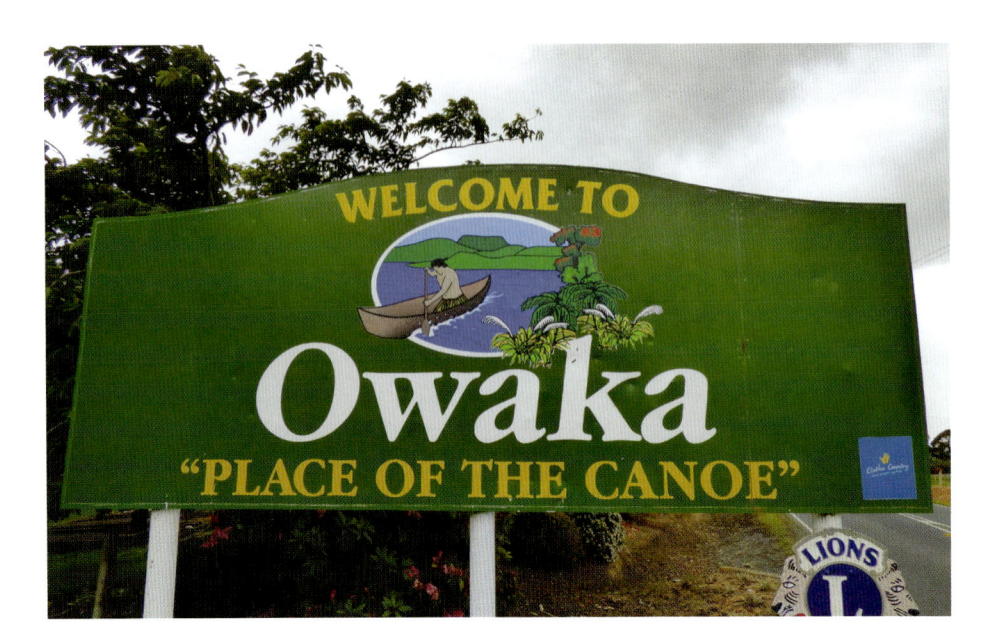

above my helmet! After a few tight and slippery bends where the bush touches the road, I ride into Owaka ('place of the canoe') and the Catlins commercial centre. The Catlins Café is an old favourite. I hang my jacket and wet gloves in front of the log fire, sip coffee and, glancing at my watch, I realise that it must be bacon and eggs o'clock. Bliss! Motorcycling is like that: from soggy misery to toasty contentment in a flash.

Back in the saddle, I head north on a damp ribbon of black for Balclutha, through the green hills, some bush-clad, some farmed, in large sweeping 85-kph bends. Somewhere along this section I pass from Southland back into Otago. I pass the turnoff down to Nugget Point (Ka Tokata), which gets its name from the wave-eroded rocks which resemble gold nuggets. For centuries this headland was an important landmark and seafood-gathering spot for travelling Maori.

I press on, for I have an appointment to keep. While I am thus engaged in brooding on schedules and deadlines and the general transient nature of things, I crest a small rise, the sun decides to show its face and the world cheers up a bit.

Back on SH1, I cross the mighty Balclutha River (largest river by volume of water in the country), which I crossed in the other direction a couple of days ago, as it came out of Lake Wanaka. 'Balclutha' comes from the Gaelic, meaning 'town on the Clyde', in reference to Glasgow. The final 80 kilometres of the Southern Scenic Route shoots me like an arrow into the heart of the Mainland's second city Dunedin, where I pull over and join the mainly Asian tourists taking pictures of the impressive train station. The first 344 mainly Scottish settlers arrived here in 1848, and that Scottish heritage has survived and is often flaunted to attract tourist dollars. For a good part of the second half of the nineteenth century and the early twentieth century, Dunedin was the nation's wealthiest city. Its name comes from the old Celtic name for Edinburgh, 'Dun Edin'.

It's a lovely stretch of highway to Palmerston, where I invest in a mutton pie, which makes an excellent hand-warmer while it lasts. Palmerston, near the mouth of the Shag River, started life in 1862 as a temporary camp for hopeful miners heading west to strike it rich in the distant Dunstan goldfields. It's only another 15-minute ride to Moeraki (which means 'long sleep') and Fleurs Place.

RESTAURATEUR — FLEUR SULLIVAN

I'm hardly through the door before Fleur ushers me to a warm corner by the fire and orders me a bowl of seafood chowder. It's delicious.

She eventually joins me at the table, but her restless energy is apparent. Fleur tells me that she came from a very hospitable family, and it didn't matter who came to her grandparents' door, the pot was always full enough for everybody. 'Well, you've certainly kept that tradition alive,' I say, gesturing to my empty bowl.

'A lot of people mistakenly think that owning a restaurant is an easy way to make a living,' she begins, 'but it's certainly not. There's a lot of pressure these days. Everyone makes good coffee, so you have to make the best. And with the huge increase in Chinese tourists, the fish must be just right, because everyone in China, it seems, knows that we have fresh fish!' She reckons that it's great when things are going well, but when things are not it can be absolutely horrible. 'You work so closely with the kitchen and front-of-house: it's your reputation that goes to the table,' she says.

Fleur is passionate about the history of food, the history of eating it and the history of growing it. Even the cooking utensils. I get the immediate impression of a passionate woman in general. 'I'm just an inquisitive person. About food. And about everything, I suppose,' she says. 'It's just a lovely thing to do. Doing this, I get to sample the good things in life and I get to meet people.'

She bought an old hotel in Clyde when she was 27, and used it as a bed-and-breakfast to get the funds to fix it up. Eventually, the restored hotel boasted, among other things, an antique shop in the old bar and a billiard room. After seven years at Dunstan House (still a thriving concern today), Fleur found herself no longer married and ended up living in Queenstown, via Invercargill, with her three kids.

THE LONG AND WINDING AOTEAROA

'I worked in good places in Queenstown,' she says, 'mostly with European chefs. When I wasn't working, I watched the chefs and learned. Some of them let me, some of them didn't. What I observed in Queenstown was that no matter how good your kitchen may be, the front-of-house can make it or break it. After four years I returned to Clyde and leased the general store, which became Oliver's Restaurant.'

Fleur teamed up with English chef John Braine, whom she'd met in Queenstown. Oliver's soon became extremely successful. Eventually it would achieve legendary status and win multiple awards, including the New Zealand Tourism Award for best boutique accommodation, and a New Zealand Historic Places Trust award for the restoration of the buildings. It also won countless food-industry awards, while Fleur herself was made an Officer of the New Zealand Order of Merit.

'We decided we'd be partners in the restaurant and in our lives, which was interesting,' she says ruefully.

Fleur was also involved in local politics. She was elected a councillor on the Vincent County Council and then on the Otago Regional Council, as well as being made a life member of the Otago Goldfields Heritage Trust.

When John left in 1992, Fleur ran the whole thing on her own for eight years, but it was so much work it was insurmountable. 'I pushed myself to the utter limit. I was diagnosed with colon cancer in 1996 and had an operation, then had chemotherapy once a week for a year, while still running Oliver's. In the end, I was turning down treatment that I had to stay in Dunedin for, in order to work, which was silly, so I had to make a decision.' Fleur decided to sell Oliver's, where she'd been for 20 years, and, 'after mucking around for a little bit', moved to the charming fishing village of Moeraki.

'You like to keep busy!' I say as a waitress brings us coffee (which is excellent).

'Well, my dad used to say, back on the farm, where we had ponds: "If you chuck a stone into the pond, just look what happens — you make ripples."'

She went on the fishing boats, and was amazed at how much of the filleted catch was simply thrown away. Always thinking, Fleur had a plan. 'I decided to make fish stock and just see how I could use it, or give it away to the Salvation Army — anything. Because with that beautiful fish stock, you only needed a potato, a bit of greenery, cabbage or watercress from the creek, and you had a lovely, nourishing meal.'

And that's what she did, with the relevant permits, from a small catering caravan. Television weatherman Jim Hickey showed a picture of it from the top of the hill, saying that while it looked a bit scruffy, Fleur was selling great soup. People had started to leave tables and chairs by the caravan, and wanted it to be open at night, which Fleur wasn't keen on. Her (now-adult) kids couldn't understand why she'd want to serve cups of tea out of a caravan. She told them: 'One day the whales will return to this place and I'll get rich!

'There was an old shed on this site at the time, and I said to myself, "I'm not even going to look." But the council was giving me grief, because now that people were sitting at tables and eating off plates at my caravan, they told me I needed a disabled toilet.'

Once Fleur's mind was made up, it was just a matter of time before her vision for Fleurs Place took shape. She was to have a huge battle over the next three years with the Waitaki District Council. It took nine months just to get the necessary permits and the definition of the compliances required to start the building. Fleur would drive the 66-kilometre round trip to Oamaru several times a week. I try to imagine the frustration. She remembers driving back after a particularly frustrating visit to the council offices. 'I heard my dad's voice saying, "Don't let those bastards beat you!", and I turned around, marched into the council office and said, "I'm not leaving until this gets sorted!"

'A lot of people think that I didn't get the required permits, but that simply isn't true. The council just kept putting up smoke screens.'

Fleur worked tirelessly with two artisan builders, Rudie and Mark, using the timber from an old shed in nearby Maheno that was due to be pushed over and burned. With various other scavenged and saved bits and pieces, Fleurs Place took shape and started to cast a shadow over Fleur's caravan, where she still worked. The finished article looked as though it had stood there on the 300-square-metre section of land for a century, which is exactly the effect Fleur had envisioned, as it was on the site of the old whaling station.

Finally, when the restaurant was up and running, Fleur's whale made an appearance and gave its blessing. She says it was amazing, as she looks out the window, remembering. 'It was a Southern Right Whale, and it went backwards and forwards not 2 metres from the rocks at high tide. It did a spout, and then it left. It was a very emotional and special moment. I had tears running down my face.'

There is a pleasant vibe in the restaurant, and patrons come and go: a steady happy chatter and chink of cutlery, even though it's a weekday afternoon. And did I say how good my coffee was?

'I don't so much love cooking,' she concludes; 'it's the assemblage, the hunting and gathering of all the parts — to be given the chance to produce good food naturally with zero waste.'

Fleur Sullivan, pioneering restaurateur, is a determined and gutsy woman and a real inspiration. She's very modest, too. Before I leave, Fleur comes outside to see my Triumph and can't resist sitting on it. I pack my signed copy of her autobiography in my saddlebag next to my venison and I'm away.

I'm alone again with the wind, the drone of the Triumph's twin cylinders, and my thoughts. I've no time to stop at the Moeraki Boulders on my right, but I've visited them a few times. These huge, smooth stone boulders have a sci-fi quality to them, like alien artefacts lying there on the sandy beach. They are in fact septarian concretions, which scientists insist were formed on the seabed 60 million years ago. In Maori legend, they were the food baskets from a wrecked ancestral waka, but I prefer to think of them as alien artefacts.

People often ask me why I travel on my own, and I like to quote a certain Leonardo da Vinci, who half a millennium ago said: 'E se tu sarai solo, tu sarai tutto tuo' ('If you are alone, you are your own man'). I have ridden in groups before and found that I just cramped the other riders' style, and vice versa. I like to stop frequently and have a wander or take a photo, and when I have a coffee I like to read or think or take notes. I usually end up riding on my own anyway, as I just say, 'OK, how about I meet you at *x* or *y* later?' Perhaps I'm just a miserable bastard, but I can live with it. Perhaps the best pearl of wisdom I remember reading somewhere was: 'As soon as you are not travelling alone, you are making compromises.'

In no time, I'm through Hampden and Herbert and merging with the 'rush-hour' finishing-work traffic in Oamaru. I never tire of another quick look at the original Victorian Precinct, the largest collection of protected heritage buildings in the country, and much of it built from the locally-quarried creamy-white limestone, famously known as Oamaru stone. I ride slowly, the wrong way up the one-way empty lane, admiring the grand old buildings and getting a ticking-off from a security guard who looks all of 15 years old. 'Do you realise you're riding the wrong way?' he bristles out of his car window. 'Yes,' I reply, and this seems to stump him. When I add 'sorry about that', he's satisfied and drives off with a tut.

Also in the Victorian Precinct is the HQ of Steampunk, whose old stone building is crammed with steel curios, amazing engines, trinkets and artefacts inspired by the likes of early sci-fi writers Jules Verne and H. G. Wells. It's well worth a visit, but is now closed, and anyway I'm heading for home.

Another hour of steady SH1 riding and I'm passing through South Canterbury's principal town and port, Timaru, having said goodbye to Otago when I crossed the wide Waitaki River. The city's name means 'place of shelter', and refers to the only safe haven for Maori waka travelling between Banks Peninsula and Oamaru.

Back on the road, I'm just riding smoothly along and resurrecting past events and old faces from my memory's vault. Once in this bubble, riding skills seem to go onto autopilot, added to the fact that the road is straight and familiar. I entertain myself, observing motorists' behaviour at overtaking lanes. There must be some psychological imperative that makes drivers increase their speed from the sedate 90 kilometres per hour they've been happy to sit on, to 110 as soon as they feel they are about to be passed. Then slow back down again at the end of the overtaking lane.

I'm very tempted to stop at Ashburton and be spoiled by my mother-in-law's hospitality, but press on and it's past eight when I park the Bonnie in the garage and finally sleep in my own bed. In the morning, I've a two-minute ride to my neighbour's house for a chat.

ALL BLACKS ASSISTANT COACH — MIKE CRON

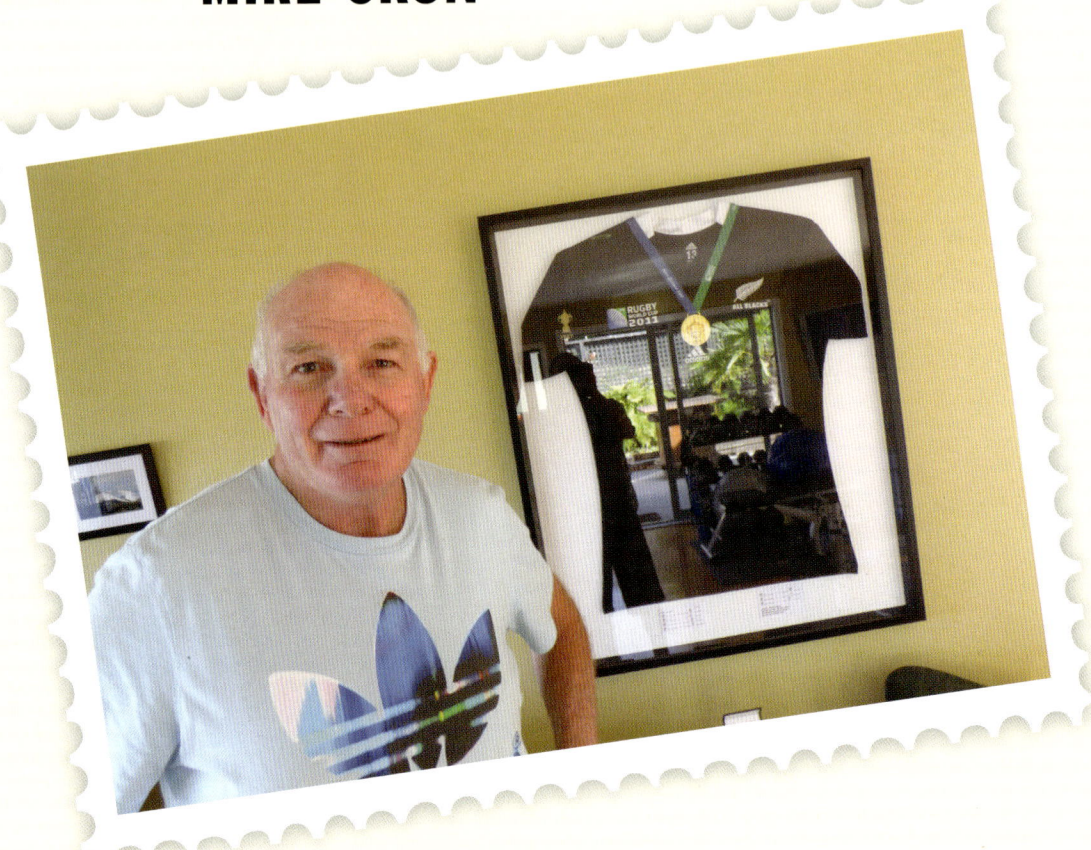

I'm sitting with a man whose knowledge of scrummaging is second to none in World Rugby, and whose innovative training techniques and man-management skills have made him widely acknowledged as the 'scrum guru'. What's more, he's a genuinely nice bloke, and, when he's not gallivanting all over the world, he's always ready for a beer and a chat down the Governors Bay Hotel.

Mike was brought up with three older, rugby-playing brothers, so it was inevitable he followed suit, strapping on his first pair of boots at the tender age of four, with the more genteel Rippa Rugby about half a century away.

His parents had a dairy farm at Kokatahi on the West Coast, just inland from Hokitika, but Mike was brought up in Christchurch, playing a wide variety of sports, as most Kiwi boys did back then.

In 1973 he joined the Police, serving his first three years in uniform, followed by 20 years in the Criminal Investigation Bureau (CIB). 'I thoroughly enjoyed my time in the Police, and developed many great friendships over the years,' he says. He became a full-time coach in 1996 after leaving the CIB.

'I played a lot of rugby, and was lucky enough to make some good representative sides,' says Mike. 'I represented Canterbury as a prop, and captained the New Zealand Colts and the Combined Services team, until at 27 my legs broke down. Today the condition is treatable and is called "compartment syndrome", which in laymen's terms means that the calf muscle swells and gets too big for the sheath. So nowadays they cut the sheath to allow the muscle out, but of course that was unknown back then.'

Mike's coaching career began in 1982, while still in the CIB, when he was asked to coach St Andrew's First XV. 'My club was Christchurch then, so I carried on coaching there, too.' Mike was a very busy amateur coach, whose reputation spread. He was soon sought-after up and down the country for his coaching expertise, as well as for his skill in assisting referees.

'I joined young, and so was only 41 when I left the Police; still young enough to go out and get stuck into life,' says Mike. 'Slowly but surely, I'd been increasing my coaching until I was doing it 40 hours a week, here and in Japan. Then I got involved with Steve Hansen here when he became the Canterbury ITM Cup and Crusaders coach.'

Former police colleague Hansen, then the coach of Wales, asked Mike to help him out with the upcoming 2003 World Cup in Australia, as a specialist scrum coach. Around this time, Mike was also working with Sanyo, later to become Panasonic, in Japan. By 2004, New Zealand Rugby had hired Mike as a full-time resource coach, which involved him travelling up and down the country assisting other coaches, mainly in the scrummaging area.

'So I worked from 2004 to the World Cup in 2011, which we managed to win,' he says. 'Initially, I turned down the role of forwards coach, as I wanted to concentrate on coaching development. A couple of months later we had another yarn and I agreed to assist, and I've been in that role ever since.' He's far too modest to admit it, but Mike's probably the reason for the ABs' dramatic improvement in their forward play in recent years. He explains the set-up to me: 'Steve Hansen is in overall charge, then there are three assistant coaches: myself, responsible for the forwards; Ian Foster, who looks after attack and the backs; and Wayne Smith, who's in charge of defence.'

Over the years, Mike has coached in 15 countries, including helping the IRB (now World Rugby) out in Dubai and Kenya. 'The phone will ring from the Islands or somewhere, and off I go,' he says. 'New Zealand Rugby have been very accommodating in that regard. I'd find myself in Munster in Ireland, and then Toulouse in France. It certainly makes for an interesting life.' As well as the ABs, Mike works with the franchises, the provinces, the New Zealand Under-20s and the Black Ferns. He reckons that rugby is a bit different to other sports as, although fiercely competitive on the field, teams are very close off it. 'We help each other and share ideas, within reason. I often have people from overseas, from all walks of life, knock on my door for a coffee and a chat.'

He's been travelling to Japan for the past 20 years, helping out from university to company teams, as well as assisting the international team when John Kirwan was coach. Mike explains that he must get written permission from the NZRU to coach other teams, and is not allowed to coach any team that is likely to play against the Super Rugby teams or the All Blacks. 'These days I can only afford about eight days a year over there, but the internet is very useful, what with Dropbox and things like that, enabling me to look at footage and offer advice from afar.' Mike says that foreign players and coaches have helped to raise the standard in Japan, but that it's very important that coaches and players go there to help the Japanese and not just to line their own pockets.

I ask him about the current state of the All Blacks. 'Well, I've been involved in about 171 test matches now. I never thought I'd be in there for one! But it's like any job, you see a lot of changes and most are very much for the better. Under Steve Hansen I think our success rate is around 91 per cent.' We both agree that that's a phenomenal statistic from a small country with a limited budget and limited players. It defies logic.

'I got a real appreciation of it a few years ago,' he says, 'when I went to upskill myself with the New York Giants, Knicks and Yankees. At the Yankees, the young boss said to me, "Do you realise that your All Blacks are the most winningest team in sport over the last 100 years, with a 74 per cent-win record?"'

Mike wonders how it can continue, and was expecting a bit of a change last year when so many big players retired. 'At the end of the tour last year, we had 19 members who didn't take part in the World Cup the year before. And we're the only country in the world that can't pick players who are playing overseas, so at the moment we have something like 70 ex-All Blacks playing overseas whom we can't select.'

I ask Mike about the highlights in his career. 'World Cups are pretty special,' he replies. 'So winning two in a row is certainly up there.' He rubs his chin and has a think. 'Another highlight for me is to coach young lads of 18 or 19, and watch their evolution into All Blacks and husbands and fathers and mature men. A highlight is simply the number of good people you work with. And I can say that I've never worked with a real arsehole. There's simply no place for them, and I think they get weeded out pretty early.'

He reckons that last year's crop of young players was probably the best he's ever dealt with, which is a big call. 'If that's what we're getting, then surely soccer and netball and hockey are getting the same? So someone is doing a good job — either the parents, the schools, the academies or all of the above. All the young men and women I coach now are smart, dedicated and eager to learn. They're just good people, and for our society I think that's great.'

Lastly, I ask Mike, which player stands out from the hundreds he has coached. His answer is no real surprise. 'Richie McCaw,' he says. 'I first watched him play when my son was playing for Christchurch Under-21s and Richie was the flanker. I'd go down on a Saturday and watch my boy play. I watched 18-year-old Richie, and I was in awe of his decision-making at such a young age. And to be involved with him in 120 of his 148 test matches, and coach him and watch him evolve into the greatest player of all time is something very special for me.'

Mike is contracted until March 2018, but talks are under way with NZRU to keep his services through to the next World Cup in Japan in 2019. 'There are three factors to consider, George,' he says. 'My health, which is good at the moment; the job is very draining. Whether it still spins your wheels every day, and if you think you're giving value to the boys. Because if you're not of value to these boys, then it's time to walk. And I know we'd all do that if we thought we weren't making a difference to these players.'

He says that he's always upskilling himself. He picks the brains of a wide range of sportsmen and -women; always looking to get an edge. From the likes of shot-putter and Olympic bronze-medallist Tom Walsh, to MMA cage fighters to the Royal New Zealand Ballet, getting tips on lifting and landing, he's constantly learning.

'The All Blacks environment is very special,' Mike says. 'We are only there for a short time, and I think it is our responsibility to pass on the jersey, so to speak, in better condition than what we got it in, and certainly not stay one day longer than intended.'

In 2016, Mike Cron was made a Member of the New Zealand Order of Merit (MNZM), but, despite his success, plaudits and accolades, he remains modest and unaffected and a bloke you'd like to have alongside you when things turn pear-shaped.

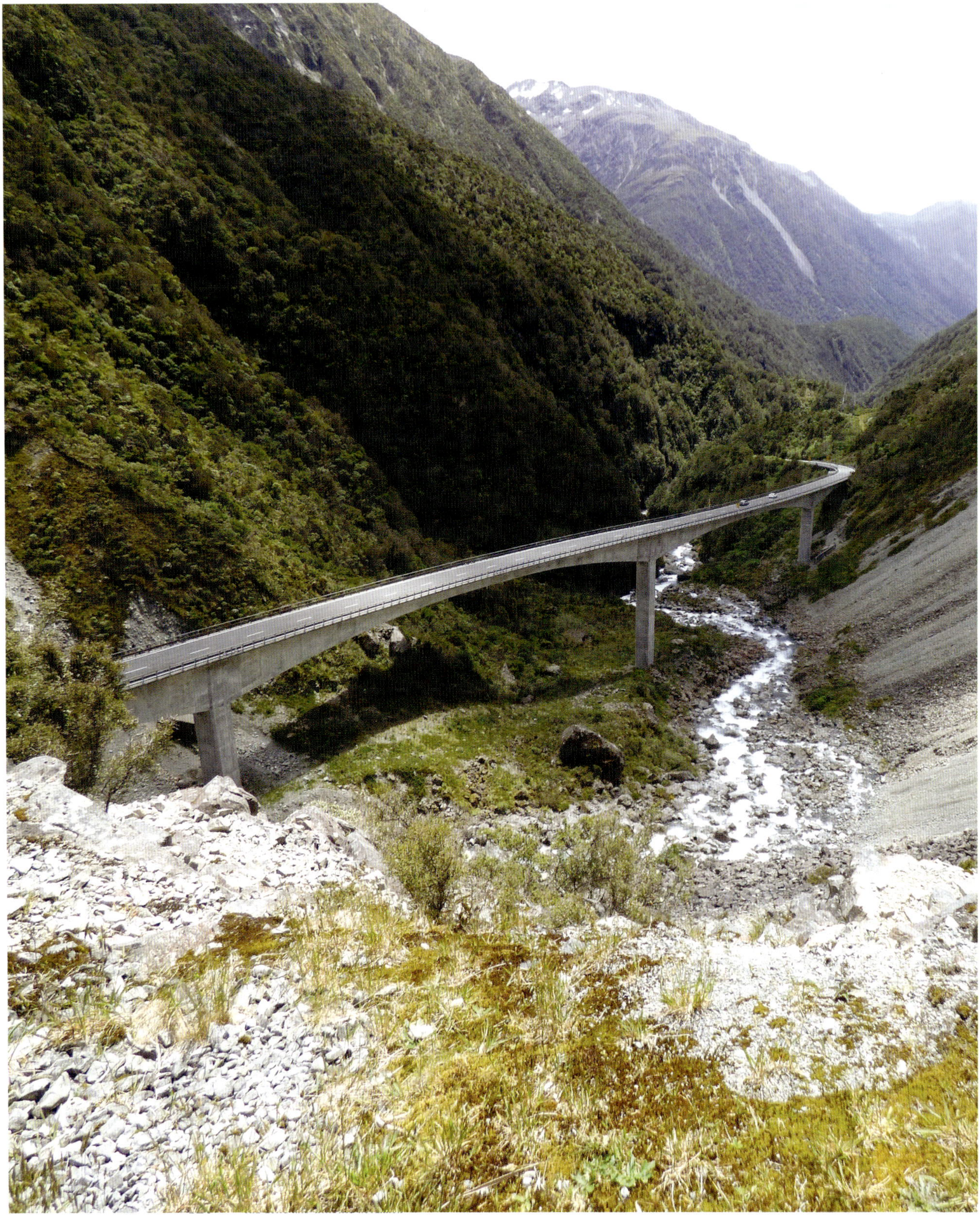

GO WEST, YOUNG MAN!
A GOLDMINER, A KNIFEMAKER AND
AN ENVIRONMENTAL ENTREPRENEUR

'Don't let the sound of your own wheels drive you crazy.'
— The Eagles

It's time to get the motor running once more, after laying a few bricks and earning a few more shekels: the ignominious need to keep the wolf from the door! I'm riding SH73, aka the Great Alpine Way, heading west for the great Southern Alps. The day lies before me untrammelled and fresh. The route this highway now follows was originally used to transport wool from the sheep runs at Flock Hill and Castle Hill to Christchurch in the late 1850s. When gold was discovered on the West Coast, the provincial government was quick to provide funds for a primitive road from the Garden City over the alps to the coast. Amazingly, this road was constructed in less than a year!

Yaldhurst Road soon morphs into SH73, as a gusty wind threatens to blow my helmet clear off my head. My map sits snugly in my tank bag, but isn't necessary, as this road goes only one way. Leaving Springfield, I wind my way up towards Porters Pass and the turnoffs to the ski fields of Porters, Mount Cheeseman and Broken River. Porters Pass is actually higher by 14 metres than its more famous cousin Arthur's, which I'm heading for. Around me now is classic high-country scenery, a conservation area called the Korowai/Torlesse Tussocklands Park, which not surprisingly protects the flora of the dry alpine environment.

An idiot in a Subaru overtakes me with inches to spare, although I'm doing 110. I watched him approach in my right mirror like a rocket, and even moved over a touch. Nothing sharpens the senses more than riding a motorcycle. You can get away with lack of attentiveness in a car. Hell, drivers text, put on make-up and eat ice creams while driving. But lack of awareness while riding, to stop being 'in the moment', could be the last thing you ever do. It's that heightened awareness required while riding, I think, that makes the motorcyclist feel truly alive.

At Castle Hill Station, I have to pull over to take a photo of the monolithic limestone rock formations. Scenes from *The Lord of the Rings* were filmed here, as well as scenes from *The Lion, the Witch and the Wardrobe*.

The new road over the alps, hacked out of this wild land with picks and shovels, officially opened for coach traffic in 1866, and the passenger and mail-service stage coaches of Cobb and Co. took full advantage of it. I picture in my mind's eye the sweating, snorting horses pulling a stage coach with often 17 passengers, across raging rivers or clinging precariously to the mountainside, while I effortlessly twist my wrist and progress serenely along the smooth tarmac.

Then, the entire trip to the West Coast — now completed in air-conditioned comfort in a lazy three or four hours with a stop for lunch — could sometimes take a whole week. It was common practice, on the very steep sections, for passengers to get out and walk.

I shoot past the Bealey Pub into the headwaters of the great Waimakariri River and huge beech forests. The Klondyke Shelter is the halfway point for the annual Coast to Coast race. I love one-lane bridges over these huge braided rivers. Instead of chaffing at the bit when forced to stop, as some motorists do, I can raise my bum off my seat, stretch and admire the magnificent scenery.

It's not long before I enter the beech forests of Arthur's Pass National Park, whose 100,000 hectares were established in 1929. The road gets narrow in places, and I really take my hat off to the drivers of semi-trailers who negotiate roads like these with such ease. I'm glad I'm on a bike and not towing a caravan.

In the café in Arthur's Pass village, I set myself up with a coffee and a pie and watch the United Nations of tourists. Outside, a group of Japanese, all wearing face-masks, are trying to take selfies (one has a selfie-stick) with a kea in the background. The kea, or mountain parrot, is said to be the most intelligent bird in the world. One guy lowers his mask to puff on his fag …

I try to get back to my book. I'm re-reading *The Night of the Triffids* by Simon Clark, the sequel to the John Wyndham classic *The Day of the Triffids*. The author has tried to write in the 1950s style of Wyndham, but has laid it on a bit thick. At times it feels as though I'm reading H. G. Wells or Edgar Rice Burroughs. It's a good bit of escapism, though. (What I'm escaping from now, however, isn't clear.)

Back in 1864, surveyor Arthur Dobson and his brother Edward blazed a track through the thick bush to the summit to discover the pass that would one day bear his name. Although 'discover' is a bit misleading, as local Maori, who told Dobson of its existence, had discovered it many years ago, on raiding sorties to the West Coast. With the discovery of gold in Westland a mere four months later, a road became inevitable.

I smile at the Japanese tourists, still busy taking selfies, and ride up to the Arthur's monument just outside the village at 920 metres above sea level. The road now descends with a vengeance, over the Otira Viaduct, which wouldn't look out of place in the Swiss Alps. Beech trees give way to podocarp pines. I then pass under another fantastic feat of engineering, which deflects water, shingle and rock slides over the road, before meandering down (slowly, as I'm stuck behind a campervan) through the Otira Gorge. The town of Otira grew from the railway tunnel settlement, whose population once numbered 600. The tunnel they dug carries the TranzAlpine and coal trains some 8.5 kilometres through the rock to emerge in Arthur's Pass.

As soon as you are over the divide, the country takes on a distinctly different aspect. Alpine scenery gives way to native bush, interspersed with dairy farms. The annual rainfall is 1500 millimetres on the eastern side of the divide, and 5000 millimetres on this side. I pull over at Jacksons, the old building that was originally a stage-coach stop. The sign on the door informs me that it's now only open for business as an executive functions venue.

SH73 now parallels the Taramakau River as it trundles to the coast, passing through the one-horse towns of Dillmanstown, Kumara and Kumara Junction, where I stop for much-needed fuel and a quick look around. A bit further on, a stone's throw from the Tasman Sea, the Great Alpine Way comes to an end and I head south on Highway 6 towards Hokitika.

'One long solitude, with forbidding sky and frequent tempest' is the way French explorer Jules de Blosseville described the West Coast in 1823, while Captain Cook found it 'unworthy of observation' and 'not distinguished by anything remarkable'. I suppose, to be fair to the great captain, he was probably a bit spoilt for remarkable sights! It is in fact a magnificent, primeval strip of land, bordered on the one hand by the cold ramparts of the Southern Alps and on the other by crashing ocean waves. New Zealanders have always treasured the idea of the hardy individual, the nuggety, stoic, no-nonsense throw-back to the original settlers. This character is perfectly represented in the 'Coasters', some of whom I hope to meet over the next few days.

The West Coast has never been renowned for its clement weather. It rains a lot here — cats and dogs and bucket-loads of wet stuff (though fortunately not today). And when it does rain, the rivers can rise to torrential floods in moments. And then there are the insects, nasty little biting sandflies that turn a normally sane man into a raving lunatic, although thankfully the sea wind keeps them at bay until you venture into the bush. It is quite mild, though, and frosts are rare.

The mass of green on my left has been shaped into a green wedge by the prevailing wind off the sea. I take in a huge breath of the salt-laden air as I cruise into Hokitika. I book into the cheap and cheerful Pioneer Hotel, having parked my bike around the back and walked through the bar, where there is one lone drinker, who looks up and nods. It's only four in the afternoon, and I find the scene a bit depressing. In two shakes of a lamb's tail, I've dumped my gear, changed and walked into town.

Jade, greenstone or pounamu is the name of the game here, with tourists wandering from one establishment to another in search of that special piece. Pounamu is one of the world's strongest materials, and it is said that the wearer of a piece draws strength from it. No two pieces are the same, guaranteeing the uniqueness of each carving. Historically, Maori shaped beautifully finished chisels, adzes and their famous fighting weapon, the patu, from pounamu. And of course the South Island, Te Waipounamu, is named after it: 'water and greenstone'.

On the beach, gaggles of tourists stand around among piles of driftwood, squint out to sea and lean into the wind. Hokitika, although a shadow of its former self, still retains a certain character and charm. It's hard to believe that during the gold rush of the 1860s, when Westland was proclaimed a goldfield, it boasted a population of 15,000 (although some say that number is grossly exaggerated). There were over 100 hotels, most of them grog shanties, strung along Revell Street.

Back on the Bonnie it's a 10-minute ride back along the coast to Awatuna, where I'm hoping Kerry has arrived home from work.

GOLDMINER — KERRY CHAPMAN

'When I was about 12, me and my elder brother found an old burnt-out AJS 650 twin in a garage in Greymouth. The owner didn't want it, so we pulled it apart and put it together again,' begins West Coaster Kerry in answer to my inevitable opening gambit. 'We painted it up, and then my brother proceeded to break every rule in the book on it. I wasn't allowed to ride it at the time.'

When Kerry was 15, his train-driver father was transferred from Greymouth to Tauranga and the family shifted north. 'I hated it there,' he says. When I ask why, his wife, Gwen, who joins us in the kitchen, says, 'In the early 1970s it was God's waiting room — full of old people.'

To escape, Kerry joined the Royal New Zealand Navy. 'Took a while to convince the old man, coz he was Army,' he laughs. 'I told him, "You guys had to walk everywhere, at least we get taken."' He bought a little 185 Suzuki trail bike for the three-hour ride to Auckland. 'But it was too small, and I kept falling off the damn thing,' he says. 'So I took my brother's advice and traded it in on a 1968 650cc T120 Trophy. Then I ended up getting married,' he says matter-of-factly. 'I think Gwen liked the bike more than me!'

I ask Kerry what he did in the Navy. 'I was a gunner' comes the reply after a sip of beer. 'I ended up Fire Control 1st class, Petty Officer Seaman.' He reckons joining the Navy was a good move. It enabled him to see the world and 'have a bit of fun'. He fetches a painting from another room, of the HMNZS *Taranaki*, a *Rothesay*-class frigate, with a list of the ports visited listed beneath. 'That was my third ship,' he points out. 'I was on HMNZS *Otago* when I started my gunnery training. When she went to Moruroa Atoll we got kicked off, because they said we were too green to burn!' Kerry was then transferred to the *Bathurst*-class corvette HMNZS *Inverell*, originally commissioned by the Royal Australian Navy in World War II, to finish his training. 'We slept in hammocks; really old-school,' he says.

Kerry served for 20 years in the Navy, retiring on a full pension, and he explains all the different financial options. He took a percentage as a lump sum, plus a sum per week that kicked in last year when he turned 60. 'It just gives me that little bit extra, so I now don't have to work a full week,' he explains.

Getting back to bike talk, I ask if Gwen rides. 'Well, I tried to teach her on the '68 Trophy when we first met. We were in Eden Park in Auckland. I hooked her on it, and she took off down the end of the field and fell over. I go racing down, coz the bike is on top of her and she's screaming. Turns out I forgot to turn the fuel on! So that was the end of her riding career. But she's been a passenger now for 42 years.'

Around 1979, when Kerry was a father to baby Vicky, a home owner in Auckland and had slowed down a bit, he realised that he couldn't fit three on his bike, but he wasn't ready to give up motorcycling. He was on leave from the *Taranaki* and Gwen had just picked him up and was heading home. 'I spotted this VW trike on Barrys Point Road,' he says, 'and I said to Gwen, "I've got to have it!" I had a wad of cash in my pocket, so I waited for the young owner to come and pick it up, and asked him if it was for sale.' It wasn't for sale, but Kerry told him that he'd leave the $2800 in his pocket for three weeks and wait for his call. The next night the phone rang — apparently, the young man had to leave the country in a hurry — and the sale was made.

'It had a 1200cc motor on the back of it, and was pretty gutless,' says Kerry, 'but I just liked the style of it. It was built by the Hog Farm for a guy to ride who'd had a bad accident.'

After a couple of years, Kerry replaced the motor with a 1300, and after an accident replaced that with a more grunty 1600 Kombi motor and SCAT racing gear. He also lightened the flywheel and replaced the little Solex carb with double 45-millimetre side-draft Webers. 'Just basic stuff,' he says, 'but it would do 11.02 down the strip, and basically the front wheel didn't touch the ground.'

'Let's just say he's a speed freak,' adds Gwen from the lounge, and tells me about their first car, a 100E Prefect. They were driving over Auckland's harbour bridge with the wipers moving achingly slowly. 'We both said, "This has got to go," so we put a Mitsubishi Gallant 1600, fully-raced motor, gearbox and diff in it,' she says.

'It could get along, then!' laughs Kerry.

Vicky was only 18 months old when the Chapmans attended their first rally, a sidecar rally in Waitomo. Gwen sat on the off-side, Vicky on the inside, with Kerry in the middle, all done up in wet-weather gear cut up from old rubbish bags. They dropped Vicky off with the folks in Tauranga, and off they went.

'I only ran my daughter over once, though,' recalls Kerry. 'We were at a VW meet for off-roaders, and I cleaned up lots of the other riders in the sand dunes, coz all of the weight was on the back wheels. Anyway, we were coming out of there and we hit a bump, and Vick went flying off and landed in front of me. By the time I'd stopped, the wheel had run up onto her legs as she lay there in the sand. I pushed the VW off her, she stood up, spitting sand, and said, "Don't do that again, Dad — it hurt!" Then she hopped back on and away we went.' At this stage, says Kerry, the Angels' (and AC/DC's) motto — 'Dirty deeds done dirt cheap' — was still painted on the VW, so they made quite a sight!

The Waitomo Sidecar Rally in 1981 was the first one of its kind, organised by Bill Reid and John Williams of BJ Side Chairs fame, and Kerry and Gwen were among the 41 founding members of the New Zealand Sidecars Register. Kerry shows me the latest club newsletter. 'We don't have a committee or rules,' he says. 'Ton Hillhorne, a Dutchman, keeps us all in line, though. He takes our subscription and organises us.'

Kerry's retirement gift to himself on leaving the Navy was a '93 Harley, which he subsequently had an accident on, and from then on didn't like the feel of. In 1996, he traded it in for a new Ultra Classic FLHTCUI, the first fuel-injected Harley, he says, in the country. 'At the time, I was a road captain in the Auckland chapter of the Harley Owners Group (HOG),' says Kerry. He attached his Hamilton-built Somerset Chair to it, and the same Harley and chair sit in his garage today. 'It's a good machine. It's done 183,000 k's. I ride on two wheels in the summer, and in the winter the chair goes back on,' he says. 'But I'm happy with it, although I wouldn't mind a VMAX come to think of it. I'm following one on TradeMe now.'

We go outside, and Kerry brings his Harley out for a photo, and under a tarpaulin reveals, of all things, a coffin-carrier. 'I've done three funerals,' he says. 'The family contact you, and you take care of the transport. You don't have to be licensed to carry a body.'

Kerry always promised himself that when he turned 55 he'd be back on his beloved West Coast, and, sure enough, in 2010 they moved back, a decision they've not regretted. He now works at a gold mine for Birchfied Ross Mining, driving an enormous 60-tonne Komatsu loader, which, he says, only takes three bucket-loads to fill up a 40-tonne articulated dump-truck. He says, 'From about 20 kilometres of where you're sitting now, there are probably 50 gold mines. They're everywhere.'

Now, happy as a clam, I eat my fish 'n' chips (wrapped in newspaper — fantastic!) on Hokitika's beach as the sun sinks over the sea. It gives me a little kick to know that nobody will ever see that sunset again.

Before I fall asleep I get a bit teary, laptop on my chest, watching the great Muhammad Ali fight Earnie Shavers on YouTube. I remember vividly watching the fight live as an 18-year-old and feeling every punch that the hard-hitting Shavers landed on my 35-year-old hero, who it was clear was way past his best. Ali, the cagey old campaigner, was way ahead on points as the bell sounded for the fifteenth round, and he knew that he simply had to survive the next three minutes to win. Shavers knew he had to knock Ali out to win, but, instead of Ali hanging on, he landed some great combinations in the closing seconds, and would have knocked out his squeaky-voiced opponent if the round had gone on for another 10 seconds. As I drift off, I imagine what could have been, had the remarkable Ali not had Parkinson's disease, and realise sadly that he's no longer among us.

After a good night's kip, I pack up and pop into Mountain Jade, where Kerry's wife, Gwen, works, and get a close look at a jade carver at work. Robert, aka 'Pook', is busy carving a beautiful piece. He's been at it for 35 years, but says that he never stops learning. Behind him stands young Tauwa, who is in his first year as a jade worker, busy 'stropping' a necklace. Conveniently attached to Mountain Jade is a great little café, where I start my day off with an excellent Big Brekkie. Good coffee, too. As I tuck in, I read the anonymously-penned poem on the wall:

It rained and rained and rained
The average fall was well maintained
And when the tracks were simple bogs
It started raining cats and dogs
After a drought of half an hour
We had a most refreshing shower
And then most curious thing of all
A gentle rain began to fall
Next day but one was fairly dry
Save for one deluge from the sky
Which wetted the party to the skin
And then at last the rain set in.

Actually, I have to confess, the only reason this party is not 'wetted to the skin' is that I chose a rare window of dryness between long periods of wetness to ride this leg of my journey, as there is nothing more miserable than a long ride in the rain.

It's only 43 kilometres to Greymouth, the commercial capital of the region. I park-up and wander along the Grey River towards the sea, past two huge cranes looking forlorn, rusting and abandoned. In 1860, the 14 chiefs of Poutini Ngai Tahu signed over 7.5 million acres of the West Coast from Kahurangi Point down to the Milford Sound and inland to the Main Divide: at 300 gold sovereigns, a snip. Excluded in the deal were 6724 acres, including present-day Greymouth. The area was known then as Mawhera Pa, and had been occupied by Maori for centuries.

Gold was discovered in 1864 in the Grey District, and diggers and prospectors poured in, making it one of the busiest ports in New Zealand, despite it having no natural harbour. Eventually, 3 million ounces of gold were extracted. Greymouth also supported the nation's major coal-mining industry until the 1920s. Just past Greymouth is neat little Runanga, the first town to be built by the government to provide houses for workers in the state-owned coal mines in the area.

In Barrytown I've an hour to kill before my next interview. I spend it down on windy Pakiroa Beach, sitting on a rock with the whole beach entirely to myself, reading *The Night of the Triffids*. Occasionally I'll look up from the page and, in kaleidoscopic flashbacks, remember all the beaches I've had fun on around the world.

As a kid, racing my mum into the freezing waves, over the cobbles on a rare family day-trip to Brighton. Trying to work up the courage to approach two stunning Danish girls as we all body-surfed on Kovalam Beach in southern India. Giving my soon-to-be-wife, Karen, a piggy-back in Cape Town. (God, I loved that brown bikini!) Making sandcastles with my beautiful, little tanned Aussie kids, Annie and Fergus, on Bondi Beach. The memories are so visceral that I put my book away, as I know I won't be able to concentrate on it again. Anyway, it's time to see if Steven is home.

BARRYTOWN KNIFEMAKER — STEVEN MARTIN

The knifemaker is famous along the coast. My son, Fergus, and I enjoyed a day here a couple of years ago, hammering, forging, filing, grinding and sanding, and proudly came away with two superb knives that you'd swear were shop-bought.

Steven eats his lunch and offers me a chip, as we chat at the table about the glittery stuff: gold. 'Spending holidays carrying heavy equipment up freezing cold, sandfly-ridden creeks completely cured me of any interest in gold or amateur gold-panning,' he begins. 'However, I do enjoy looking for jade, and this beach here at Barrytown is famous for the jade pebbles that wash up on it.'

Steven and partner, Robyn, bought the land here on the main coast road 25 years ago, with the intention of making a living from the tourist traffic, but without a clear idea of how, although Steven was already a successful businessman in the textile industry in Wellington. 'We originally bought half a dozen or so houses in Greymouth and rented them out,' he says. 'We very cunningly bought them at the top of the market, spent a fortune on them, then sold them at the bottom of the market. We're probably the only people in New Zealand not to have made money out of a real-estate transaction.'

The idea of knifemaking came out of the blue when Steven was walking along the beach one day and came upon a piece of steel he thought he could do something with. He brought it home, made a big bonfire, and fashioned a not-so-good knife, which, he says, got him keen on the idea. I ask him whether he had any previous experience in this field, and he shakes his head. 'I did have experience in textile engineering, but this was a completely different kettle of fish.' I marvel at his inquisitive nature, as I'm sure most readers, like me, would have simply walked past that piece of metal on the beach!

'It turned into a business,' Steven goes on, 'because the lady next door had taken in German WWOOFers when her relationship fizzled out and things were a bit tight. When she needed a bit of privacy, she sent the volunteers over to me, telling them "The guy next door makes knives, and I'm sure he'd love to see you." So I could have done a Donald Trump and put up a big fence, or I could start a business out of it. I did the latter.' (WWOOFers are people sent by the World Wide Opportunities on Organic Farms network to have homestay experiences on organic farms, where they work in exchange for their accommodation and food.)

At this stage, Steven had made a few knives but hadn't forged any. He explains: 'There are two ways of knifemaking. The first is called stock removal, where you get a piece of steel and take away everything that doesn't look like a knife. That's what most people do. It's slow and tedious, but you must start off with a good piece of steel. The other way, of course, is forging, where you heat the steel to high temperatures, adding extra carbon from the coals, and heat-treat it however you want it. It's far more interesting, a lot more fun and much quicker, and out of very ordinary steel you can make a great knife blade.'

Usually, Steven tells me, for a skilled artisan, making a knife (let alone over a dozen) would require 20 or 30 hours' work, and the finished item wouldn't be any better than the knives produced in a day at Barrytown. And I can speak from experience that transforming the length of steel you have in the morning, and looking at it sceptically, into the quality knife you end up holding in your hand at day's end is a remarkable metamorphosis. Steven's skill isn't just in the process of knifemaking, though, it's also in his ability to make people feel welcome and at ease, and keep them entertained with his one-liners and anecdotes.

Being small, the business is limited in the kind of advertising it can afford, so word-of-mouth recommendations contribute greatly to its continuing success.

Steven dips a sausage into chilli sauce and continues. 'So the WWOOFer experience proved to me — and this is fundamental — that people were more interested in the experience than the finished product. I mean the finished product mattered, but the experience of making it mattered a whole lot more.'

Interestingly, there are nearly as many women as guys who come through, and all-male days almost never happen. Women come individually or in groups, and, says Steven, invariably make better knives. 'Women are easier to work with, and they pay attention,' he says. 'I think because it's so foreign to what they normally do. It's like us doing a needlework course — we'd probably pay attention. But of course blokes know everything about knives and all things mechanical!'

It didn't take long before the knifemaking business really took off, and Steven and Robyn have been flat-out ever since. Initially, with tour buses, then word-of-mouth, and then with information sites on the internet. Featuring in *Lonely Planet*, which used to be the traveller's bible, didn't do the business any harm either. 'And of course with the internet came the feedback,' says Steven around a mouthful of chips. 'I think the internet has been a damn good thing for tourism in general. It's weeded out the people who were disasters, and gives a pretty good assessment of what's out there. There is usually a good reason for tourists to say unflattering things.' Steven excuses himself to answer the phone — another booking — while I pinch one of his chips.

'I used to take groups of 14,' continues Steven, 'but I found that it wasn't fair on them or me, so now 12 is our absolute maximum. And even that can be pretty stressful, believe me.'

Incredibly, Steven has overseen the making of over 20,000 knives, with knives now residing in 108 countries. And at one time about two years ago, there were Barrytown knives at the North and South Poles. Two people took their knives on an expedition to the North Pole, while a group of scientists took their knives down to the permanent base at the South Pole!

But just as amazing was the visitor Steven and Robyn had recently. Spaniard Iñigo Tena was not only a knifemaker himself, but he also hailed from exactly the same longitude and latitude — just on the exact opposite side of the globe. Neighbours, but as far away as one could get! 'The funny thing is,' laughs Steven, 'if he wanted to get further away from us, he'd have to climb a ladder, because when he walks out the door, whichever direction he takes, he's getting closer. You'd be surprised who's visited us here. Sooner or later, everyone turns up on your doorstep.'

I ask Steven if he ever gets sick of making knives. 'Only now with my health issues,' he replies. 'I get a lot of pain from my bladder cancer, which I've had now for three years. I've had a knee replacement, which was a great success and I'd recommend it to anyone, and I'm waiting to go in and get my other one done. I was all set to have it done the following day when the surgeon rang and said that they'd looked at my biopsy and my need for cancer surgery was greater. And I was all set to go again when I received another a call to say that I had a heart condition which needed fixing, so my knee had to wait. The heart's now been fixed. I remember I had been feeling dog-tired all the time, but the instant I woke up from the heart operation (they basically stop and re-start it), I felt like a new person and the sun shone again.'

That procedure was carried out only four weeks ago — the surgeon and the anaesthetist had both met Steven while knifemaking — and he is hoping it will be third time lucky for his knee replacement. This time he plans to leave the phone off the hook and just turn up at the hospital as planned.

Steven seems very fatalistic about his illness and ailments, and remains optimistic about his prognosis. His stoicism and determination are humbling. He says that, according to an American insurance guy he spoke to recently, his treatment would have cost millions in the States, and so he's very grateful to be living in New Zealand and the West Coast, in particular, where his treatment has been of such high quality. 'So, considering what we get back from the health system, we pay bugger-all,' he adds.

I ask him how long he can see himself going on making knives. 'I look at it two ways, George,' he says. 'I still enjoy it, and more so now that we're doing only two or three days a week. Also, while we're still doing it, we're not spending our retirement savings. And I'd like to keep doing it until I pitch face-first into the furnace one fateful day!'

Steven says it was hard not to get depressed when he discovered his cancer had returned after the first operation. 'But,' he says, 'I found the ideal cure on the internet to rid me of my depression completely and keep me happy for the rest of my life. It was as obvious as the nose on my face: simple.' I'm intrigued and urge him to continue.

'All I had to do was go out and buy a late-model Aston Martin convertible, capable of doing 180 miles an hour, which I did, and so now I don't worry about any of that shit. And Robyn didn't mind, because she said if I died she'd make a very attractive widow in it.'

We go outside and Steven shows me his toys. A late-model Can-Am Spyder and a lovely old red Austin Seven. But it's not until he lifts another garage door and reveals his pride and joy that I realise that he wasn't joking about the Aston Martin!

Heading north again, I had intended to stop at the Punakaiki Rocks, for another look at the eroded limestone that resemble piles of pancakes, but it's like Piccadilly Circus. The number of campervans, hire cars, tour buses and pedestrians comes as a bit of a shock, and I just keep riding. Obviously, I can't be anti-tourist, because here I am touring. (I prefer to think of myself as a traveller, though, snobby bugger that I am.) Punakaiki Rocks is the second most popular tourist destination in the country after the Huka Falls, and the West Coast Road has been voted the ninth best drive in the world.

Tourism West Coast chief executive Jim Little warned recently in *The Press* that communities could simply not cope with the demands tourists put on infrastructure. (Punakaiki has only 30 ratepayers.) Perhaps the answer is a fee or levy for visiting these tourist hotspots. Some Chinese tourists were asked what they thought of this idea, and they said they didn't have a problem with a levy, as the Punakaiki Rocks were so cheap for such a beautiful place.

When in 1847 explorer Thomas Brunner stumbled out of the bush, having taken 18 long months to battle through the wilderness from Nelson in search of less-disputed land for the new colony, the spot where Westport now stands today was a small Maori pa. Brunner and his party were so hungry towards the end of his trip that they were reduced to a diet of fern roots, and even ate the dog. I haven't time to look around Westport, as I'm heading all the way to the end of the road — Karamea — but I'll be coming back this way tomorrow anyway.

North of Westport, riding with the ghost of Thomas Brunner on SH67, the coastal plain between mountain and sea narrows and the road runs very close to the sea, crossing many small rivers, lined with whitebaiters' huts. This land of fern and low scrub is known as 'pakahi', and is often unfarmed. The forest seems untouched, but that's not so. Forests like this once rang with the sound of birds, but are all but silent now, thanks to rats, cats and stoats.

I was hoping for a quick coffee in Granity, but the nice little café I remembered is now closed. Hector is the next seaside hamlet, named after the rare Hector's dolphin, which is found in the area. At the mouth of the Mokihinui River with its collection of little baches, my road turns right and heads inland towards the rainforest-clad hills. The curving and swerving up and over Karamea Bluff soon begins, now in brilliant afternoon sunshine, and I shift between third and fourth gear endlessly. The narrow road wends its way around the bluffs of the Radiant Range, up to the high point of 420 metres, where I can pull over and admire the views. Flax, nikau palm and cabbage trees surround the thin ribbon of tarmac. It is a glorious, twisty ride, but I'm glad it's dry, as I know how challenging this ride is in the pouring rain.

I duly arrive in Karamea, 'the West Coast's best kept secret', sitting like an island in the middle of the Kahurangi National Park, New Zealand's second-largest at over half a million hectares. The cows look very contented here, as though they belong, a bit like how sheep look in Central Otago. With the area's high rainfall and mild climate (it boasts the warmest climate in New Zealand), there is no need for artificial irrigation. The first Europeans to call the area home were goldminers in the 1860s. Farming became a major industry, also timber, flax and gold mining. Today the major industry is dairy farming, and you can certainly tell.

Prior to European settlement, Maori were using the river mouth as a resting place and food-gathering source, as the huge piles of pipi shells that have been discovered testify. It has been suggested that Karamea was a seasonal camping spot for Maori en route from the North Island to more southerly West Coast rivers and their sought-after pounamu.

In 1874, several shiploads of hardy pioneers arrived here from Nelson, although prospectors and surveyors passed through before this. In the early 1900s, the huge heaps of shells (middens) were crushed with machinery to provide lime to fertilise paddocks. Up until the 1929 Murchison earthquake, Karamea did in fact have a functioning river port. The huge quake caused whole hillsides to collapse into the gorge and headwaters. The silting up of the river reshaped the waterway and made navigation very difficult. A wharf at nearby Little Wanganui continued to operate, but coastal trading gradually gave way to trading on the unsealed road over the trusty Karamea Bluff.

Anyone who wants to continue north must walk for four or five days along the Heaphy Track, before taking the road the 34 kilometres to Collingwood.

I pull into Rongo Backpackers, which is hard to miss with its rainbow-painted exterior. Last time I stayed here I came very close to smothering a Canadian backpacker in the dorm, whose snoring was beyond belief, as he slept blissfully, spread-eagled like a giant starfish on the top bunk. I had told this to owner Paul (whom I'm going to interview in the morning) in an email, and he thought it prudent to book me my own room this time!

ENVIRONMENTAL ENTREPRENEUR — PAUL MURRAY

Next morning finds me chatting to Paul in Rongo's kitchen as he makes coffee for us. He's a great talker, and would I feel make a great politician, although I'm not sure he'd thank me for the suggestion. 'The Buller region is facing some serious economic challenges,' he begins. 'In the past year we've lost 40 per cent of our jobs, what with Solid Energy closing, Holcim Cement relocating to Timaru and the dairy industry looking a bit wobbly.'

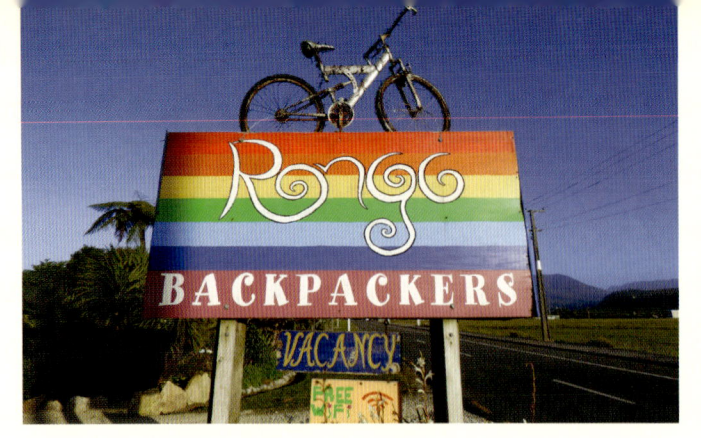

I have a feeling I won't have to do much talking, which suits me fine! Paul continues as hostellers wander in to make breakfast: 'Central government are finally listening to us and getting behind tourism promotion. Governance on the West Coast is controlled by people who support the extractive industries, so tourism has been somewhat neglected.'

There's an interesting dichotomy here, because for many people Karamea's appeal is its isolation, which is also its main problem. Most tourists come down from Nelson, bypass Westport and go straight to Punakaiki. 'Our job is to identify an iconic attraction up here that will attract tourists into Westport and then here,' says Paul, sipping his coffee. 'And we have it in the Oparara Arches, which are on the same level scenically as the Punakaiki Rocks and the Fox and Franz Josef glaciers. Currently, only 10 per cent of tourists visiting Punakaiki continue up to Westport, and only a fraction of those make it up the cul-de-sac to Karamea. If that number were to increase by only 15 per cent it would be a game-changer for the area.'

There has been serious discussion recently about building the long-debated 50-kilometre road from Little Wanganui to Tapawera. The Ministry of Business, Innovation and Employment have looked at the road proposal, and have said that they require a viable business plan. That is: if this is the cost of the road, what will be the return?

We move to some comfy couches outside, overlooking the beautiful hills. Paul points off into the distance: 'Apart from the Oparara Arches, there is the Heaphy Track mountain-bike promotion to bring people here in the winter months,' he says. 'There's already a 45-kilometre track to the Arches, an old gold-mining route, which really is a latent asset. Trouble is, when people walk in they have to use the same path back out.'

Australian-born Paul (he grew up on Kangaroo Island in South Australia) spent

146   THE LONG AND WINDING AOTEAROA

10 years as a journalist in Tokyo, working in a windowless office behind a computer for 'ridiculously high wages', but always thought he could do something more meaningful with his life. He was good at his job, worked hard, but came up against the glass ceiling that many foreign workers hit in Japan.

I ask Paul how the whole Rongo thing started. ('Rongo' means 'peace' in Maori.) 'Well, I met my wife, Sanae, in Tokyo,' he says, 'but her father, who was very traditional, didn't like the idea of her knocking around with a *gaijin*, and I was *persona non grata* to him. I was basically driving a wedge between her and her family, so we broke up. It was a very tough one, because we loved one another.'

So Paul came to New Zealand alone (he'd already purchased 80 acres of native bush near Karamea), and six months later Sanae bravely defied her father and met up with him here. Her father basically said 'Don't bother coming home.' Two years later — Sanae's mother had been working on her dad — the couple are invited back to Japan to meet the parents.

'So, we get back to Tokyo,' Paul says, 'and I've got dreadlocks down to my shoulders, I'm six foot three and a wild-looking bastard, so the first thing the dad says is, "Oh, my God, you're huge!" After he'd had his bath, the old boy hands me a beer and suddenly launches into this long, eloquent, apologetic speech about how happy he is that we're in love and welcome to the family: and I was the son he never had!'

But all the time he's giving this impassioned, formal and dignified speech, his balls are hanging out of his pyjamas! 'I wondered if it was a simian display of authority or something,' Paul laughs, 'and if I should hang my balls out, too!'

Paul and Sanae now have two kids, and the Japanese grandparents love them to bits.

So, back in New Zealand with his new wife, Paul started a movement called the LivingInPeace Project, which evolved, he says, from the street marches that took place around the world to protest the 2003 invasion of Iraq. 'I actually believed that for the first time in history,' he says, 'the peace movement would stop a war. But it didn't happen.'

The LivingInPeace Project concentrates on the *quality* of life rather than the *quantity* of life. In Tokyo, Paul had plenty of quantity, but when he came to New Zealand he made a conscious decision to concentrate on the quality. 'The LivingInPeace Project, of which Rongo is a big part, has four elements to it,' he explains. 'There's art, travel, permaculture and education.'

There is an Artists in Residency programme at Rongo, where in the quieter winter months free accommodation is offered to artists from all over the world. The artworks are left here, and at the holiday baches down the road, though it's not a stipulation, and the substantial collection helps to contribute to the colourful ambience. 'Now,' says Paul, 'we're actually running out of wall space.'

Travel, Paul reckons (and who could argue?), is very beneficial to personal growth and the best educator there is. Travel is very different to tourism (as any traveller will tell you — often!). He sees tourism as expensive entertainment and quite damaging to the environment, although I do point out that it's essential to many areas of New Zealand. Another dichotomy.

'Tourism is boring,' says Paul, 'but if you actually slow down and experience life in another country for a period of time, you learn a lot. In Japan, I learned who I was. Growing up on Kangaroo Island, things were very insular. Everybody knew who you were, or thought they knew who you were, and you ended up living your life to other people's expectations. D'you know what I mean?' I nod, as I know exactly what he means and empathise totally. He goes on: 'In Japan, I didn't feel compelled to be anybody but myself.'

So Rongo caters to travellers, and the Farm Baches, which are quaint retro-70s Kiwiana, cater to domestic travellers. 'They're not luxury accommodation,' he says, 'they're baches, and that's what a lot of Kiwi families enjoy.' And I can attest to that, as my wife and two kids stayed there a few years ago and loved them. Interestingly, about 90 per cent of those who stay in the baches are Kiwis, and about 90 per cent of those who stay in the hostel are from overseas. Rongo offers a transport service for those finishing the Heaphy Track or to the other scenic attractions nearby.

Permaculture is an important part of the LivingInPeace Project, too. Rongo has a 7-acre farm where they grow food which is made into meals for their customers. 'We are trying to apply the principles of permaculture in the whole business,' says Paul, 'to make it more energy-efficient, more environmentally responsible and socially equitable.' I ask if he's aiming to be carbon-neutral.

'We're already there,' he replies. 'When I bought my 80 acres, I was inspired by a guy called Douglas Tompkins, co-founder of the North Face and Esprit clothing brand. With the millions he got when he sold those companies, he went to Chile and bought almost a million hectares of virgin forest with the express purpose of preserving it.' Paul is so glad he bought land where there are 1000-year-old rata, because he's sure that, if he hadn't, it would be another dairy farm today. That land represents the project's carbon sink. 'We had carbon audits done on our business for five years in a row,' he says, 'by Carbon South out of Christchurch, and after everything was considered they found that we sequestered more carbon than we were responsible for, so we're ahead of the game.' Paul is obviously very passionate about this subject. 'Just think, George, if big corporations like Apple followed suit — we could save the Amazon rainforest!'

The fourth element of Paul's philosophy is education. 'Here at Rongo we cater to the sons and daughters of the most affluent people in the world. These are the 10 per cent who can afford to travel. So, the young people who come here will be the captains of industry and the leaders of the future. I know that the things we're doing here have had a marked influence on a lot of these guys. Particularly the WWOOFers, who are the real travellers and get involved and really experience life.'

Rongo offers many workshops and classes in the winter months. Paul tells me how appreciative he is of the seven paid staff and the WWOOFers and everyone else who have helped Rongo evolve over the years, with limited resources, to what it is today.

Before I leave, Paul (aka 'DJ Crap') shows me his funky radio shack at the back of Rongo. It's from here that Karamea Radio (107.5 FM, and now SoundCloud — www.SoundCloud.com/RongoBackpackers) is hosted and broadcast, as it has been for the past 12 years. There are community service announcements, and if there is an event in town it's promoted. People can also contribute to it with creative content and even their own radio shows.

'I'm not trying to change the world,' says Paul, 'I'm just trying to change myself, and if that influences someone else, then that's all we can hope for.'

P
P
WILLOW STREET
BACKPACKERS
MOTUPIPI ST
Motueka
60
Collingwood
Pohara
Totaranui
TASMAN
National
Park

THE TOP END: A QUAKER, A COLLECTOR AND A BIKER

'The open road, the path of greatness. It's at your fingers.'
— Kings of Leon

Clouds gather on the horizon like popcorn as I watch Karamea disappear in my mirrors. I've another long ride ahead of me today. Back in Westport I watch the world go by as I enjoy bacon and eggs on the main street. Across the road and down an alley is The Carving Shed, where I go to chat to owner Hohepa Barrett, who's having a fag outside. Business has been brisk, he says, as we stand outside his little shop, which opened five weeks ago. 'People can come in off the street with any idea of a carving pertaining to them,' he says, 'and I'll carve it for them on MDF or show them how to do it, and then nugget it with polish, so they have their own original Maori wood carving.' He excuses himself as he has customers, and I wish him well.

I'm now back on SH6 — I don't think there's a state highway that passed through more varied and spectacular scenery than this one — winding up the Buller Gorge to Inangahua. After singing the praises of the road over to Karamea, I feel I must ease off on the superlatives, but the Buller Gorge makes it hard. Man, what a great road! I remember watching *World's Greatest Motorcycle Rides* recently on the Discovery channel, and heard Henry Cole sum up my feelings in a nutshell. He said, 'In New Zealand the destination is something you shouldn't hurry to. Being on the road here is something to cherish; something to savour. To ride quick is to miss the whole ethos of this land: the pure pleasure of being at one with yourself, your bike and your quite stunning surroundings.' Wise words, I thought, but then he *is* a middle-aged Pom!

Inangahua Junction is where the Inangahua River meets the Buller, and it made headlines in 1968 when a 7.1 magnitude earthquake killed three people and residents were evacuated. The Maori name for whitebait, 'inanga', gives its name to the river and the settlement. The simple wooden hall, built in the early 1930s, doubles as the museum, and offers a good reason to have a little wander.

The road keeps following the river, now the Upper Buller Gorge, between the Lyell Range on my left and the Brunner Range on my right. Countless twists and turns deliver my Triumph and me to the Rivers Café in Murchison.

Since the massive 7.8 Kaikoura earthquake in November 2016 and the closing of SH1 between Picton and Kaikoura, traffic has been diverted this way, and it's very noticeable. I'm not accustomed to the crowds, traffic and queues, and it makes me realise how lucky we are, knowing that this is only temporary.

A young couple with a lively toddler and a sleeping baby in a bassinette arrange themselves apologetically at the table next to me, where I'm engrossed in *Dalva* by Jim Harrison and sipping a long black. They're apprehensive and ask whether they are bothering me. 'Not at all,' I reply, 'been there and done that.' As I leave, I tell the couple that actually the happiest days of my life were when my kids were small, although I didn't realise it at the time. Back on the road I cogitate on the truth of what I'd said: that the happiest time of my life was not being single and fancy-free, travelling the world in the 1980s, but working six days a week, paying off a seemingly huge mortgage and bringing up two kids in Sydney. Funny that!

More glorious riding along my old favourite SH6 brings me to the Motueka Valley Highway turnoff. I happened upon this great stretch of road while tiki-touring around the top of the South Island with the family many summers ago.

The burbling Motueka River appears on my left from time to time, and I have the road virtually to myself. In country like this, the road tends to parallel the course of the river: the lines of least resistance. The whole valley is liable to flooding, and locals have endured some bad ones over the years. In 1983 a visiting motorist from Wellington spent the night trapped in a poplar tree above the raging flood waters. In the nineteenth century, gold panning was particularly popular immediately after a flood. Fishing is very popular today, especially for brown trout, with many forms of accommodation and tours geared up to catch this fish. I pull over in tiny Ngatimoti, switch off the engine and consult my map. The verdant valley walls press close. The first 'highway' up the Motueka Valley was the actual river itself; canoes and boats being the vehicles. There were of course many tracks made by Maori passing through the valley hunting.

The first European settlers moved here up-river from Motueka, where they had landed in 1843. When they arrived, they were greeted with solid beech, totara and rimu forest. They didn't have horses, so had to grow everything using hand tools. Their harsh lives would have been unimaginable to twenty-first-century residents. Imagine cutting the forest down using an axe and a saw, and burning the logs to create a clearing to sow your seeds. These days some of us moan when we have to put out the rubbish or mow the lawn! It was particularly difficult for those on the west side of the riverbank, as the first bridge in the area wasn't completed until 1894, and widened for light traffic in 1916. Before this, punts that ran along a steel cable attached to pulleys were used as ferries.

In motion again, I ride past more tall hop vines, which are trained onto poles and wire frames. The scaly cone-like fruit is kiln-dried before being used to brew God's nectar. All too soon the little highway comes to an end in Motueka. It's the kind of valley that you'd leave from on a glorious quest and return years later, battle-scarred and triumphant and retire Hobbit-like to pipe and slippers, growing vegies, fishing for trout and bouncing your grandkids on your knee while recounting your adventures.

Motueka is another top spot, but I've not time to tarry. This area is renowned for its market gardens and fruit-growing, as well as providing the nation with most of its hops and tobacco. Just past Motueka, the tortuous (if you're towing a caravan) Takaka Hill begins. The road takes me through 14 kilometres of tight bends to a height of almost 800 metres. It then plunges down into Golden Bay, synonymous with sun, sea and camping, and refuge for artists and dreamers. On the way down I pull over a couple of times to enjoy the views over Tasman Bay. On my right is the beautiful Abel Tasman National Park, established in 1942, and the smallest in New Zealand at 19,222 hectares, where the forest is slowly reasserting itself after early logging. Just before Takaka, I turn left up a gravel road and soon find Tugela Farm and my next interviewee.

QUAKER — ALBIE BURGERS

Like most people (I'm guessing), I'm not sure what being a Quaker means, and I'm keen, as we sit in Albie's living room sipping his home-brewed beer, for him to enlighten me. I pick his South African accent immediately, as I've spent some time there, and actually met my wife, Karen, there.

'People have the image of funny hats,' softly-spoken Albie begins. And he's right. The image I have is something akin to the Amish, riding a horse and trap and dressed in black. 'The main thing that drove me towards Quakers was the statement on peace. Where it talks about denying all forms of armed conflict and finding it totally unacceptable. That was what really struck me as its main tenet. Quakers vary enormously, and you'll find that there are some who don't fully believe in that peace testimony, but most do.'

It would appear that some 'cherry-pick', as is the case in most religions. But is Quakerism a religion? I ask Albie. He explains that the roots of Quakerism are Christian, but that most Quakers in Golden Bay don't believe in God as portrayed in the Bible. They talk more about the spirit and the light, and he points out that a couple of his Quaker friends are also Buddhists. 'They're double-dipping,' I joke, and he agrees with a laugh. 'We believe that everyone has something that is good inside them. An inner light.'

In New Zealand, there are approximately 800 members and about an equal number of attenders (those who attend meetings, but haven't made the final commitment). Meetings in Golden Bay can vary from 2 to 30 people, and are held at people's houses with a shared meal once a month. Quakerism can vary from country to country, with some being more evangelical than others, like in the United States, where some groups have a paid pastor, who preaches from the pulpit.

'Quaker meetings for worship start with a group of people sitting around in a circle, with the first 45 minutes or hour in total silence,' says Albie. I pull a face, not understanding. 'It's to allow the light to come in,' Albie explains. 'If a person has something pressing to say, he simply stands up and speaks into the silence, then sits down and nobody responds. And the meetings work on consensus. We don't have voting as such.' He pauses, gazing out the window into the paddocks before continuing. 'Everybody speaks their mind while the others listen. It's very difficult to listen. When everyone has had their say, the clerk — anyone can be the clerk — says what they think is the consensus, and if there is disagreement the discussion may go around again until a final consensus is reached and the clerk can write it down and call it a minute.'

Sometimes the meetings go around and around, and very occasionally, if a person simply cannot agree, they will 'step aside', rather like abstaining. It's clear that Quaker meetings can take a long time. I ask Albie if Quakerism is a family affair.

'Well, my wife is a Quaker and my children have had a Quaker upbringing. They've been to Quaker camps and things like that, but they are not practising Quakers. When children turn 16, they can make up their own mind. Our children have turned away from it, but they may return,' he shrugs. 'It's up to them.'

Albie was born in Cape Town, and around 40 years ago, when the political system in South Africa became too much to stomach, he and his wife, Felicity, came here. 'White people who didn't agree with the apartheid regime were considered almost traitors,' he says. 'So if we had stayed, life would have been very difficult. It wouldn't have been a nice environment to bring up kids, so we left and found a wonderful home here.'

And it is indeed a wonderful spot to live. Albie and Felicity's comfortable home (shifted down from Collingwood) sits amid 50 hectares of green wood and pasture.

Albie was a teacher when they moved here in the 1970s, as there was a teacher shortage at that time. When I ask him what he taught, he replies, 'children', then goes on to say, with a glint in his eye, how much he loves it when people ask that question, as his answer often bamboozles them! 'I taught high-school kids,' he says, 'and on my very first day all of the staff were gathered together for a pep talk and we were told, "Now, remember, you aren't going out there to teach Maths or Science or English — you are teaching *children*." And I've tried to carry that with me.'

There was a teaching vacancy in the small town of Ohura, on the Forgotten Highway in the North Island, where Albie and his family went and were welcomed with open arms. 'It was an area school,' he says, 'with kids from six to university age, and the playground was like one big family. It was wonderful.'

After a couple of years in Ohura (which is now a ghost town of only 120 residents), they came to Golden Bay for a vacation and fell in love with the place, which I think wouldn't be difficult. Albie reckons the principal at Ohura wanted to get rid of him, furnishing him with a glowing reference, so when a vacancy came up in Golden Bay they shifted here.

Albie retired from teaching about 15 years ago, and is now a trim and fit 68. 'We try to do the self-sufficiency thing here,' he says. 'We have a large vegie garden which Felicity takes care of; I do some of the weeding. We try to keep fit with plenty of tramping, but there is always something to keep us busy here.'

They started out with 100 goats, which they milked to make cheese, but after calculating that they were getting about 50 cents an hour for their labour, they realised it was crazy. They then changed to dry stock cattle and sheep, but this year decided to sell the animals and lease out the 20 hectares of grazing. 'It was very liberating,' says Albie. 'Now we can hop into our electric car and just go!'

He has always been something of an inventor, and, after working on the hot-water problem for years, has finally come up with a workable system. 'We now have hot water coming out of our ears for us and the rental cottage,' he says. 'I also had a play with the wind and built myself a huge panemone.' I point out that it sounds like a nasty operation, but it is, Albie assures me, a windmill with a vertical axis of rotation that goes around horizontally, unlike a propeller that has the axis of rotation pointing straight into the wind. 'It isn't as efficient as a conventional windmill,' he says. 'I built it for no other reason than that it was beautiful. I thought I was building something unique until I discovered that the Chinese had been using them for the past 800 years.' The sails were painted blue on one side and red on the other, and generated nothing but beauty, which, let's face it, isn't a bad thing. Albie said he could sit and watch it for hours!

The Burgers also take advantage of a small spring in the hills above the property, which runs through a pipe at about 1 litre per second, to generate hydro-electric

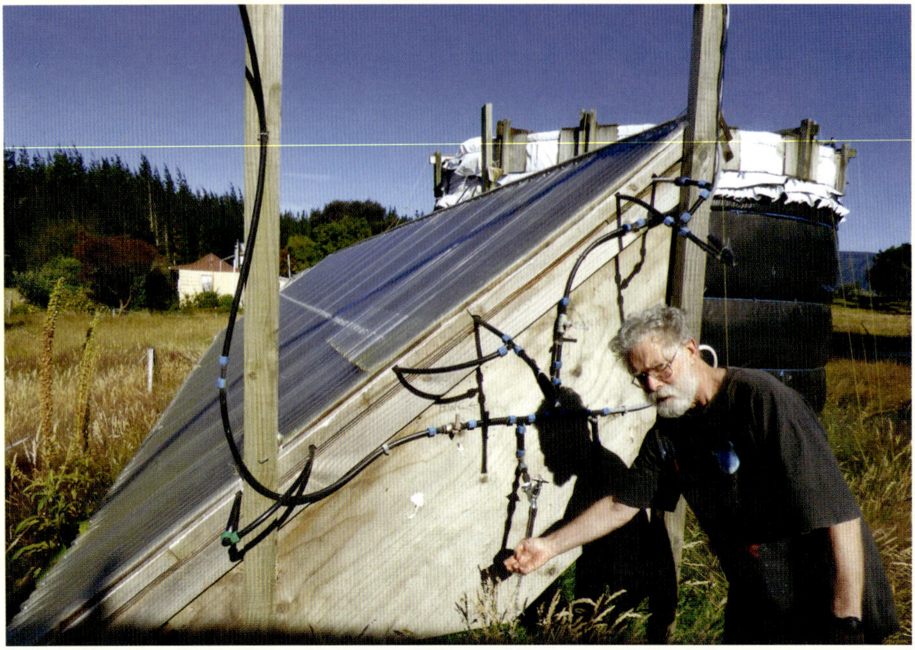

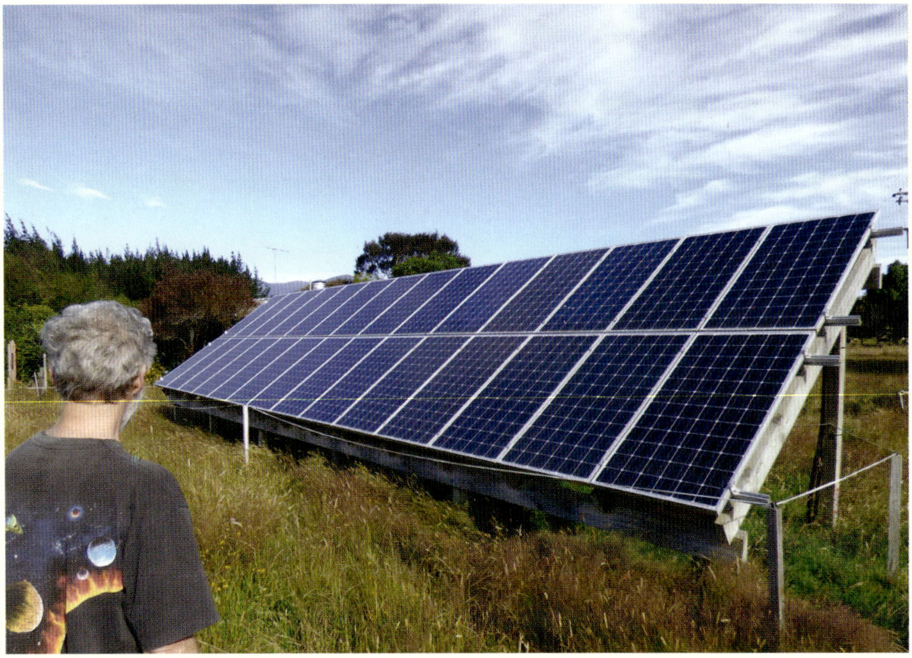

power and charge up a truck battery. 'It only generates 20 watts,' he points out, 'but it's enough to power reading lights, like the one behind you and all around the house.'

They went solar in a big way when they bought 28 photo-voltaic solar panels. 'We used a couple of local guys as consultants, one of whom had learned all about them in Australia. I dug the holes and passed him the spanner and hammer. The PV panels provide us with more power than we could possibly use, and we sell our excess to the grid. We haven't got batteries, so at night we grudgingly buy power back.' Albie's rationale is that they use the grid as though it were a battery that they don't have to buy and replace.

The solar power also goes into charging up the two electric vehicles in the garage, where we now go. The near-new Nissan Leaf was only recently purchased, and driven from Auckland back to Golden Bay. 'It can store about 20 kilowatt hours, giving it a range of 135 kilometres,' Albie explains. 'We were impressed by the number of charging stations available, and the fact that it took only 20 minutes to fully charge the car. And if we can find a caravan park, then we have ourselves a filling station, because we just plug into the socket. The government is not helping people get into electric cars with any incentives, but then again they aren't putting up any barriers either.'

Albie then tells me to get in the driver's seat and we go for a spin. Apart from the lack of noise, I could be driving a normal petrol vehicle, and I'm very impressed, especially when he tells me to plant my right foot to the floor and the acceleration feels equal to that of any normal car. The future, I'm sure, is electric.

More of Albie's thoughts and inventions can be seen on his webpage, www.esypsy.co.nz. It's been fascinating meeting him, and I feel a tad wiser than I did an hour ago. As I ride off I wonder how much longer I'll be riding a petrol-fuelled motorcycle!

Leaving Albie's farm, I turn left for the short ride to the house of my mate Des Molloy, which is on the other side of Takaka, near the popular Pohara Beach. I've had a tiring day in the saddle, and I'm glad to sit down with Des and his wife, Steph, for dinner. Des, who featured in my last book, *Living the Dream*, is an interesting character, and I joke with him, saying he could feature in this one under the title 'Stories Des forgot to tell me'. In the morning, Des takes me on a little pushbike tour before we meet up with Steph at a local café for breakfast. Before heading back over Takaka Hill, I take a stroll around the colourful Main Street of Takaka, with its beautiful young vacationers. Looking very alternative, they're dressed in twenty-first-century hippie chic, complete with dreadlocks and bare feet. Everything is funky, organic and rainbow-coloured. And God, they make me feel old!

Takaka Hill was always a barrier, and isolated Golden Bay from the rest of the world, apart from sea access. I cruise along the main street of Motueka, a more conservative version of Takaka's, but still colourful and following exactly the clearing burnt through the dense bush by the first settlers.

It's now time to put my superlatives away for a while, because the road from Motueka through Richmond to Nelson — sunniest town in New Zealand — is mostly straight and in excellent shape, and the scenery is only average, although I suppose if you beamed me here from the UK's M25 on a cold, foggy day I would be in heaven. But then I must get them out and dust them off (the superlatives, I mean), as the 50 k's of SH6, as it snakes up and over the Whangamoa Saddle and through the forested hills of the Bryant Range, are simply superb. The bends are not as sharp as Takaka Hill, making it a faster ride, all the way down to Rai Valley, where my circadian rhythms nag me into stopping for coffee at the Brick Oven Café.

Past the picture-perfect Pelorous Bridge, where vacationers are jumping from rocks into the river, I pull over at tiny Canvastown and look at the display of mining machinery and tools. In 1860, Mrs Pope discovered specks of gold while doing her laundry in the Wakamarina River.

Originally called Wakamarina, Canvastown was named (as you probably guessed) after all the tents that sprung up with the subsequent influx of gold miners.

Just down the road, Havelock is one of the gateways to the wandering waterways of the famous Marlborough Sounds. Apart from green mussels, Havelock is famous for being the birthplace of Ernest Rutherford in 1871. Ern would later become the first successful alchemist when he fired alpha particles at nitrogen atoms to produce oxygen atoms.

I decide to ride the Queen Charlotte Drive to Picton, but soon realise that it might be too much of a good thing. There are so many 35kph bends on the narrow road, with no opportunity to admire the view up the Sounds, that I almost get motion sickness. Picton is a pleasant resort town, as well as being the terminal to the North Island. It was named, interestingly, after a British hero killed at Waterloo. Queen Charlotte Sound delivers me almost to the door of the Tombstone Backpackers, a motorcycle-friendly, relaxed place run by Gary and Niki, and located, not surprisingly, by the cemetery and overlooking the docking ferries. After dumping my gear, I head down through Blenheim to Seddon, where I've an appointment with Ron.

Welcome to...
HAVELOCK
GREENSHELL
MUSSEL CAPITAL
OF THE WORLD

ANCHOR SHIPPING & FOUNDRY Co LTD

258 Home of...

The Dangerous Kitchen
CAFE · RESTAURANT · BAR

COLLECTOR — RON HEBBERD

Ron is an affable gentleman of 80 years. His pride and enthusiasm for his bike collection (Ron's Toy Shed) is obvious as he gives me the well-practised tour. Before November 2016, Ron says he'd get two or three in a day and then nothing for a fortnight. Ron's wife is also a collector, as the shelves full of sewing machines behind him testify. He tells me that about 30 of his bikes fell over and three doors got stuck in the catastrophic 7.8 Hanmer earthquake. 'That's what happens in earthquakes,' he says simply.

Ron got into bikes as an apprentice car mechanic in Blenheim, back in 1953. 'After I'd been working for 12 months and cycling to work from Renwick, I bought myself a brand-new 500cc Royal Enfield Bullet. Two years later I got the accessory for it,' he shows me a photo of a young girl sitting on his bike. 'I've still got the accessory, but I've no longer got the bike.'

He saved the money for his Royal Enfield by shooting possums. At the time the government paid a bounty of 2 shillings and 6 pence, tax-free, for two ears and a strip from the possum's back. 'That would have been a nice little earner!'

'Yes, it was,' says Ron. 'Actually, I used to make more money shooting possums at the weekend than I'd make during the week. Over here,' he says, showing me various engine pieces, 'are the result of 40 years of blow-ups. They're not mine, like Burt Munro; they're the jobs that came into the garage. The terrible things people did to their bikes.' He shows me rockers worn away to almost nothing, sprockets with teeth worn completely off, and other bits and pieces of tortured metal, each with a tale to tell.

Back in the day, Ron rode competition motocross on an old converted road bike, before getting into trials-riding when he opened his workshop here in Seddon. There's a great black-and-white photo showing Ron, with half his bike stuck in the mud. 'I've been around and I've done some silly things,' he says, pointing to photos of him riding through flames and standing up on his seat. 'I used to go to the A and P Shows,' he says, 'and this was the best way to be noticed.'

We move on to the bikes. 'This 1913 three-speed New Hudson with cane sidecar is a runner. And I'm only the second owner!' he says proudly. Ron didn't inherit the bike, but bought it before he married. However, when he was cleaning the dust off the original cane sidecar he started to blow the cane off, so had to take it easy. 'I gave it eight coats of two-pot, and lined the inside with plywood. It took me 400 hours to restore it all.' I can only admire his skill and dedication.

In the corner sits a wheelchair made after World War I. 'It was made for men who were strong but had lost both legs,' he explains. 'You pump these two levers here,' he demonstrates, 'and it has two ratios.'

What I like about Ron's collection is that the items are not in mint condition, but show the patina of age and the scars of use. 'I like them the way they are,' he says. 'I'll get around to mending that one day,' he points to a ripped seat. He can't lift his arm up far to point, as both rotator cuffs are shot — motorcycle prangs. I'm guessing that Ron has a multitude of tasks that he will 'get around to'. We then admire an old electric bike, a Peter Pan. 'I can find nothing about it anywhere on the internet,' Ron says, 'but it's factory-built and I'm pretty sure it was made in Japan. The power pack is a starter motor. And see the little emblem on the toolbox? Well, that is moulded into the rubber pedals, so it's obviously been a production bike.'

There's a little Honda with the motor built into its back wheel, a row of old farm bikes, and the first of the three-wheelers with the huge tyres vulcanised to the rim like an aircraft. 'When you got a hole in your tyre, you bought a new wheel,' says Ron. 'They came out in 1972, and the tyres were so wide that the bike actually floated, and poachers would float them across rivers in the back country.'

Rare models like Buffalo come and go in a giddy parade as we shuffle around the shed and Ron shows off his encyclopaedic knowledge. I spot a green Yamaha DT360 in the corner and nod towards it, admiringly. 'I'll fix that up one day. They only made them for one year,' the font of knowledge tells me. '1974. The next year they changed it to a 400.' Next to it is a rough XT500, which I also admire. 'A roughie,' he says, 'but you can't expect too much for $80!'

Next is a lovely Yamaha YDS3, a 250cc that Ron tells me was the first Yamaha 250 to achieve 100 miles per hour. 'They then jumped to YDS5 because the word "four" and "death" sound very similar in Japanese,' says Ron. 'And that 175 Harley trail bike over there by the two Benellis was just too rough and I had to re-paint it.' We see DKWs, CZs (Ron demonstrates the dual-purpose kick-starter/gear lever), and Indians, then stop at a row of weird-looking farm bikes called Mountain Goats.

Moving on to the next room, we pass two mannequins by a work bench 'working' on a bike. 'These are my mechanics,' says Ron. 'I don't pay them much — a bottle of beer occasionally — but they don't get much work done.'

First up is a Yamaha AG farm-bike collection. Then we pause by a lovely example of an old Yamaha TX750, which he rides to rallies occasionally. 'Would you ever sell something like that, Ron?' I ask.

'No,' comes the reply, 'because it's in the collection. If I get an extra, I might.'

I'm then transported back to my teenage years by a 'Fizzie' or Yamaha FS1E, which Ron allows me to sit on and wallow in nostalgia for a few seconds. These mopeds were all the rage in the UK in the 1970s, and had the ability to be powered by pushbike pedals. In normal riding operation, these were rotated forward to act as motorcycle-style foot-pegs. I tell Ron that my mate had a Puch Maxi moped when we were 16. 'Well, we called them "Push" in New Zealand, coz they always broke down,' he replies.

In the corner is an Ariel Square Four that he's working on at the moment. 'I just got it started, after buying it 42 years ago in a box,' says Ron. 'The oil flow isn't big enough, but a brand-new after-market Morgo oil pump arrived last week from the UK, so I'll put that on and sort the oil flow, and then put a sidecar on it.'

Next down the line is the first of the YZ Yamaha motocross bikes built for purpose at the factory. 'Yamaha made the first "trail" bike as we know them in 1968,' the font continues. 'Nobody made them before that.'

Then a beautiful fully-faired Yamaha Police bike with the most comfortable-looking saddle. 'That needs a new cam chain,' he says, 'and the battery packed up, so I had to ride something else. But it's nice to ride.'

Beside that is the classic pocket rocket: an RD350. 'They were the bike when they came out,' he says. 'When I was involved in racing back in '73 I got the factory-listed speed out of it, which nobody else ever did. The biggest secret to making them go fast was to set your carburettor up, set the gap in your points for your timing, then go and ride 10 k's. Then come back and do it again until you come back and it's perfect. And that would be worth 2 or 3 miles per hour, and that makes a big difference on a race track.'

We chin wag for a bit about Ron's writing (having penned books on the history of the local area and motorcycle clubs in Marlborough) and the bikes we regret having sold over the years. 'Well, when I got short of room, before I built this extra shed, I started selling stuff. I just couldn't fit 'em in,' Ron says. 'Suzuki RV 90s, Stingers, 125 twins …' He sighs a regretful sigh. 'Anyway, they've gone. Breaks your heart!'

Ron sold his Seddon Yamaha dealership in 2004 to an American 'who thought he knew everything, didn't want any advice from me, and lasted only 15 months'. Ron had enjoyed 39 successful years in the dealership! He still attends National Vintage Rallies and wins trophies. His wife, he says, 'has gone off riding motorbikes since the throttle got stuck and she went into a concrete wall in Vietnam recently'.

Meeting Ron and having a personal tour of his 'toys' has been an absolute treat. His shoulders are stuffed and he can't kneel because of two knee replacements (he had to raise the saddle on his current bike because he couldn't bend his legs enough), but Ron reckons there's a good few years of collecting and tinkering left in his tank.

I head back up the eerily empty road to where Gary is hopefully waiting.

BIKER — GARY HUSBAND

Gary and I sit on stools sipping quiet ones in his workshop beneath the backpackers. 'As soon as I turned 15, I got my licence and bought myself a 1972 Suzuki T250 Hustler,' says Gary, 'which was a huge improvement on the Victa scooter that my dad had bought for me to hoon around the farm on. That was followed by a Yamaha XT250 for a bit of trails riding, and then in 1985 I went overseas.'

By then a qualified electrician, his first stop was Brisbane, with a stint as maintenance man in a shopping centre, but soon got sick of the routine. 'I flagged

the job, the girlfriend, the car and the flat, bought an XT500 and headed north.'
I tell him there could be a song in that and we laugh, as he gets us another beer from his little fridge in the corner. Did I say his workshop was well-appointed?

'I contracted as a sparky for a while on Hamilton Island, and used to leave the XT, hidden behind some bushes, on the mainland. When I needed a break from partying, I'd come back, wander around the bushes until I found the XT, kick her in the guts and go off riding for the weekend. The old single-thumper was a great machine; I loved it.' Gary says that once he actually fell asleep while riding the XT. Worse for wear after his farewell night on Hamilton Island, he finally found the bike in the bushes, mounted up and headed for Townsville from Airlie Beach, having had no sleep, and gave himself a bit of a fright when he found himself on the wrong side of the road. He remembers, 'I shook myself awake, found a creek to douse myself in, then carried on to Townsville.'

In Cairns, Gary found work on a prawn trawler, working night trawls. He reckons he didn't make a huge amount of money due to some breakdowns which spoiled the prawns, but mainly did it for the experience. 'I was assigned the job of finding a new cook, which I relished,' says Gary with a grin. 'So I went down town and found a suitable recruit, who it turned out couldn't cook to save herself!'

After three months of shrimping, Gary dusted off the venerable XT and, with the Swedish 'cook' now on the back, put it to good use, riding off-road up the Cape York Peninsula. 'In Bloomfield, an Aboriginal reserve, I had to knock on a few doors to find some gas, as everyone seemed to be having a siesta,' he says. 'After I'd fuelled up, four locals emerged from the bush, very drunk, swigging what looked like meths and asking for a lift to Cooktown. Things got a bit ugly when they tried to grab my girlfriend, who started screaming. So, I gave it some throttle and literally dragged a couple of them down the track for 50 metres before shaking them loose and making a getaway! Around the corner was a collection of old Fords and Falcons which had all probably run out of gas.' Gary carried on to Cooktown and had a great time, as it would appear he has a penchant for doing. London now beckoned.

Gary was soon eating up the miles on his Honda CX500 and earning the 'folding' with LASER Couriers. 'Dispatching was a great, adrenalin-fuelled job, and the more drops you did, the more drops you were given. It was a lot of fun.'

One of the spots Gary lived in while in London was in a squat in the Nigerian High Commission building in Bayswater. 'About 20 of us lived in this building with the permission of the Nigerian High Commissioner himself, who told us he knew we were living there, but as long as we took care of the building it was fine and he'd even leave the power on.'

Gary then bought the superb four-cylinder, high-performance Yamaha FJ1100, with touring Europe in mind. He crossed to Dublin on the FJ, and rode up to Belfast to hang out with his mates in Omagh for a while, before touring around Eire and

THE LONG AND WINDING AOTEAROA

returning to London. He then picked up a cricketing mate who wanted a lift to Paris, the next destination. They had a great time in the City of Light, being shown around by a couple he'd met on the Channel ferry. 'It was great being shown around by a Frenchman, and we were treated like kings,' says Gary. 'Next night, we hit the town on our own and it was the complete opposite — the Parisians gave us the cold shoulder.'

Bidding *au revoir* to his cobber, Gary carried on down to the south of France, boiling his brakes in the process, due to some hard riding on the superb roads. Then on to Italy, enjoying the tunnels through the Alps. 'I remember I was doing about 160kph through one of the big curved tunnels, and a hell of a pool of water had formed ahead from a leak. All I could do was pray and keep going, hang on and clench my sphincter! I got through unscathed, but it was a bit of a "moment".'

From Italy, Gary hopped around the Greek islands, before touring Turkey, including a ride across the top of Syria. 'Back in Istanbul,' he says, 'the girl who was travelling with me got pretty sick, so we had a few days there before heading up through Yugoslavia and eventually back to the Beerfest in Germany for the third time, which may have been one too many, and so back to London.'

The Yamaha performed admirably on this 10,000-mile trip, with Gary only changing the oil when due. Apart from the clip on the chain-joining link, which he used a bit of Kiwi No.8-wire ingenuity to fix, he had no mechanical problems. On one long, dry stretch of smooth tarmac in Turkey, Gary's eyes lit up. He opened her up, and the FJ managed an incredible 238 kilometres per hour, which with a pillion and gear is pretty impressive!

Next stop for our Kiwi adventurer was America, where he spent the next couple of years. He started out touring the northeast with a mate who'd bought a Buick Riviera in New York, before driving down to Miami, Florida. Gary, a qualified construction diver and fisherman, fell in love with Key West immediately, and decided to stay for a while. 'I got work for three months, diving, snorkelling, driving a glass-bottomed boat and giving commentaries on things I knew nothing about.'

In Miami, Gary bought an inline-4 Suzuki GS1100GK. 'I meandered west through Louisiana,' he says, 'in and out of Mexico, through Texas, up to the Grand Canyon, Las Vegas and across to San Francisco. Then down the California coastline and the Baja Peninsula, before another jaunt through Texas. Finally, I rode to LA, where I sold the bike and flew back to New Zealand. It was a big trip where I did ridiculous miles. Outside the cities, I found the American people really hospitable.'

Back home again on his parents' farm, Gary of course needed a bike. His experiences in the States had him leaning towards Harley-Davidson, and it wasn't long before he was the proud owner of an FXR Super Glide. He grew to love it, and in the next 10 years clocked up 78,000 kilometres on it. 'By then, Niki and I had a couple of kids and I wasn't riding it much,' he says, 'so I sold it for the same money I'd paid for it.'

Gary's next bike is very familiar to me, as Gary's and my mate Tim owns it. The Yamaha SRX600 was a bit of a change from the Harley, and it wasn't long before Gary was pining for something with a little more grunt. 'I spotted this Buell on eBay for sale in Albuquerque, New Mexico,' he says, and nods to the 1200cc sports bike in front of us in the workshop. 'I bought it via auction just before it closed, and very nearly didn't get it as I was cursing and struggling with our dial-up connection.'

At the time, Gary was assistant manager at Cardrona Ski Field. (He has, he tells me, spent a total of 24 years working on ski fields and has clocked up thousands of hours of snow-mobile riding.)

He had a ski-lift conference in Colorado coming up in five months' time, and anxiously counted down the days. Accompanied by wife Niki, he finally got his hands on his Buell after many nervous convolutions and setbacks, where he thought he'd been swindled. 'It was a huge relief when I finally fired her up in a storage unit in El Paso, and Niki and I rode it to Colorado, where I attended my course and Niki flew home. After another great ride along Route 66, I shipped the bike home from LA.'

Gary says that he can't imagine ever selling his Buell Lightning, as riding it gives him such enormous pleasure. 'It just loves to cruise at about 95 miles an hour, or around 150 kilometres an hour,' he says. 'That's its sweet spot and it'll do that all day.'

→ 45
SURF HWY
Opunake

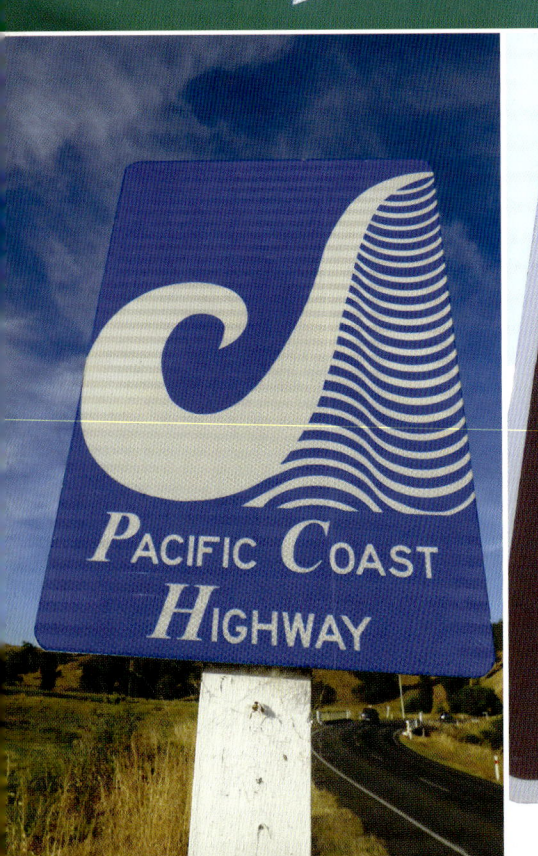

Pacific Coast Highway

Adventure Highway
TURN RIGHT
300 m

PART TWO: TE IKA A MAUI/ NORTH ISLAND

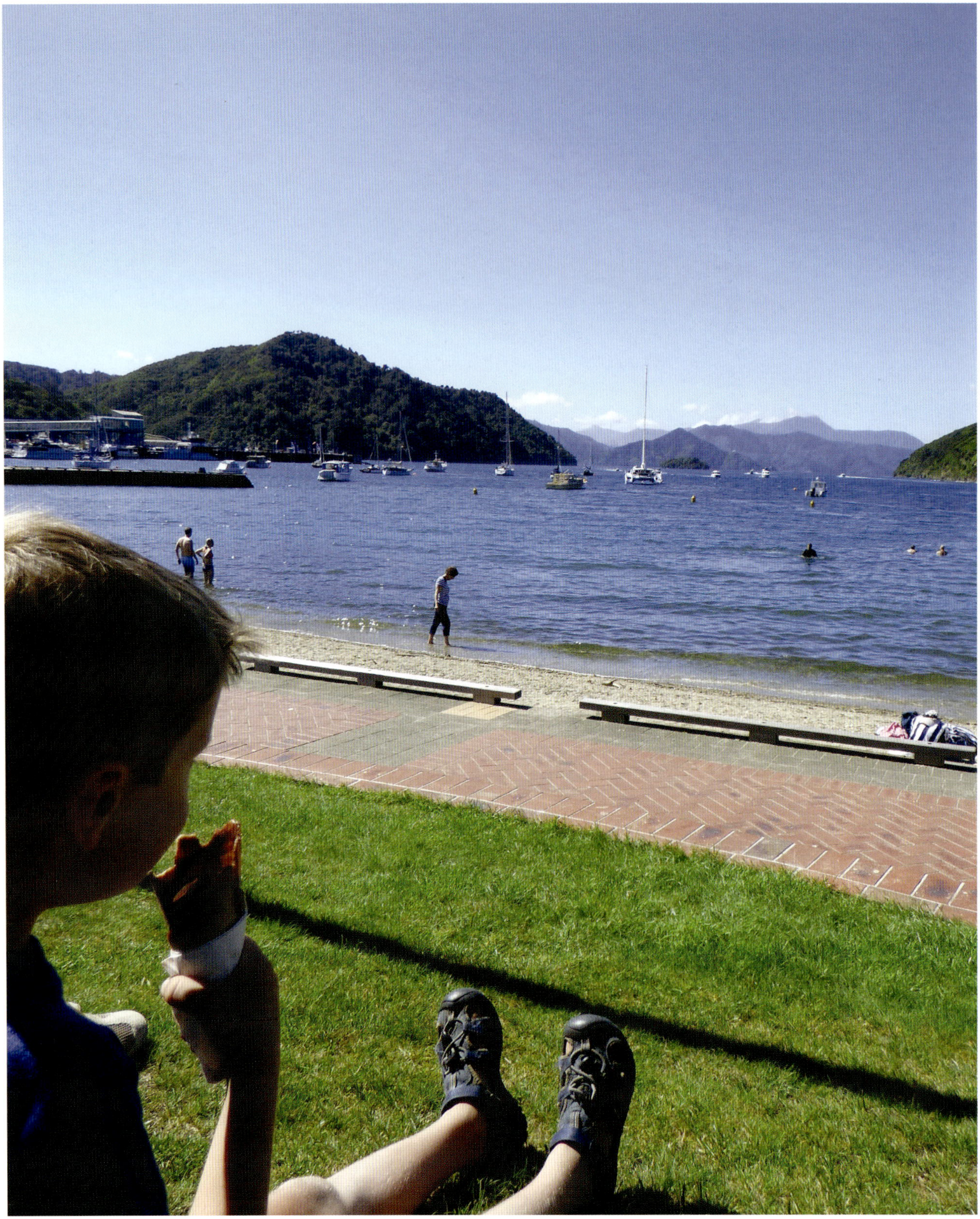

ACROSS THE WATER: A CRAFT BREWER AND A NAUGHTY NANA

'It's a highway song. You sing it on and on.'
— Blackfoot

After a couple of weeks back home in Governors Bay sorting stuff out, seeing a man about a dog and doing a bit of dry-stone walling, I find myself back in Picton on a sunny, blustery morning. I enjoy a relaxing day just poking around down on the waterfront, in a great secondhand bookshop, and downing more coffee than is reasonable. There's nothing like a ferry crossing to get the adventure juices flowing and fill your head with Quixotic notions. And the longer the crossing, the better, so far as I'm concerned. I finally get the thumbs-up and ride up the wet ramp gingerly, with feet down as outriders. I strap the Triumph securely, once more admiring its vintage flair, in the bowels of the *Aratere* (Maori for 'quick path'). The good ship *Aratere* sailed to Singapore in 2011 to undergo refurbishment, including new propellers — and returned 30 metres longer!

I stand on deck with the wind in my thinning hair, watching the Mainland shrink and remembering past sea crossings. Mainly across the English Channel or North Sea. It's a time to take stock and reflect; a time to plan the future and a time to indulge in an orgy of reminiscing. A long ferry crossing can act as a pause between chapters, figuratively and in my case literally. After finding a good seat, I lean back contentedly and think fondly of my motorcycle below. I've had her for three years now, and have put over 30,000 kilometres on the clock. Actually, rather than plagiarise myself, following is the piece I wrote in Issue #131 of *Bike Rider Magazine*, entitled 'Procrastinate No More!'

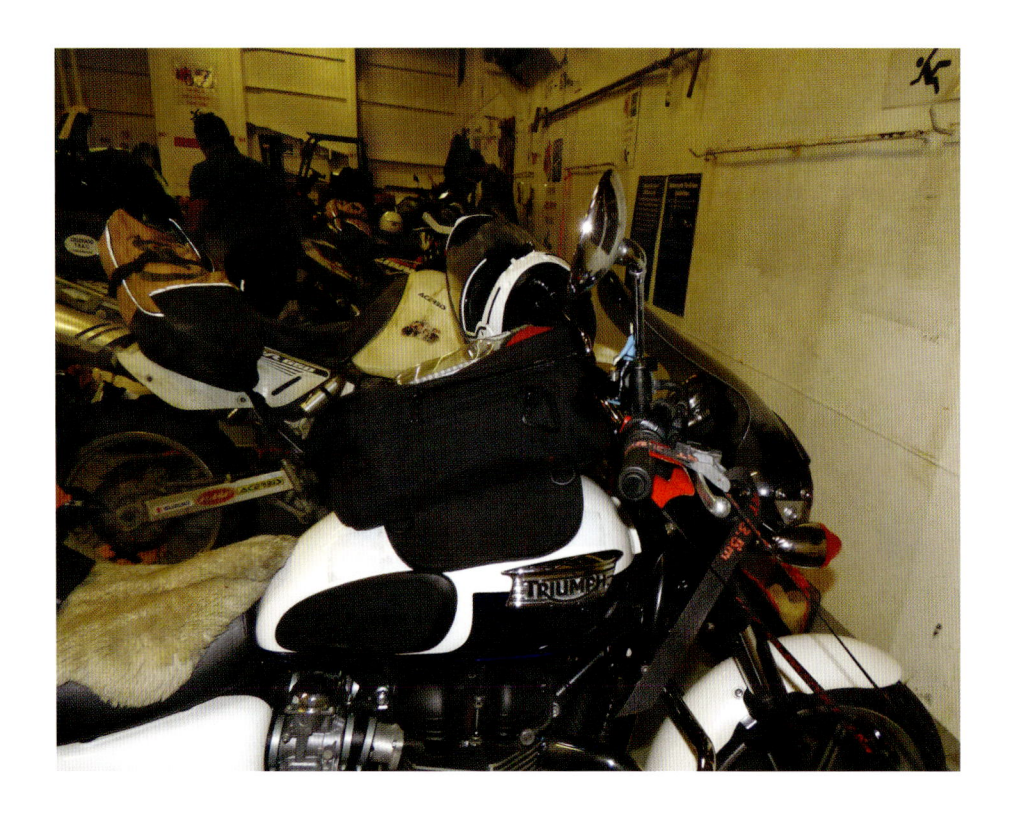

Buying a new bike. There's no feeling quite like it. In a way, the anticipation is almost as good as the reality. There's the agonising over the financial decision. 'If only I had the money …', or 'If I could just persuade 'er (or 'im) indoors', or 'Well, things are a bit tight at the moment and we're supposed to be upgrading the kitchen with Smeg appliances this year.' Or you may just be a bit of a tight-arse like me and still be overly careful with your hard-earned.

A kind of epiphany came to me the other day (as many good ideas do) while I was cruising around the Port Hills on the KLR. I figured that if I was lucky enough to be able to ride bikes for another 20 years (taking me into my mid-70s) and if I traded in for a new model every other year (well, that's the theory) then that would give me only 10 new bikes before I hung up my helmet. Which, let's face it, is a somewhat sobering, even depressing thought!

Over Thai curry and prawns that night I sighed plaintively, while describing my dilemma to my dear lady wife, while trying not to overdo the sad, resigned look. 'Well,

what are you waiting for then, you plonker?' she replied. Bless 'er cotton socks.

Now I'm sure we all have an idea of what our next bike would be. God knows there is enough variety out there. So, next time I was in my favourite coffee shop I wrote down a list of requirements for my new steed.

I didn't need a huge motor. Most of those CCs would be superfluous for my kind of riding. But then I'd endured years of struggling over passes with underpowered machines, so we'd go with what today is termed a 'middle-weight', but back in the day was a stonking big bike. I've never been a sports bike guy, preferring an upright riding position. So it would have to be a 'cruiser'.

It had to have that classic look; a nice bit of eye candy. I preferred wide-ish bars and a reasonably low seat, and the bike had to have only five gears. (I can be a bit lazy that way. And I sometimes forget what gear I'm in with only five!) I liked a decent-sized tank, too. I knew I wouldn't need one as gigantic as my KLR's, but at least 15 litres so you could do a good few k's between fills.

And though I was quite partial to single thumpers, a nice parallel-twin would probably hit the spot. Before I'd completed the list, I had screwed it up into a ball and was heading out the door, realising that my list was merely confirmation of the bike that had been hovering inside a thought bubble above my helmet for ages. What I needed, of course, was a new Triumph Bonneville!

Triumph, the oldest manufacturer to still be in business today, is as iconic as a warm pint of best bitter or a pot of jellied eels, and as English as a double-decker bus or toad in the 'ole. As cool as Steve McQueen (yes, I know, he wasn't English, but he did like Triumphs), and as substantial as W. C. Grace.

Let's face it, as you get older, repetition can make some everyday things a bit ho-hum; a bit boring. But no matter how jaded or blasé one becomes, there's still nothing quite like picking up your new motorcycle.

The tedious paperwork and last-minute instructions from the dealer are complete. You can be excused for a few butterflies in the old tum as at last you settle into the saddle and fire her up.

I now let out the smooth-as-silk clutch, and the 68 British horses and I, teetering together on that thin line where gravity meets centripetal force, are away. I have opted for the basic Bonnie (an A3) with a smaller front wheel and no rev-counter. My white-and-blue model is reliable, solid, understated and worthy of the proud Triumph badge.

The lights change, causing me to brake sharply (daydreaming), and I'm pleased to note the single disc brakes seem responsive enough. I give her a bit of a blast *on the motorway and smile at the noises coming out of those pea-shooter pipes. This bike was made in England, just like myself, lending to the whole ownership experience an almost visceral 'feel good' factor.*

But it's not just the smooth twin that puts a smile on my dial. Today, astride my spanking-new bike I head for the Port Hills across a once devastated Garden City which is now clearly showing signs of re-birth.

Long May We Ride.

The backpackers is no distance from the terminal, and in no time flat I'm all squared away. I'm a bit nervous about leaving my bike on the street, but I've no choice. In the morning, I watch the scurrying commuters through the window of the café around the corner from the Beehive as I tuck into a Big Breakfast. Each person immersed in their own bubbles, with their own memories, aspirations, fears and untold stories. I'm spoilt for choice café-wise, as apparently Wellington has more of them per capita than New York. Wiping the egg yolk from my mouth, I hit the road. I quickly re-acquaint myself with the rules of city riding, and, having learned to ride in London, it comes naturally. The trick is to be positive in your lane-splitting: confident, but not rude. And a hand raised in apology occasionally doesn't hurt either. I head for the Basin Reserve and a small craft brewery that is tucked away behind it.

CRAFT BREWER — ANNIKA NASCHITZKI

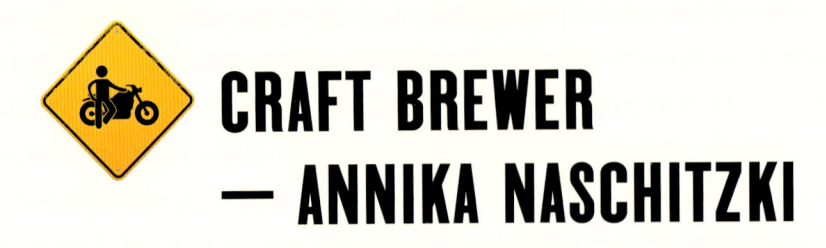

Inside, I sit with Annika, owner of Tiamana Brewery, at a stainless-steel bench, surrounded by buckets, hoses, pipes, tanks, kegs, bottles and pallets. All very neat and ship-shape. You could say that beer runs in her blood (I had to get that in!), for in the 1970s and 1980s her father, back in Germany, was himself a brewer, working at Schultheiss, one of the oldest breweries in Berlin.

'But I certainly didn't expect to become a brewer myself,' she says. 'I studied

Sociology, and trained as a specialist in designing and making websites more user-friendly.'

Annika came to these shores to get away from 'stuff' after a break-up seven years ago, initially for a holiday, but she fell in love with the place, while falling out of love with Germany. 'An Italian-American friend of mine used to run a pizza place in Arizona, and wanted to go into business with me and start up a frozen-pizza company. She said the pizzas here are awful, and we must make them better! She also suggested later that, as I was the daughter of a German brewer, then why didn't I become one myself, what with the growing popularity of craft beers in New Zealand? So, I said to myself, "Why not?"'

At the time, Annika's parents were visiting, and on long drives touring around the South Island she had plenty of time to quiz her father on the subject of brewing. She returned from that trip determined to become a brewer, and I get the impression that Annika is quite a determined young lady. 'So, before my dad left, we bought a home-brew kit and started making beer,' she says. 'But I wanted to make it a business first and foremost. I thought it would be a perfect combination of history, business and what I'd really like to do. I'd been advising businesses for years as part of my job, and so wanted to show how a business could be run. I basically wanted to practise what I'd preached, and show that integrity can work in business. I didn't want to make huge amounts of money; I just wanted the beer to be good.'

Despite not having a diploma in brewing, Annika found it relatively easy to get help and sound advice for her venture in Wellington. She puts it down to the fact that Kiwis love an underdog and someone willing to 'have a go'. She goes on: 'Craft beer is not big over there. People in Germany are very much in the grip of marketing. It's all about the historic purity of their beer.'

Apparently (and amazingly to me), there is a law in Germany dating back to the 1500s that says that beer can only be made with four ingredients: malted grains, hops, yeast and water. *Reinheitsgebot* is the collective name for these regulations in Germany and 'the states of the former Holy Roman Empire'. Which explains, Annika points out, the domination of the German market with Pilsner-style beers. 'There's no way I could have become a brewer in Germany.'

Annika tells of a brewer friend in Bavaria who put lactic sugar into the brew to make milk stout, and had trucks pull up outside, take her entire stock away, and fine her €25,000! Apparently in Bavaria it's illegal to interfere with the old brewing custom, whereas in other parts of the country you can make it, but just can't label it as beer. You must call it a 'fermented alcoholic beverage'.

Growing up, it was ingrained in Annika that German beer was the best in the world. And I must admit to having been brainwashed into assuming that was the case, too. She continues: 'In the 1970s the importation laws were changed, so suddenly beers that were not considered pure could be imported. So the big German brewers had to fight it. They did this with massive advertising campaigns, describing the new beers as chemically botched, impure and liable to give you hangovers. And it was incredibly successful. These lies were embedded in people's heads, and are still there today. Having said that, though, I think the base standard is higher in Germany than here. An average, generic beer is I think superior to the average beer here in New Zealand.'

When Annika started her brewery five years ago, even her friends asked her what beer purity laws she was breaking! 'I told them those laws are bullshit!' she says. 'It's all bollocks!' And I tell her how impressed I am with her use of the English language.

'In reality,' she continues, with a nod and a smile, '60 ingredients are allowed to be used in beer. There are fillers and filters and silicones, anything but natural. But the idea is that they don't stay in the beer. The idea is to trickle them through and catch proteins. What these ingredients make possible is the fast, large-scale production of uniform beer that all tastes the same.'

As a small brewer in New Zealand, Annika can argue that she makes more interesting beers than the big brewers do, despite the fact, she points out, that the big players are getting on the bandwagon, buying up different craft-beer brands, trying to stay relevant in an area that they initially struggled with.

'I don't use anything that isn't natural,' says Annika. 'I don't use anything people don't need.' I want to know if your hangover will be less if you avoid the chemical-filled beers. 'Well, it's all about fermentable sugars and the length of them,' she replies. 'Longer chains make it harder for yeast to turn into nice, short-chain alcohols, so it may be true, but I'm not a biochemist. But I'd say I'd be wary of drinking a lot of sugar-filled beers like the big brewers make. To me, those popular sugar beers taste flat like cardboard, like flavoured water. Look, George, I wouldn't criticise anyone for not drinking craft beer, but I think it's good to have the variety out there.'

Annika's Tiamana Brewery produces 800 litres in a double-brew day of 14 hours. It's small even by craft-beer standards, but she says it's the right size for her to start. She shares the premises with Canadian Llew Bardecki who produces Wild and Woolly craft beer. 'And he looks wild and woolly, too,' she says. 'He owns those two fermenters, and I own these two. This one is called Hildegard and this one Helga, after big German opera singers.'

When she started out she admits to being a bit scared. Her pizza friend from Arizona had gone home, so basically she was on her own. 'For me, what always helps is planning and spreadsheets, so I sat down with my calculator and asked myself, "What will it cost to run a brewery? How much will I have to make? And what will I have to sell the beer for?"'

She worked with a real estate agent looking for a suitable space, but it was fruitless and nothing was happening, until it was suggested she talk to Llew, the wild-looking Canadian guy. 'So, we met,' says Annika, 'and it was weird, worse than a blind date. And quite stressful, as we would both be investing a lot of money. But luckily we were well-matched, and we soon found this place with a great landlord and each bought half of the assets. We are very different personalities, but work well together.'

During the two years it took to set up, Annika was busy experimenting with brewing at home. She was under no illusion that it would be an easy ride, and was prepared for a steep learning curve where she knew she would make many mistakes along the way. Annika read a lot of books, talked to many people and visited many breweries. She also continued working in her well-paid contracting job for the government during the process, so she didn't have to go into debt to start her venture, which she says is quite unusual. 'That's why I started small,' she says. 'I didn't want to go into debt. People told me that I had to produce 2000 litres in a double-brew day to be viable. And I can see that now, but with more volume comes more problems, too. I remember the first few weeks of brewing here when it all seemed so overwhelming. Although there are only four basic ingredients, so many little things can impact the way the final product tastes. It's all about the palate; your understanding of tasting and evaluating your own beer. Now I think I could fly blind in this brewery.'

Annika clears her throat, and I suggest that she might need a drink! She is a great talker, and proceeds to blind me with brewing science — ratios, enzyme temperatures, water pressures and beer balancing — without pausing for breath or referring to notes, before giving me a tour of her equipment. And it's not just brewing. Annika is a one-man-band, so must move and stack the 60-kilogram kegs herself, which she ably demonstrates. She then lines up her new beer labels, which she designed herself, of course.

In two years Annika must move out, as earthquake strengthening will take place. She tells me that she is now in the process of selling the whole brewery business, and the buyer will then take over the lease. When it's sold, Annika would like to go into contracting, and pay other people to brew her beer. 'I want people to think about business and not brewing,' she says. 'When you own a brewery, you must remember that you are running a business. The accounting, the legal crap, certifications and designing. As most people in my position will tell you: it's 10 per cent brewing, 20 per cent cleaning and 70 per cent business.'

She started a blog called 'The Brewer's Daughter', and wrote the only post, called 'So you want to start a brewery', which received over 10,000 views.

I'm sure anything Annika does will be successful. She is high-energy and one smart lady. I wish her well — and it's not until I'm back on my bike that I realise I didn't ask for any free samples. Doh!

NAUGHTY NANA — JO MORGAN

I'm talking to Jo over a cuppa in the kitchen of her and Gareth's lovely home in Wellington's Oriental Bay. Growing up in Invercargill, she got her first bike at 15, having saved up the money from working after school. 'It was a Suzuki and looked like a motorbike, but was only 50cc, a scooter really,' she begins. 'I realised very rapidly that it wasn't enough, and a couple of years later I'd crept up to a simple two-stroke Suzuki 350.' Jo tore it to bits and played with it, teaching herself the rudiments of mechanics, even taking the cylinders down the street to the local bike shop to see if they could bore them out to a 400. She was soon the proud owner of another two-stroke, this time a Suzuki T500. 'It seemed incredibly long, and was an odd-handling bike. I used to ride it from university in Palmerston North down to Invercargill in the holidays. I'd do the trip in one hit, as I was a poor student. Sometime I'd end up sleeping under hedges and things.'

I'm thinking that's a hell of ride to do in one hit. Aloud, I say, 'That must have been pretty unique back then.' And at the risk of sounding sexist, add: 'It wasn't exactly a girlie thing to do.'

'Well, there were no cops on the road. The road itself was the limitation,' she replies, 'especially at night. There were a few exciting moments. But I've never done the girlie thing, though I am getting better. I can do both now. I remember looking very butch at times; I didn't have very big boobs, which probably helped.' And we laugh.

Jo rode regularly until her first child, Sam, was about six months old, and one of the financial decisions was to sell her bike. But, she says, husband Gareth promised her that he'd buy her another bike one day. There was quite a gap between rides, until one day, after a good year financially and when the youngest of their children was four, Gareth turned up with a big, shiny, red Harley. 'So,' says Jo, 'I pushed this beautiful piece of machinery into the kitchen, and it was so heavy. Gareth said, "Well, if you're not going to ride it, then I will," so I told him that he'd bought it for me and he should go and buy his own.'

Which he promptly did, and the couple proceeded to enjoy many rides on their Harleys, enjoying the early days of the Harley-Davidson Club in Wellington.

In those early days, explains Jo, the club was transitioning from a gang culture to the mainstream, mid-life-crisis affair it is today. They experienced many great rides where they'd end up in a gang's headquarters for a beer, with double barbed-wire fences and chained-up Rottweilers. 'And often I was the only woman rider, and I'd occasionally hear comments like, "What a waste", but I never felt uncomfortable, though maybe I should have.'

It provided them with a great network of like-minded people, and, as she points out, that's one of the great things about motorcycling: it breaks down barriers. She recalls breaking down once in Central Otago. 'This gang member came by, picked up my bike, and stored it at their headquarters for a few weeks while I went back to Invercargill. I remember asking him if it would be safe, and then felt a fool when I picked it up — inside a fenced compound, with patrolling dogs. Of course it was safe!

'There are just a lot of good people out there,' she continues, 'and we've found that all over the world. We'd arrive tired, dirty and hungry, obviously on a mission, and people take you under their wing, either put you up or show you where you can pitch your tent.'

I completely agree with Jo. Perhaps it's the fact that you are so exposed on a motorcycle, that strangers can be so sympathetic and helpful — and perhaps not so helpful or friendly if you rocked up in a four-wheeled vehicle.

Jo and Gareth enjoyed a couple of organised commercial bike trips overseas in India and Bolivia, which really lit the fuse for the idea of independent motorcycle trips.

'We soon discovered how labour- and bureaucracy-intensive these trips are. You certainly need time and planning. On our first independent trip, the Silk Road, we all did first-aid courses and had the right number of spares. That first trip, involving three and a half months' riding, really got us hooked. It was also good for Gareth to break out of the work culture thing, because he is basically a workaholic.

'And on the African trip we all carried IV fluids as well. I was in charge of medicine, but obviously couldn't carry 10 kilograms of fluids, so we all carried 2 each. We knew everyone's blood group, and we had giving sets and receiving sets.' Jo maintains that she's not particularly well-organised, and that it's Gareth who does the organising and then delegates.

'But it's amazing how the little things crop up,' Jo says. 'On our American trip we thought we were safe with 90-day visas, until we discovered that that included travelling in the West Indies, Mexico and Canada, so we suddenly had to do an emergency flight to Europe in order for a new 90 days to start.'

Jo has always enjoyed fixing things and getting lost in the mechanics of tinkering. Husband Gareth always says that she is the mechanic on a trip, although other members of the team often vie for that position. And a list of their motorcycling trips is very impressive. Jo shows me a huge world map on the wall, with pins highlighting the routes to all parts of the globe. I, like thousands of others, have read and enjoyed the many books detailing these adventures, from the 2006 *Silk Riders* to the 2014 *Kimchi Kiwis*. Jo thinks their most recent biking adventure, through Indonesia, doesn't really warrant a book.

'But with mechanical issues, two brains are often better than one,' Jo continues. 'When I'm on a trip with just Gareth, I'm definitely the mechanic, because Gareth's just not interested, though that's not to say he's not capable. I'll often ask him for a bit of muscle, like if we have to get a tyre off. I'll tell him to jump here or jump there. But there are techniques, like using the side-stand on the bike to break the bead, and things like that. If you have a good teacher, you're fine; you only have to be shown.'

Jo and Gareth haven't finished with motorcycle adventuring. They are busy planning a massive trip in 2018, starting in West Africa, riding through part of North Africa, Turkey, up through Georgia into Kazakhstan, Russia and Mongolia, and ending up in Japan for the Rugby World Cup. I'm very jealous.

'At the moment, though, I'm totally distracted,' says Jo, and beckons me around the corner where another map along with a list is pinned to the wall. The list is of all 24 mountains in New Zealand of 3000 metres or over, which are all part of the chain that forms the backbone of the South Island. She promptly crosses off Mount Vancouver, which she knocked off a couple of weeks ago, making 20 out of 24! According to Wikipedia, there are in fact 26, but, as Jo points out, a couple of those are mere shoulders of Aoraki and Tasman. And who am I to argue?

It's an amazing accomplishment for someone who only started climbing five years ago. I ask how technical the climbs are. 'It's definitely technical. Life-or-death stuff every second day. It makes motorcycling seem tame,' she says.

Jo says that for her it's very much a 'learn as you go' thing. She has been with the same guide, Wolfgang, for all her climbs. 'He does the technical stuff, but of course I have to follow and do the climb, and put up with the falling rocks and things. There's just the two of us. In fact, he hasn't climbed these remaining peaks either, so it's really exploration as we try to work out the routes. Our last one, Mount Vancouver, is the fourth-highest peak in the country, and yet we couldn't find anyone who'd climbed it.' I find Jo's mountaineering feats amazing, and I'm sure there are not many other grandmothers doing it!

'It's very sobering being in a white-out or stepping over crevasses 50 metres deep. But it's so like motorcycling, I think. You must concentrate always, and every now and then something random happens: you've got a rock you have to avoid, or the weather can turn to custard. It's that whole thing of risk management.'

Jo is a remarkable woman and I take my hat off to her.

High Risk Route

THE WAIRARAPA AND HAWKE'S BAY AND A VETERAN BIKER

'Working on the highway, all day long I don't stop.'
— Bruce Springsteen

I leave Jo's lovely home with drizzle threatening, and head north with the traffic up SH2. After a quick lunch at an uninspiring place in Upper Hutt, the drizzle begins as I start the climb over the Rimutakas. I must concentrate, as the road is narrow in places and greasy, and the wind has picked up. The Rimutaka Hill Road, which reaches a height of 555 metres above sea level, is only 14 kilometres long, but changeable weather, even in summer, makes it challenging. It was marked out in 1843, and a rough road opened in 1856 for the wagon trains of primary produce between Wellington and the Wairarapa.

Before the arrival of Europeans, these hills were heavily forested and no doubt filled with birdlife. I imagine the scrub-covered hills would be pretty bleak on a cold winter's day. It was from the summit of the Rimutakas that the first Maori (Rangitane) to settle the land to the east looked down onto the shimmering lake below, and named it Wairarapa, or 'glistening waters'.

I'm excited because the part of New Zealand from here to Gisborne, where I stayed with my new in-laws 30 years ago, is all new. The drizzle stops as I roll into Featherston, formerly known as Burlings after a pioneer settler. It was renamed in 1854 after Dr Isaac Featherston, Superintendent of Wellington Province. It's then a quick ride down the length of SH53, over the Ruamahanga River to Martinborough, which sits in the middle of a plain and so gets a bit of wind. It was laid out with military precision by Sir John Martin, who used over 1000 acres of his own land on which to build the town. From where I sit in the handsome central park, the streets radiate out in the form of the Union Jack. Everything looks very pleasant, and I have to pinch myself or I'll think I've been beamed to a village green in the Cotswolds. But wine is what Martinborough is really famous for, especially its award-winning Pinot Noir and Sauvignon Blanc.

The guy I've come to interview has changed his mind at the last minute, so there's nothing to do but shrug philosophically and head back up the long and winding to the next one, which is in Wairoa. My other interviewee in Napier has also pulled the plug, for medical reasons, so it seems I'll be riding rather more than I'll be asking questions on this leg of my journey. Ah well, it beats laying bricks!

I head up a minor road to hit SH2 at Greytown, oldest town in the Wairarapa, founded in 1854 and named after Governor Sir George Grey. Greytown and Masterton were in fact the first planned, inland towns in New Zealand. Tall trees and tastefully restored wooden buildings pass by as I accelerate out of town. Just east of the main road is the tiny settlement of Papawai. While the Maori land laws were being formulated, Papawai was Ngaruawahia's main rival for the centre of Maori influence. Carterton, just up the road, is another little charmer, surrounded by tidy farms. It was completely destroyed by fire in 1859 when it was a tiny timber town surrounded by forest.

I cruise around the centre of Masterton for a bit, looking for accommodation. The town was named after Joseph Master, who organised the Small Farm Scheme in 1854, which assisted settlers to purchase farms in the area. The motels are too pricey, the backpackers is full, and I'm sick of stopping and taking my gear off so I don't look like a visiting alien. I'm overheating and I've decided that Masterton doesn't fit into my Goldilocks Zone for towns, being a little too big. I clunk the Bonnie into gear and press on. North of Masterton, the brown hills contrast sharply with the green flatlands. I ride through the occasional stand of poplars and oaks. Dairy herds of Friesians and Jerseys dot the landscape, mixed with herds of Romney and Southdown sheep.

My next interview is a fair way off, so I figure I'll get as many miles in today as I can. About 50 k's more of SH2 brings me in the early evening to Eketahuna. The name means 'to run aground on a sandbank', as this was as far south as a waka could navigate the Makakahi River. Scandinavians settled here in 1872, carving the town out of the Seventy Mile Bush, a forest that stretched from Mount Bruce to Takapau. The town was briefly known as 'Mellomskov' or 'heart of the forest'.

The Eketuhuna Inn is nothing luxurious, but it's unpretentious, the sheets are clean and I can have a beer and a chat with the locals, mostly farmers. Highlights of the Australian Open are playing on the TV above the bar. Federer's classic thriller against old rival Nadal.

'He's 46, you know,' the barman and owner says to me as he dries a glass.

'No, he's 35,' I reply.

'Twenty-three Grand Slams,' he adds.

'No,' I reply, 'I think he's only got 18. It's Serena who's got 23.'

He walks away without another word, and I feel it's time I hit the sack before everyone thinks I'm a smart-arse!

After a stroll around town in the morning, it's time to pack up and head off. When touring on a bike, my favourite times of day are always the 'leaving' bit and the 'arriving' bit. Obviously there's the bit in the middle, which can be OK, occasionally awesome, but never mundane. It's all in the lap of the gods. I behold my loaded bike with an optimistic stare: the whole day ahead seems to radiate promise and I want the clock to stop right here. Threatening clouds are left behind as I fuel up and head north with logging trucks and utes. The road takes me through gorgeous valleys, beautiful farmland and little towns I didn't know existed. Pleasant little communities like Pahiatua, just going about their business. The main street here is very wide. It was built to allow railway tracks to run down the middle, but this plan didn't eventuate.

Riding towards Woodville, dozens of wind turbines gradually grow in size away to my left and make a marvellous sight. The Tararua Wind Farm sits on 700 hectares of farmland, at the northern end of the Tararua Range, between Woodville and Palmerston North, and its 134 turbines have a capacity of 160 megawatts. Woodville, is … well, woody, with lots of wooden houses and shops. Somewhere between Woodville and Dannevirke, with cloud sitting on the Ruahine Range like icing on a cake, I cross into Hawke's Bay. It reminds me of crossing from Canterbury into Marlborough on the east coast. Suddenly the hills look browner, more parched.

In Dannevirke it's time for breakfast at the Red Sky Café. The lack of any ambience is compensated for by good coffee and bacon-and-egg pie, as well as a bit of flirting with the jolly ladies behind the counter. Dannevirke was settled by sturdy Scandinavians who hewed out their farms from the dense forest. Dannevirke means 'Danes' work' (as in 'Danes' creation'), and is named after the defensive wall that used to stand between Saxon lands and the Danish peninsula.

The sun has now burned off any remaining cloud, and the heat is building as I put some miles under my belt and blast up the largely straight stretch of SH2 into Hastings. Hawke's Bay is basically the fertile Heretaunga Plain with the rolling hills that rise up to form the spine of the North Island to the west, and the Pacific Ocean to the east. It didn't take Pakeha long to see the farming potential here, and they soon set to, and the region was 'stamped, jammed, hauled and murdered into grass', as naturalist Herbert Guthrie-Smith eloquently put it.

Hastings looks very English with its profusion of gardens. It's one of New Zealand's youngest towns, achieving city status as recently as 1956. It was razed by fire in 1893 and again in 1907, and then was mostly flattened by the 1931 Hawke's Bay earthquake. Despite its attractions, the traffic and general business do not encourage me to linger, and I twist the throttle and ride another 10 k's to Napier.

Napier is a town I've heard much about, but never visited. The earthquake that flattened Hastings literally tore this city apart and then set alight its largely wooden buildings. Thus, the city was rebuilt in the Art Deco style of the 1930s, using cement to avoid another firestorm, re-creating the look of one of Hawke's Bay's oldest settlements. Before the earthquake, Napier was almost completely surrounded by water; after the quake, vast areas of the seabed were lifted above sea level.

It's stinking hot as I park on Marine Parade in the shade of one of the many Norfolk pines which at night are festively aglow with fairy lights. I've only seconds to get my gear off before I spontaneously combust. If you'd beamed someone into the centre of Napier, they could be excused for thinking they were in LA or Saint-Tropez. That is until they wander onto the beach to discover what looks like black pre-mix instead of golden sand, and no topless beauties. But that's no criticism, because I think it's a top spot.

Leaving my gear on my bike and thinking 'to hell with a parking ticket', I stretch my legs around the main drag and then, forsaking coffee, I wander into the Provincial Hotel where a bubbly barmaid hands me a cold shandy and tells me it's 33 degrees outside.

In the saddle again and feeling a bit cooler, I'm back on SH2 heading for my next little chat in Wairoa, another town I've never visited. The best thing about New Zealand roads is that, simply looking at a map, you never know what you're going to get. It's a bit like Forest Gump's box of chocolates. The road out of Napier turns out to be another cracker, with everything a motorcyclist could want. Long, fast straights, sweeping 80kph bends and plenty of twisties going up hill and down dale keep you interested. It's still hot, and near Raupunga I pull over at a picnic spot and sit in a rare piece of shade with my back against a tree to cool off. Taking off my boots and socks is bliss, as is the soggy sandwich and bottle of water I remembered to buy, which are stowed in my tank bag. I revel in the peace and silence — apart, that is, from the chorus of the cicadas. A nice bloke in an electrician's van pulls up and shares my shade for a bit. He, too, owns a Triumph, and we talk bikes.

Wairoa, the quiet little town I now ride into, means 'long water', and is named after the wide, genteel river which is navigable for shallow-drafted boats for many miles. The area has been farmed for a long time. In fact, Maori grew wheat, maize, kumara and taro back in the 1870s. It proved to be something of an Eden, for, along with their crops, Maori hunted pigs and goats from the dense bush, as well as enjoyed plenty of fish and shellfish. I'm surprised to find a lighthouse on the riverbank, and quiz the lady who makes me a passable flat white on the main street. 'It used to be on Portland Island,' she says. 'They used to light it up every night.'

I once more sit in the shade of a tree, one of many Phoenix palms, and read for a bit, while also watching kids on the opposite bank swinging off a rope to drop, laughing, into the river's cool, green depths. I'd love to join them.

VETERAN BIKER — MIKE LITTLE

Mike has just arrived home from work to find me waiting for him in his backyard. He's in possession of a steely gaze and big workman's hands, and is wearing a wide-brimmed straw hat. At 80 he's still fit and strong and working hard. After a cold drink, he gets his work boots off and we sit in the shade for a chat.

At 14 Mike bought his first motorcycle from an old chap who ran a market garden in Hastings. The 1926 Indian Prince cost £7 10s, the cash consisting of a 10-shilling note and lots of coins, as it represented the savings from his paper round. 'I was riding it to the river one Saturday,' says Mike in his deep baritone, 'when the local traffic cop stopped me, eyed me up suspiciously, and said, "Has this bloody thing got a warrant of fitness?" "No." "Don't suppose it's registered either, is it?" "No." "Well get the effin thing home then before I kick your arse!"' After that introduction to motorcycling, Mike never looked back. One of his earliest biking memories was riding around the South Island over 60 years ago, on a Royal Enfield wearing an army greatcoat and a pair of flying goggles.

His father was a builder in Hastings, and Mike completed his carpentry apprenticeship there. 'The carpentry kind of morphed into general building. At one time we had 36 men on the payroll. We were into heavy engineering, too, and soon realised that, instead of hiring cranes, it was better if we bought some for our own use. We discovered that it was easier to hire out cranes and drivers. We also got into heavy haulage and demolition, with a couple of bulldozers and excavators.' It sounds like Mike has done it all. 'Yep, I've done just about every bloody thing! Had four cranes here at one time, even prospected for oil at one stage,' he adds matter-of-factly. These days, Little Crane Hire (he's kept the company name the same —

that way he can still use the old stationery) sells oils and lubricants, timber and plywood, and hires out scaffolding.

Mike's always been practical, and started working, collecting and tinkering at an early age. While still living at home he built himself a Model T Ford from bits and pieces of wrecks parked-up all around the district. 'My mate and I would go door-knocking after school, asking if we could have parts from their old Model Ts sitting in the yards. If they said "yes", we'd take them; if they wanted paying for them, we walked away.' Apparently when you bought a new Model T it was delivered to your door in a crate, and part of the crate formed the footboards. One guy had the original crate, but told Mike he couldn't have the car but could have the handbook on how to assemble it. 'You could do the whole job with the one spanner,' says Mike, 'and I've still got the bloody thing somewhere.'

After returning home after a seven-year absence, Mike was shocked to find that his father had used all his collected bits and pieces to fill in an old open drain which he says was the sole remnant of the original river. Amongst the 'junk' used as fill was a Model T truck, a 1937 Square Four Ariel with a set of Dowty Oleomatic forks on it ('a pig of a thing to ride'), an Army Indian and a 1939 Royal Enfield. 'It had belonged to a chap who didn't come back from World War II, and his family had hidden it away,' says Mike. 'I bought it well after the war, and it had virtually zero miles on it. I remember I was riding out towards Pakowhai one day and started to overtake a very slow-moving truck, which chose that moment to turn in front of me. All I could do was go with him and I hit the kerb, which pushed the forks back under the bike, and I ended up in the middle of a bloody rose bush.'

Mike had a huge collection of machinery which ended up in the drain, but he seems philosophical about it, although I imagine time has eased the pain considerably. It wasn't long before he started collecting again. I resist the temptation to ask him to list the bikes he's owned, as we'd be here all day and he'd probably not remember them all anyway! 'We had a 1927 four-valve Rudge, which we took from one end of New Zealand to the other to various rallies and things. It's now owned by a policeman in Invercargill. It was a lovely bike.'

Over his many years of biking, Mike's belonged to the Royal Enfield Owners Club, the Norton Owners Club, the Indian Owners Club, the Gisborne Classic Club, and the Hawke's Bay Classic Club. He still rides, and plans on going to the Bi-annual Vintage Motorcycle Rally in a couple of weeks' time at Waitomo, where he'll be on his Army Indian. 'That bike sat here for 25 years before I restored it,' he says. 'It's a 741 model, and was one of the last registrations in 1942. They only manufactured them for two years.'

Mike uncovers and drags out a beautifully restored 98cc 1951 James Superlux Autocycle, and wheels it outside into the sunlight. The purple and sky-blue tank is gorgeous. I ask Mike how long it took to restore. 'Thirty years,' he says with a chuckle, 'because, for a start, you couldn't buy tyres for them. I also struggled to find a headlight. I finally got that one from a guy in Masterton, who had gone with his father to the tip in order to dump his James and thought he'd keep the headlight for a memento!'

Mike's partner, Gail, loves to ride motorcycles, too, and is, says Mike, a very good rider. She's clocked up 130,000 k's on her BMW R80, but hasn't ridden for a while. Her CB350 is sitting in the workshop waiting to be fixed. 'She wouldn't be seen dead on the back of my '96 Honda Gold Wing, so she rode her own,' he says. 'But the Gold Wing was a superb piece of engineering. It made you lazy, as all you had to do was put fuel in the tank and air in the tyres.'

Mike suggests we go to his workshop to see some more bikes, and as we drive he points out landmarks, giving me a running commentary. Mike's lived and worked here for 50 years, and has obviously seen a lot of changes. He tells me that after his apprenticeship he was called up for three years of military service, or CMT (compulsory military training). 'I certainly didn't want to be there,' says Mike. 'I was paid a ridiculous amount of money; about 10 shillings a day. It makes me laugh now, because I didn't want to do anything — and that's what happened: I didn't do anything. And the less I did, the more they promoted me! I was in the tank regiment training up in Waiouru, in those horrible little British things with a two-pounder gun that the Germans blew the shit out of. The engineers were flying about the desert in American tanks with the radial aircraft motor in the back and the turret cut off.'

Every year they had fortnight-long camps. To dodge parades, Mike would go in with the advance party and put up the tents, then stay there with the rear parties and pull the tents down. 'The first one I went in I was promoted to corporal, and the next one I went in I was promoted to sergeant. The guy who was meant to be the vehicle officer for the camp was bloody useless and got things into a dreadful state. A three-tonner vanished and was found at the top of the North Island. He'd peel off and go drinking in Taihape, until MPs [military police] picked him up. It was interesting, because he later became an assistant to the Governor-General. So I became the new vehicle officer, and as such I could requisition whatever vehicles I wanted.' Naturally, Mike requisitioned four motorcycles, and he and his mates had a ball riding up and down the hills on the 741 Indians. He also put an Austin ambulance to good use, sleeping in the bunks in the back, while the others had to camp. 'Yeah,' laughs Mike, 'that was the time I got promoted to staff sergeant.'

Little Crane Hire's premises are part-workshop, part-man-cave and part-museum. Inside, Mike shows me his part-completed 1939 MAC Velocette and his rejuvenated yellow Army Indian. Mike, despite his advancing years, has no intention of hitting the rocking chair. In his office, he tells me about his latest project. He plans to import and distribute the new Black Douglas Sterling, a bike that looks for all the world like it's a century-old autocycle, but is in fact a new retro model powered by a 230cc Chinese motor. The company is owned by Italian entrepreneur Fabio Cardoni, and the bike is designed by Englishman Benny Thomas. It sounds very exciting, and I wish Mike luck with it, as back at his house I don my gear and hit the road again.

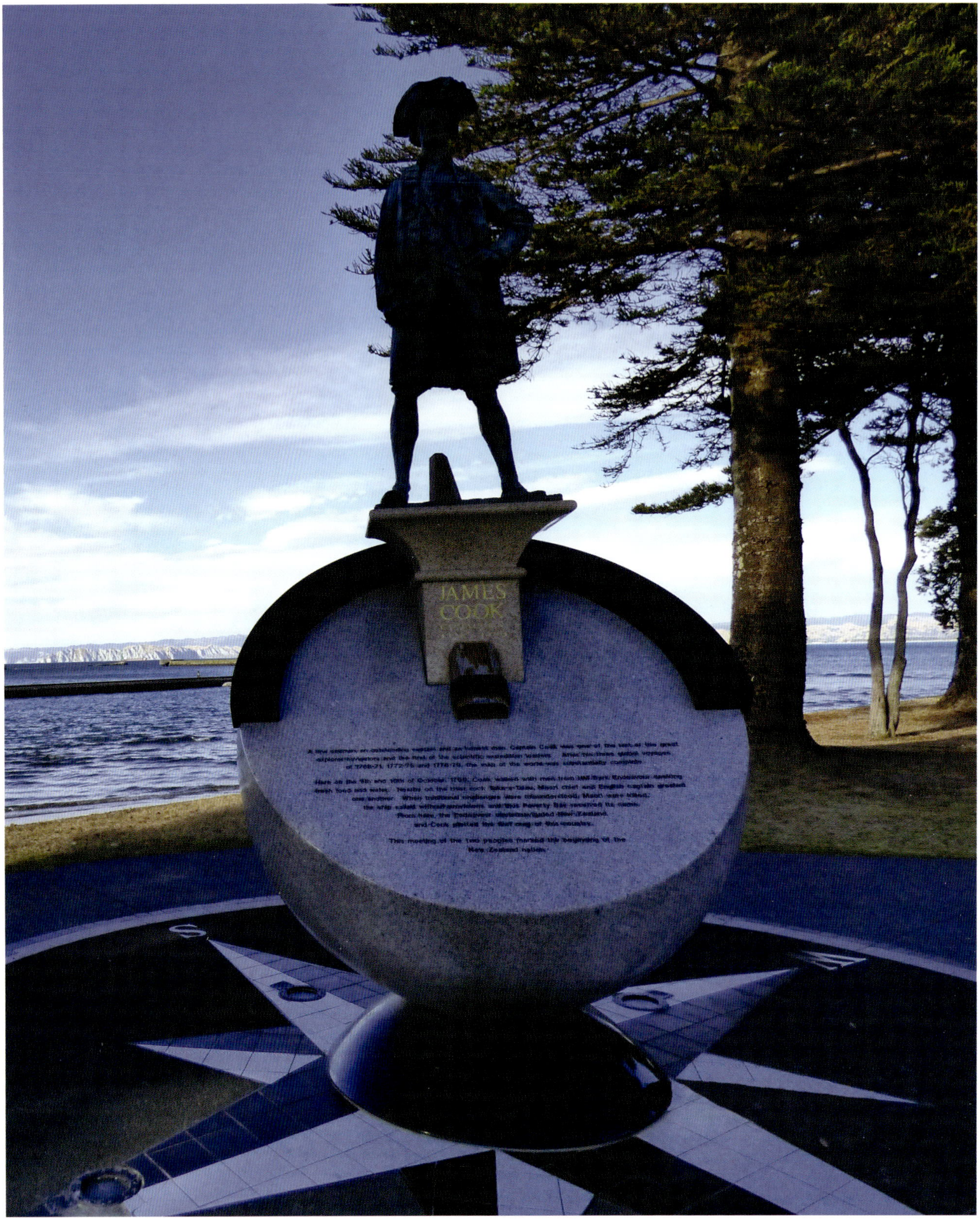
JAMES
COOK

POVERTY BAY AND WESTWARD

'Give me the highway, Lord knows I love to roam.'
— Vince Gill

I enjoy a fabulous evening ride from Wairoa to Gisborne. The sun is at my back and it has cooled down. I arrive in Gisborne, the East Coast's only city, just on dark, and am anxious to find a place to stay after a long day on the road. I try a couple of motels, but find them too expensive. The last time I was here was 30 years ago, visiting my in-laws in the suburb of Kaiti, and it's there I unerringly ride to, for I remember there was a YHA hostel there. With more luck than judgement, I park my bike around the back of the hostel and claim the last bed in the place. After dumping my gear, hitting the shower and crossing the street for a Chinese takeaway, I'm a new man.

Gisborne, prosperous hub of this fertile district, is situated right on the coast at the confluence of three rivers — Taruheru, Waimata and Turanganui. Hence, it's often described as the 'city of bridges'. It also has some great sandy beaches, which are popular with surfers. Most famously, of course, it was Captain Cook's first sight of New Zealand. In 1769, a cabin boy called Nick on board the good ship *Endeavour* spotted the promontory, which we now know as Young Nick's Head. Millions of words have been written about the details of Cook's landing by far more skilful writers than me, and, besides, I haven't got the room. Suffice it to say that in the 1860s much bloody fighting took place in this region, with Maori objecting to European settlement.

In the morning, I'm mightily displeased to discover that the guy I came to Gisborne to interview — the very reason I'm here — has forgotten all about our appointment and is somewhere up on the East Cape! I read recently that the Dali Lama is a keen advocate for banishing the emotion of anger, saying 'That shit will kill you.' Not his exact words, I'd imagine, but His Holiness did say that being angry all the time will considerably shorten your life. So, taking a deep breath and mumbling 'homm, homm, homm', and with a less-than-sincere grin (read 'grimace') plastered on my face, I shift up the gears and head out of Gizzie.

I console myself with the interesting fact that I'm in the first city to see the light of a new day. My ire is also soothed by the Gisborne-to-Opotiki road. I regret cutting off the East Cape to the north of me, but promise myself to ride it another day. I share this beautiful stretch of SH2 with more logging trucks and not much else. I ride through small, mostly Maori settlements, dairy farms, market gardens and more vineyards, to arrive mid-morning in Matawai. This tiny town has a feeling of isolation far stronger than many South Island towns in the middle of nowhere. Maybe it's because the wild East Cape is on my right, and the rich carpet of rata, tawa and beech that make up the Urewera National Park — the largest in the North Island at almost 200,000 hectares — is on my left. I pull over at the only café for a very average flat white, and chat to a biker from Yorkshire riding a Kawasaki W800 who's over here for a summer's touring.

Then it's time to dust off the superlatives once more as I ride the Waioeka Gorge, through the Urutawa Conservation Area. The roughly 50 k's of bends following the river through natural bush are simply stunning. It was around here that Maori leader Te Kooti, guerrilla fighter, prophet and founder of the Ringatu Church, hid for months during skirmishes in the Land Wars.

Through Opotiki, I pull over at Waiotahi Beach in the sun for a spell, and drink in the view of the sparkling ocean and two old-timers in floppy hats, fishing in a little 'tinny'. Joining SH30 and heading for Rotorua, I pull over at tiny Taneatua to photograph a Maori flag fluttering proudly in the stiff breeze. The house is very run-down, and car bodies litter the front yard. Before I can turn the engine off and get my camera out, a pitbull with a big studded collar explodes out of nowhere and charges at me, and I just manage to clunk the bike into first and weave a wobbly escape!

At Lake Rotoma my coffee antenna twitches, so after fuelling up I park outside the Old Trout Café. My instincts are good, and so is the coffee and all-day Big Breakfast. I eavesdrop on a 'one that got away' story from the next table, and discover how big recreational fishing is around here.

Looking back on last year, I realise what a tumultuous year 2016 was. I mean, who would have thought that Britain would have voted to leave the European Union and that a billionaire tycoon with dodgy hair and an even dodgier tan would become the most powerful man on the planet? We certainly live in interesting times! As well as losing Muhammad Ali in 2016, we lost another big influence on my formative years: the genius that was David Jones, aka David Bowie.

I re-run a miserable Saturday afternoon from over 40 years ago through my head. I'm trudging home beneath leaden skies on the long walk back from Hounslow High Street in the drizzle. 'How did the human race come to this?' I ask myself for the umpteenth time, as I try to find anything pleasing to the eye in traffic, puddles, old dears pulling their little shopping trolleys (trundlers) past shopfronts selling tacky rubbish nobody needs. A middle-aged bloke with a terrible comb-over exits the betting shop ahead of me, and grinds his fag out under his shoe with a look of despair on his face. He's obviously just 'done his dough', as my dad (no stranger to that feeling) would say.

But I manage to push these thoughts aside, for inside my W. H. Smith's carrier bag (two bags actually, to keep the drizzle off) I have David Bowie's new album. In the 1970s a new Bowie album was a momentous event, anticipated and looked forward to for months. I vividly remember my excitement as a spotty teenager, walking home with the new *Diamond Dogs* album, then in the sanctity of my bedroom reverently placing the needle on the vinyl.

As I lie on my bed, the mono sci-fi strains of 'Future Legend' wash over me, and I'm transported to a post-apocalyptic, Orwellian future of urban chaos which fits my mood of the day perfectly. The artwork on the gatefold depicts Bowie as a reclining half-man, half-dog hybrid, with his genitalia airbrushed out. My mate and fellow Bowie fan, Roy Smith, told me later that there were some rare copies in circulation that had escaped the censor's airbrush and had his full bollocks on display!

I'd been a devotee of David Bowie since my Aunty Marion (at my request) bought the 1969 album *Space Oddity* for my thirteenth birthday and set my imagination on fire. I must have spent hundreds of hours, as now, flat on my back drinking in those weird, otherworldly lyrics and temporarily leaving behind my boring world.

The response elicited from my dad was predictable. 'What a load of bleedin' rubbish,' he'd sneer if he happened to hear Bowie on the radio. My mum, a master at not rocking the boat, bless her, was less scathing. 'As long as you like it, Georgie,' she'd say.

Big brother Malcolm I think secretly liked Bowie's music, but couldn't quite reconcile his macho image with Bowie's claims of being bisexual. Or the lurid tales of sexual high-jinks involving Mick Jagger and Rudolph Nureyev being caught in a wardrobe with Ziggy Stardust. I wasn't too comfortable with that image myself, to be honest, but could happily brush it under the carpet.

I found it amazing that not everyone shared my obsession with Bowie, who I was sure at first was in fact an alien walking amongst us and not from South London at all. How shallow the pop tunes of the Top 20 sounded, compared with Bowie's. I'd sing along to 'The Supermen' from the 1970 album *The Man Who Sold the World* at the top of my lungs, then shake my head in wonder.

Bowie made it OK to dream about living a life without cans of lager, greasy fish 'n' chips, Tesco supermarket clothes, orange Austin Allegros, *Crossroads* and *Coronation Street* and horse racing on the tele, and endless trudges along grey streets, desperate to find something of interest.

Halfway through 'Rebel Rebel', I hear my dad come home. Afternoon 'shant' down The Castle complete, he would have weaved his drunken way home in his old Vauxhall Cresta, stopping off at the bookies for a flutter on the gee-gees, of course. I picture the scene downstairs as Mum brings his chicken, chips and peas on a tray to where he'll be reclining like a lord on the sofa, glued to the three o'clock at Aintree. 'Here you go, babe,' I hear her say, and picture her fake smile. I turn the volume down to hear better. If it isn't to his satisfaction, he's been known to throw the whole plateful against the wall in a fit of rage. His worst nightmare would be to find a hair in his meal. That would be time to make a dash for the nearest exit and lay low for a spell. Fortunately, the meal must have met with his approval. Maybe his horse has even won for a change. Someone is yelling up the stairs: 'Turn that bloody rubbish down!!' Looks like Dad's horse didn't win after all. I wearily turn the volume down and lie back down with a sigh, my hands behind my head, staring at the ceiling. I fall asleep in this position, waiting for the rest of my life to begin …

Back at Lake Rotomo, it's 2017 and life's good as I enjoy a relaxing ride into Rotorua. I hate breaking up my journey, but sometimes life gets in the way and I must leave the bike with friends while I fly back to Christchurch for a while, to write up notes, plan my next leg and lay some more bricks.

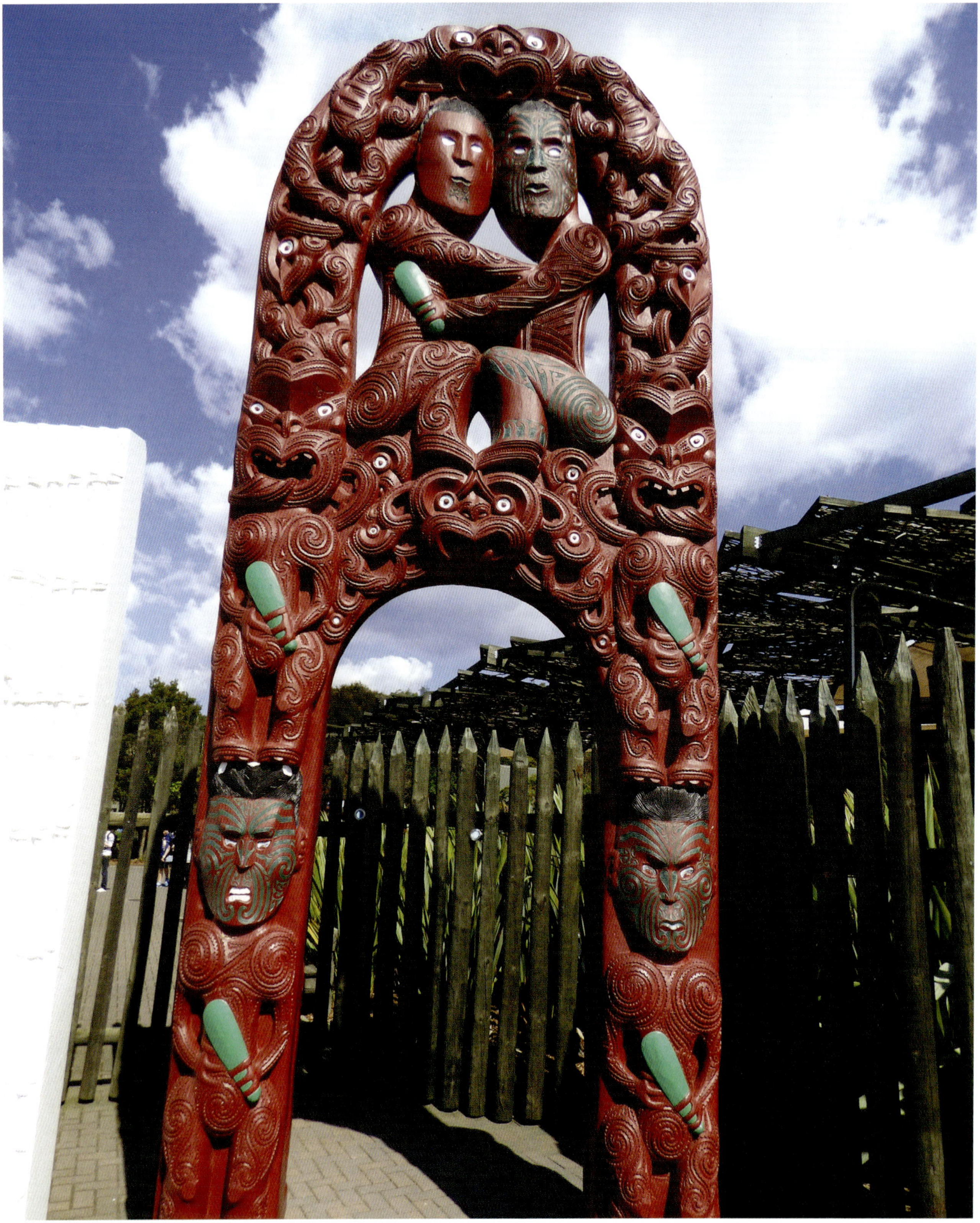

THE MIDDLE BIT: A RED DEVIL, A RACING LEGEND, A 'BUELLIGAN' AND A CRAFTSMAN

'Ain't you come a long way down ... this old road.'
— Kris Kristofferson

Three weeks later, I'm back in the saddle. I've had an action-packed time at home, working, writing and spending a week fighting the Port Hills fires, along my fellow Governors Bay Brigade members, paid firefighters from town and DOC. Interesting times indeed!

The city of Rotorua, famed for the smell of hydrogen sulphide, the natural gas whose smell resembles that of rotten eggs, sits on the southern shore of the almost circular lake of the same name. One of the Maori names for Rotorua is Whangapipiro, or 'evil-smelling place'. The lake measures 16 kilometres across, making it North Island's second-largest. Mokoia Island out in the middle was formed by slowly oozing lava.

Rotorua is the renowned heart of Maori culture, but puts me in mind of Queenstown in a way, with its long strips of motels and motor inns and everything geared up to relieve you of your tourist dollar. And, like Queenstown, it's popular with adrenalin junkies in search of 'adventure tourism'. You can still relax with geothermal and mineral beauty treatments or just soak in a spa — natural spas have been popular here for 160 years. Get away from the tourist spots, though, and you'll see how multicultural Rotorua has become.

It would have been nice to get a full night's sleep in the Rock Solid Backpackers last night without fear of my pager going off, but that luxury wasn't forthcoming. I swear — not for the first time — to never stay at a backpackers again, as the young party animals kept me awake until the wee hours. I'm so tired in the morning that I squirt Head and Shoulders onto my toothbrush. And not getting dandruff on my gums is no consolation for the lingering taste of shampoo. I make a mental note to attempt to drown it in coffee.

Leaving the hostel in the centre of town, I twist the throttle once more and head northwest. As I roll on the gas, I feel the tension of the previous week peeling away like exfoliating layers of stress from my psyche. It feels good to be back on the road: in this case, State Highway 5.

It's quite a cool morning, but I resist the urge to flick my heated grips on. All is green, with steady traffic through the Mamaku Forest and Fitzgerald Glade, to the town of Tirau, established in 1870 as a military post. There are a couple of great coffee shops calling out my name, but I must content myself with a quick stroll down the main road as I have an appointment in Hamilton. I chat with a group of elderly trampers who have stopped to photograph the Big Sheep and Wool Gallery which is cleverly shaped like a ewe and a ram and made of corrugated iron. Just down the road, the information centre is similarly themed as a Big Dog.

Out of town the road becomes SH1 again, and soon morphs into the Waikato Expressway, a super-efficient but still incomplete river of tarmac that makes me feel as though I'm back in Europe. I bypass Cambridge, which is a shame as I've never been there, and enter the city of Hamilton, then surprise myself by riding unerringly around the nationally acclaimed gardens to Graeme's house, with only a vague idea and rough map under the see-through plastic of my tank bag.

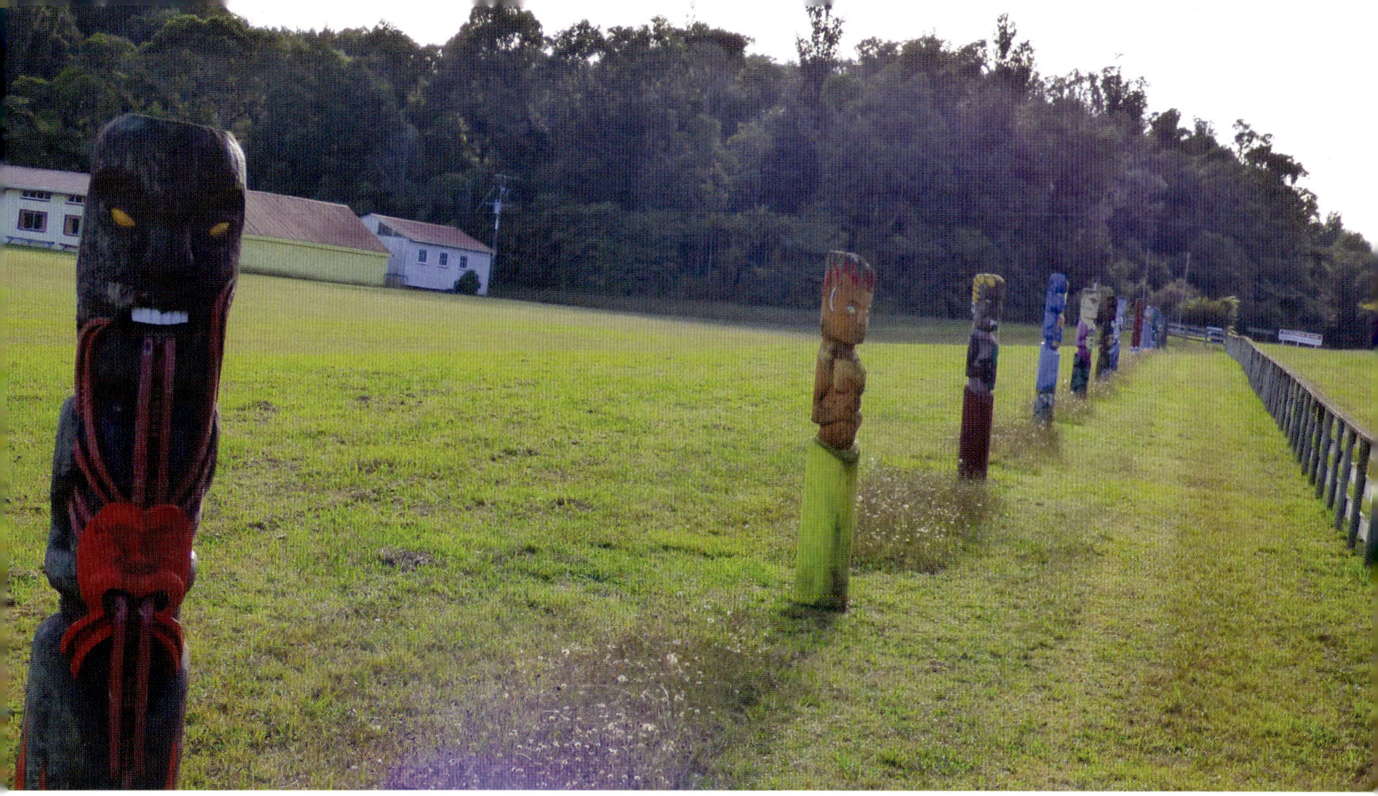

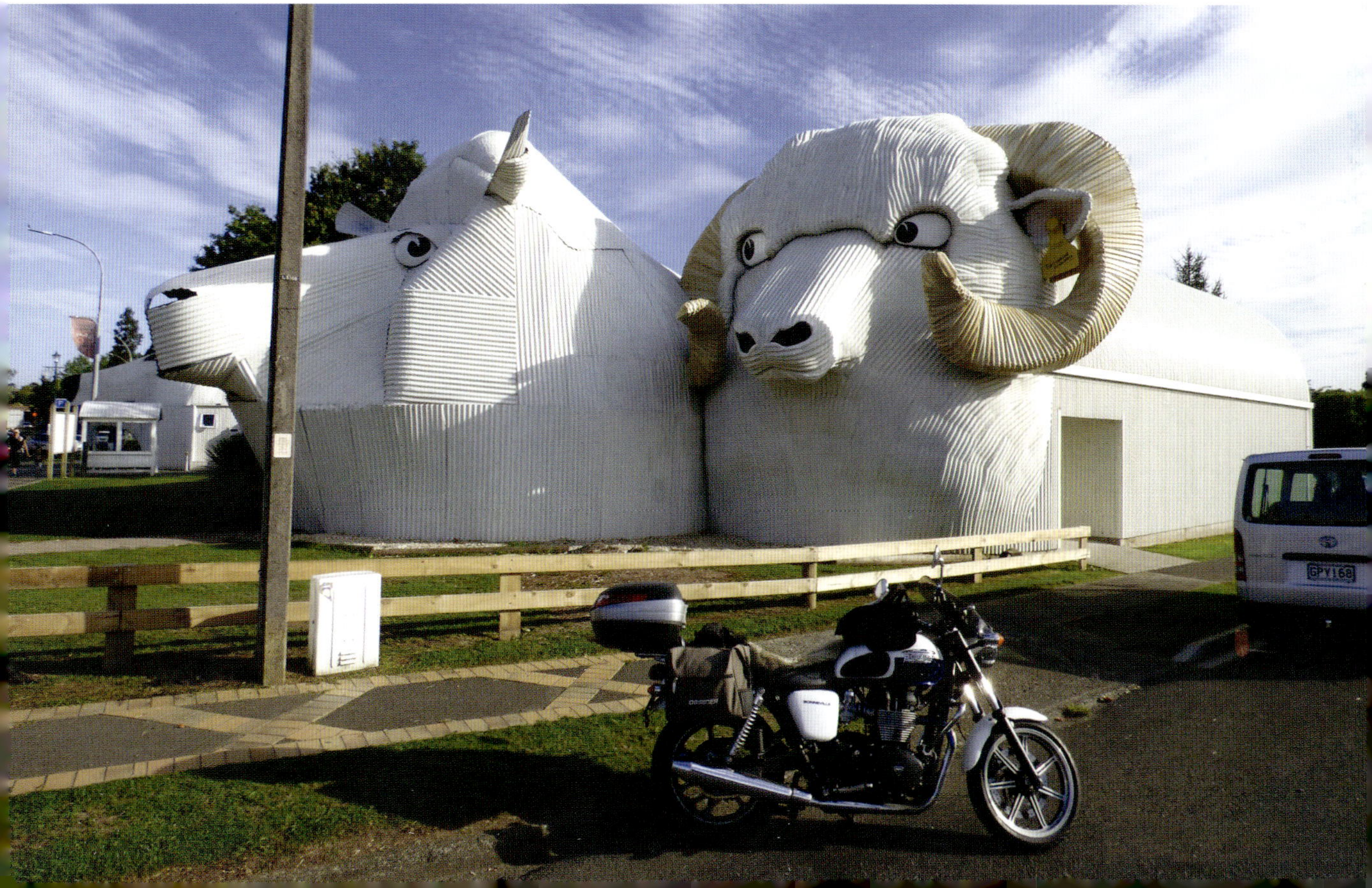

RED DEVIL — GRAEME COLE

Graeme, a panel-beater by trade, opened his shop Cycle Torque here in Hamilton in 1989, after working on motorcycles at home in his spare time. In 2000, sick of insurance agents and time-wasters, he closed the doors and moved operations to his house, where he's been working ever since. But calling Graeme a mere panel-beater would be like calling Gordon Ramsay a cook or Bill Gates a businessman.

'In that time, things have changed a lot,' says Graeme, sipping a black tea in his kitchen, 'what you're working for and what you're working on. It's not so much bikes that I work on these days, it's bits and pieces like gearboxes and wheels. There are fewer and fewer people these days who can fix anything.'

He's a rare breed. There really isn't much Graeme can't fix, and if he can't fix a part, he'll have a crack at making a new one. 'I'm always learning, though. A big part of my job is substituting a part from another bike that might fit. For example, a piston or a valve or piston rings. I change things around and modify them. It takes time and a bit of cunning.'

Graeme reckons some customers simply don't appreciate the time that goes into some of his fixes. Often he'll get an engine or gearbox where previous owners have 'had a go' at it, and his first job is to undo the harm they've done, before he can even think about fixing the problem. 'Most of the imported stuff from the US is good to work on, but some of the Kiwi stuff, where the owner has taken a hammer and chisel to it, can be a … challenge.' Graeme grins, and I feel that he's restraining himself from using more colourful language! 'Yeah, so that's what Cycle Torque is all about,' he continues. 'We employed people before, but I find I work best on my own. It's probably a subject I shouldn't say too much about!'

Graeme advertised initially, but says that in recent times it's all word-of-mouth. 'I get work from everywhere now — a motor from Gisborne, a gearbox from the West Coast — but word-of-mouth seems to work. We go to the occasional swap-meet to buy and sell. The big one at McLeans Island in Christchurch is a beauty.'

This year Graeme and his partner, Rosanna, plan to travel down in their camper bus, which is parked-up just below us, and have a working holiday, travelling to four swap-meets in four weeks.

A Ducati pulls into his driveway below us, and Graeme excuses himself as he goes down to talk to a customer. Ten minutes later, the phone rings and he takes time to give some free advice on some technical problem or other. 'Sometimes it's busy like this,' he explains, resuming his seat.

Graeme got into motorcycling as a young bloke with the purchase of a Yamaha 125 twin from Boyd's in Hamilton. He gradually progressed to eventually own the model he craved: a Triumph Bonneville. (I tell him he has good taste.) On the way, he had to sell his Honda CB350 to pay off his speeding tickets. 'With my dad's guidance,' he says, 'I bought through tender this 1973 Bonneville that had been in a fire, and spent the next six months stripping it and rebuilding it. There were no parts available at the time, because the bloody Meriden factory in the UK was always on strike. So we learned how to make our own speedo and throttle cables, and fabricate bits and pieces. Then we painted the tank (which had almost exploded) with a vacuum cleaner.' At the time, Graeme was working at a car-wreckers, which he says helped sorting out cables and bearings, etc. 'Yeah, so I wreaked a bit of havoc around the place on that Triumph.'

His next project after selling the Triumph was to build a chopper. 'My parents were probably not too impressed, but I built this chopper from scratch. I bought a Matchless 500 twin motor and gearbox out of the paper, and shoe-horned it into a Triumph frame. I'd met Rosanna at that stage, and we'd go everywhere on the chopper.' With only a gallon-and-a-half tank, they couldn't go very far or very fast, but they had a lot of fun on it. Making it was a steep learning curve, and Graeme says he'd make three or four cock-ups before getting something right.

We now move on to the topic of racing, and Graeme's initial reticence turns to enthusiasm. Around 1980 he got wind of a big race meeting at Pukekohe. 'So, we jumped in our 100E Prefect and off we went,' he says. 'I still remember driving this three-speed up the Bombay Hills at about 12 miles an hour with steam pouring out the bonnet. You could park on the hill then, because they were using the club circuit in the New Zealand Classic Club Register. I thought, "Wow, this is for me", and told myself I'd be back with a bike the next year.'

Bill O'Brien had been around forever, and had raced Douglases in his day. It was from the bits and pieces in Bill's shed that Graeme bought a chrome G12 Matchless frame he thought was pretty cool. 'Looking back,' laughs Graeme, 'it was bloody horrible!' With a trailer-load of Matchless twin parts purchased from a mate in Te Kuiti, he managed to cobble together a bike to race at Pukekohe the following year. 'Just like that,' I say, as I'm always impressed by others' mechanical ability and desire to just have a go.

'Look, George,' he says, 'it was a huge task, but with that youth and enthusiasm, nothing was going to get in the way. It was just gonna happen.' The bike smoked and leaked and bits fell off, but it didn't matter. Graeme was just happy to be competing. 'And that,' he says, 'was the start of it all.'

One thing led to another after that, and, as Graeme puts it, 'It just captures you. It gets its hand around your throat. I didn't give a toss if I raced my Matchless in Superbikes or Formula 2, I just wanted to race. I spent a lot of time at Baypark over Mount Maunganui. That's all houses now.'

Once, Graeme picked up race-kit cams for his motor, and stuck them in to race in Gisborne. He then discovered that he could only go half a lap at a time, so had to pull over every half-lap and fill up! But, undeterred, he'd fix the latest setback and resolutely move on to the next one.

Over the following years, Graeme became more heavily involved in the sport, always reading up in magazines on how to improve his bike's performance, persevering, and always striving to learn more. One of his regrets was not getting into Japanese bikes, he says. The phone rings again, with the request to rebuild a chap's gearbox in a week. Graeme tells the caller that he'll do his best and give it a shot. He strikes me as one of those guys who's always happy to help and doesn't like saying 'no'.

Now, back to the story. Graeme then started building his own frames. Featherbed was the thing to have for Classic Racing, so one Saturday he and his mate Mark Hatton set about building a pipe-bender and jig. With the new frame, they set about building a new bike. 'Didn't know anything about releasing agent for the fibreglass bits, so I was using dripping,' he says, 'but in a week the complete bike with the Matchless twin in it was up on wheels, painted red (I was sick of black bikes), and in 10 days it was ready for racing. I worked around the clock. Rosanna would yell down to me when breakfast was ready; then I'd go off to work, panel-beating. A couple of times I was caught asleep sitting on the toilet or curled up in the boot of a car!'

People would tell him he was wasting his time riding a Matchless, but Graeme was starting to get good results, and, like a latter-day Burt Munro, was spurred on. He remembers well his first win at Napier, when he beat Wellington's Jim Dews by a wheel-length — 'and Jim didn't take any prisoners,' he says. He loved it all: street racing, hill climbs and bench sprints. It was an obsession. One year he raced in 15 meetings! Graeme financed everything himself, and owes a huge debt of gratitude to partner Rosanna, who supported him, with their two boys in tow, through thick and thin, disappointments, crashes and wins, and the sacrifices she made to help him succeed.

Over the next hour, Graeme entertains me with his hair-raising racing tales, some with him 'swinging' — hanging off the side of a sidecar for grim death. He also built a BMX bike, which his elder son raced with some success at the New Zealand Championships. 'It all sounds a bit ruthless, but I just had this tunnel vision. But without Rosanna it would have all fallen down a hole. The things she's had to endure over the years are simply incredible.'

Nowadays he doesn't ride much at all, saying it just doesn't light his fire any more. Graeme and Rosanna now travel the Classic Racing circuit with their Red Devils Racing Team. 'Racing fans would probably be aware of the little red Triumphs,' he says. 'It all started when I built a red Triumph 3TA, and then another one for my son Nick to race the following year.' Now there are 15 of these little Red Devils competing on the circuit. As well as the Red Devils, Graeme acts as spanner man for Nick, who has had success riding a Kawasaki Superbike, competing here and overseas.

As I take my leave, another motorcyclist shows up at the workshop below with a faulty part. I leave Graeme, a passionate man who lives and breathes bikes, hammering at his vice, fixing another problem as I head up the road to Huntly to meet my next character.

RACING LEGEND — GINGER MOLLOY

I'm sitting with Ginger, who is looking trim and fit for someone not far off 80 years, in the lounge of his Huntly home. He's also getting around well for someone who only three months ago received a new knee.

Ginger arrived in Huntly as a three-year-old when his father, who had been gold mining in Otago, moved here to mine coal. He bought his first bike for £30 in 1953, a 125 Royal Enfield. But the 15-year-old apprentice mechanic wasn't too impressed. 'It was a shit of a little bike,' he begins. 'I didn't have any tools to tighten up the flywheel, and I was forever pushing the damn thing down to Roberts Bros. Motorcycle Shop.

'I was about 15 when I raced at the Raglan Aerodrome,' says Ginger. 'I rode a 1937 Triumph Tiger 70 that had been converted to a TT carb and ran on methanol. I came second in the New Zealand Championships on it.' Incredibly, young Ginger had to organise everything himself, including transporting his bike to meetings. 'A Speedway rider, Lenny Jelaka, would charge me two and six to put my bike on his trailer to go to miniature TT.'

At the time, Ginger was having problems at Smith's Garage where he was apprenticed. 'The mechanics were on limited time,' he explains, 'and wouldn't give me any work, so I basically had to teach myself. George Smith, my boss, wouldn't let me leave, so when I was 17 I faked an injury, telling him that I had dermatitis on my arms from washing parts in the kerosene.'

Ginger left and started work in the nearby coal mines, trucking underground, pushing coal skips and no doubt enjoying the pay rise. 'I remember the very first time I heard an explosion, I just ran!' he says. 'But Huntly is simply riddled with coal.' He nods out the window. 'There's more here than we'd ever need.'

Young Ginger treated himself to a new 350cc BSA Gold Star DBD for the princely sum of £200, and, with the addition of a car, raced all over New Zealand. 'I had a lot of success on that,' he says. He did all the mechanical repairs himself — a financial necessity — learning as he went.

These race meetings, before the likes of BEARS and CAMS, were largely organised by private clubs, such as the Auckland Motorcycle Club, and many featured cars as well as bikes. As Ginger improved and progressed up the ranks, so his bikes improved. 'I bought a 500cc Gold Star from Harry Lowe, who'd been racing in England,' he says. 'That put out 46 horsepower, which was pretty good back then, and I raced both BSAs with great success.'

In 1961, through importer John Dale he also bought a Matchless G50 that Kiwi John Farnsworth had been racing

226 THE LONG AND WINDING AOTEAROA

on overseas. Despite making a splash on the racing scene, Ginger was never sponsored in New Zealand, although he says some riders were. He continued working at the mines until 1962, while also earning money on the race circuit as a one-man-band. 'Sometimes I'd make £30 in prize money over a weekend,' he says.

In February 1963, Ginger went overseas. 'I sailed on the *Fairstar* and took my G50 with me,' he says. 'That's where I met my wife, Claire, who was from Australia and heading for Canada. Instead, she got a fast trip around Europe.'

Ginger's first race was at Silverstone in England, where he entered in the 250cc class, borrowing flatmate Gary Williamson's Honda CB70, complete with racing tyres, megaphone, streamlining and no air filters. 'It was a freezing cold, wet day at Silverstone. There were six of us sitting in the back of my Ford Thames van with a camping gas-stove going all day. We went out and practised in the wet, and Jim Redmond was the quickest on his Honda Four at 2 minutes and 12, and I was second fastest at 2 minutes 12.1.' On race day, in the dry, Redmond managed to get down to 2 minutes, but Ginger couldn't better his time. 'I proved to myself that I could ride well in the rain,' he says.

Ginger had written to all of the European race organisers from New Zealand, but says when he received the replies he couldn't understand half of them! 'I took my letters to a translating school, and they wanted £10 to translate each one! I told them to just tell me where the race venues were, I didn't need it translated, but they wouldn't, so I bought myself a map of Europe.' He soon figured it out anyway, racing at Snetterton and winning on a 196cc Bultaco: 'Everyone told me the two-stroke, single Bultaco would seize, but it turned out to be the best motorcycle I ever had.'

He then won on the old wartime airfield at Thruxton, where organiser Neville Goss had told him: 'If you are as good as you say you are, I'll pay you £60 for a win or £40 if you don't.'

Claire then joins us, kindly making us a cuppa with some welcome nibbles.

Ginger continues: 'The first time I raced in Schleiz, East Germany, was 1963, and I remember getting to the border with Claire and friend Gary. I remember the barbed wire and mine fields and the sign saying *You are leaving the American Sector*. This Stasi, secret-police guy came out demanding our papers. He did some pointing and I did some pointing, and he sprayed us and we were through. He'd sprayed us all with disinfectant to kill the cultural poison from the West! The atmosphere was quite oppressive, with armed guards everywhere. I remember on Sunday, race day, there were huge queues, and we discovered these people were queueing up for oranges and apples, which had been brought in to make things look normal for the Western cameras. They used to get 350,000 spectators on race day at Saxon Ring in East Germany,' he says. 'Now that's a pretty good crowd. But the average East German was fantastic. Passing through the villages we saw the loudspeakers on street corners, broadcasting Communist propaganda.'

And so Ginger's successful European racing adventure continued, funded, he says, entirely by 'start money'. I ask Claire if she accompanied Ginger on the circuit. 'Yes. By then I owned the Bultaco and half the 7R, the 350 AJS racing bike!'

Ginger, along with his mate Gary, then headed down to Spain and the Bultaco factory in Barcelona. The boss, Señor Francesc 'Paco' Bultó (the name 'Bultaco' came from the first four letters of his surname and the last three letters of his nickname), had been reading up on Ginger's success, and took his Bultaco away to the workshop, returning it, all fixed up and in mint condition for the knockdown price of £150. Ginger took the re-vamped Bultaco to Madrid for a 40-lap race. 'I just nipped through on the second-to-last lap to overtake Johnny Grace, who raced for Bultaco, and came third behind two Montessa works riders.'

Johnny Grace asked Ginger to call into the Bultaco factory, where he was invited to join the works team and ride a 125 at Saragossa. 'They put a factory six-speed 125 motor into my bike, and I raced with fellow Bultaco riders Ralph Bryans and Ramon Torres.' After Ginger's coming third, Señor Bultó made Ginger part of the team, providing free bikes and spares, and paying him after each race report. 'I was very happy. There were plenty of riders who were envious of my position,' admits Ginger.

He'd race with the little Spanish manufacturer from 1964 to 1970, winning the World Championships in 1966 at the 250cc Ulster Grand Prix, then finishing third in the World 125cc Championships, fifth in the World 250 and 300 Champs in 1968, and in 1969 finishing sixth in the 125 class. In 1970 Ginger finished second in the 500cc World Champs, riding his Kawasaki H1R.

'By 1970, Claire wanted to come home — we married in 1964,' Ginger says. He spent a bit of time at home before visiting Claire and their three daughters in

Australia, and then heading off to the USA. There, he raced the big two-stroke triple Kawasaki H1-R 500, coming second that year in the World Championships. 'At Talladega,' he says, 'where I won that day, I went through the speed trap at 146 miles per hour after I'd worked on the expansion chambers to make it rev to 12,000. I remember a young Kenny Roberts was in that race, as well as Kel Carruthers and Cal Rayborn, riding Don Vesco's Yamahas. Kel came second, and Cal came third.'

Ginger points at my T-shirt, which has *The World's Fastest Indian* on it. 'I rode on that bike,' he says. 'In 1960 at Teretonga. Peter Pawson and I were there, and this funny old guy comes running up to these two girls and chased them away. We didn't know it was Burt Munro at the time. After the race, he took us back to his place, and it was just like in the movie. An old double tin shed, full of tools, with a bed in the corner and dishes everywhere. He showed us a con-rod he'd made from a rear axle that he'd taken three months to make! He was a character, Burt.'

Ginger continued racing through the 1970s in New Zealand, Australia, Asia and the US, while being kept busy setting up motorcycle dealerships in Hamilton and Huntly. 'I was kept busy doing all the bookwork,' chips in Claire, 'and running flat-out between the two shops.' They sold the businesses in 1980.

Eight years ago, Ginger took a tumble at home, fracturing his skull. Ironic when you consider the near-misses in a lifetime of racing. In 2014, he was inducted into the Motorcycle New Zealand Hall of Fame. 'I still raced here and in Australia after the accident,' he says. He was still winning races when he stopped for good at 73. 'I was confident in myself, but wasn't confident about the other people.'

I reluctantly swap the cool of Ginger and Claire's house for the heat and traffic. It's very apparent I'm in the most populous area of the country. I pull over by the Waikato River, New Zealand's longest at over 400 kilometres. There's a picnic table in the shade of a tree, which I can sit at and write some notes. Across the river is the Huntly Power Station with its 150-metre-tall chimneys. Operated by Genesis Energy, it's capable of generating 31 per cent of the nation's electricity needs, and naturally draws the ire of environmentalists.

The trouble with efficient roads is that they are sometimes a tad boring, as is this next section, heading for the big smoke. I turn off the Auckland Southern Motorway at Drury, and the 30 kilometres of two-lane country road to Waiuku prove more to my liking. Then it's up the Awhitu Peninsula where I'm to stay with friends. Oh, the bliss of getting out my riding gear, having a cool shower, followed by a large sandwich and a cold beer!

I'm treated royally at Judy and Richard's, who insist I stay with them again on my way back down in a few days' time. Eggs on toast, good coffee and an early start see me join the giant conga line of steel, plastic and rubber commuting into work.

Once more my lane-splitting skills are put to the test, as I pass slowly but steadily between lanes of frustrated motorists, crawling along or gridlocked.

Memories of London return. Weaving my way to the red light and being joined by a line of dispatch riders, fellow road warriors exchanging nods. I'd be on my Honda CX500 or CB400, off to a building site somewhere, Stabila spirit-level strapped to my back and tools in my panniers. On a cold morning, we'd all have our gloved hands wrapped around the hot cylinders of our engines. There were two tricks to this. The first was not burning through the leather of your gloves, and the second was knowing when to pull the clutch in and clunk into gear before the lights changed and a double-decker bus or a black cab rammed into the back of you.

I soon reach the Manurewa (a name I have trouble pronouncing) off-ramp, and, with the aid of a map with directions Judy has printed from her computer, I find Debbie's house easily.

'BUELLIGAN' — DEBBIE CURLE

Vivacious, bubbly and enthusiastic (her, not me!), Debbie is bursting to tell me her story. She says that, unlike many of her fellow riders, she didn't grow up with motorcycles. In fact, she wasn't at all impressed with her introduction into the biking world, when as a 16-year-old she rode home on the back of a co-worker's bike. 'I absolutely hated it,' she says, 'not being in control.'

About a year later, she accompanied a friend's son to pick up his new Yamaha 225 TT trail bike from a dealership on the Great North Road. 'I hadn't thought any more about bikes since that awful pillion ride, but then I spotted this beautiful blue-and-yellow DT175 and I just fell in love.' As it was close to Christmas, she asked her dad for an interest-free loan to purchase the little Yammy. He reluctantly agreed after Debbie said she needed it to commute to her new job. 'My new job (as an apprentice photo-lithographer) started in two days, so I literally had two days to learn how to ride it. My friend Dale showed me the basics, and it was like "Yahoo!" And I've never looked back.'

Needless to say, it wasn't long before the 'Buelligan' had her full licence. 'I had to sell my Yamaha to get the money to go overseas,' Debbie says from the kitchen, as she puts the kettle on. 'Everywhere I went in Europe I found myself photographing Harleys. So naturally, when I came home a couple of years later, I went straight to Red Baron. Although I'd had my heart set on owning a Ducati, the salesman — the same one who had sold me my trail bike — persuaded me to buy a red Harley 883 Sportster.'

Debbie's dog Rocky is bothering us, so she gets up to give him his breakfast.

She loved the little 'Sporty', and toured all over the country on it, despite the bike's tiny 'peanut' tank that has you stopping for fuel every five minutes. She remembers riding to a HOG (Harley Owners Group) rally in Dunedin and becoming mates with a group she had met along the way. From then on, she rode regularly with them. She says, 'We called ourselves "The Stragglers", because we'd always take the longest route and would have a session every night. The ride to the rally was often more fun than the rally itself!'

She then made the natural progression up to the 883's bigger cousin, the 1200 Sportster. 'My new bike had more power, but I somehow preferred the 883. I think it was simply the great memories of the journeys I'd made on it that made it so special.'

Then, tragically, Debbie's partner died at the age of 32 from a massive heart attack, and she inherited his bike. 'So I decided to trade both bikes in for a big-block Harley,' she says. 'Namely, the 1440cc Night Train, all in black.' But racing legend Graeme Crosby at Shaft Motorcycles knew Debbie, and thought a fast-cornering bike would suit her riding style to a T. He said, 'Have you thought about riding a Buell?' Before you knew it, Crosby had picked up the two Sportsters and dropped off a yellow Buell that had belonged to veteran rider, Doug Kaye.

'I took the 1999 X1 Lightning — my mum had christened it "the yellow peril" — for a test ride to visit a mate in Waitoki, and when I was turning it around I dropped it in the mud. All the weight was at the front, but I just managed to pick it up.'

'Adrenalin,' I say, and we laugh.

'So, I rode it for the weekend,' she continues. 'I took it through the Karangahake Gorge in the pissing rain, and it handled so brilliantly. Like a dream. So, I said, "Yep, this is me", and went back to Shaft's on Monday and signed the papers. They knew that I wanted it painted black, and it so happened that a customer had just brought in a black 2000 model, so we did a straight swap of all the paintwork.' Debbie toured everywhere on that bike. To Buell rallies, HOG rallies, touring with The Stragglers ('sometimes a bit painful sticking to 110–120!'), riding on her own, in pairs or with other groups. She simply loved to ride.

That bike, which she's ridden an amazing 180,000 k's on, still sits in the garage, although it's since been fully customised. 'She's my baby,' Debbie says, 'and I'll always keep her.' She had clocked up 160,000 kilometres really quickly, and reckons it was costing her a small fortune to keep the bike serviced with a service interval of only 4000 kilometres. 'So I thought I really need to retire her from everyday riding.'

Her riding companion, Andy Jameson (AJ), would fly up to Auckland, and they'd often take out a couple of demo bikes from Amps Motorcycles for the day. They took the new Buell 1125R out for a demo ride but didn't like it at all. They later discovered on the Kiwibiker forum that someone had previously taken the bike out for a review, changed all the dampener settings, stuffing up the handling, and the shop had forgotten to set it back to the factory settings.

A year later the pair took the Buell 1125CR out for a demo ride, and when they returned, they looked at each other and agreed that they simply had to own one. But not just any one — they wanted to own the demo bike they'd just thrashed.

'But I couldn't get rid of the X1 and AJ couldn't part with his XB,' says Debbie. 'So that night I rang him and told him of my cunning plan: to co-own the bike.'

This means the running costs of the Buell CR, which currently sits in Debbie's garage, are split down the middle, except for tyres, which are sorted out by who's doing the most k's. Every year either Debbie or AJ rides the bike to the annual Buell Rally, where it changes garages for a year. Whoever is dropping off the CR will then fly back home. Sounds like a great system. 'Yeah, we're on the same page as far as doing little bits and bobs to the bike, and it works out really well.'

After Debbie's mum died in 2013, she heard that a friend of hers from the Buell Club was selling his 1125R, the bike which she originally hadn't liked but had since changed her mind about. 'Don't even advertise it!' she told him on the phone. 'I want that bike.' So, flush with inheritance money, Debbie flew straight down to Wellington and bought it. 'But,' she says, 'it's given me no end of grief with its Italian electrics. Erik Buell was aware of this and was going to fix the problem with the next model, with retrospective parts made available, but then Harley ditched Buell. So Buell replaced the faulty parts under warranty with the same parts.' The last Buell — number 136,923 — was manufactured in October 2009, with CEO and engineer Erik Buell going on to found Erik Buell Racing to support privateer racers. 'He eventually started producing bikes again,' Debbie says, 'but they're called EBRs, as he couldn't use the Buell name.

'But, God, I've had some amazing rides,' she continues, 'especially with AJ. We've developed this rapport over the years. When we do the Coromandel loop, with all those tight bends, it's so hard to see what's ahead. If he's ahead of me, he'll overtake a car and his indicator will blink if it's safe for me to follow him, so I'll overtake on a blind corner, completely trusting that nothing's coming. AJ and I have been to a lot of rallies together, as I have with my friend Gwenda from down south, whom I also introduced to Buells.'

Debbie has a thousand stories from the road, as you'd imagine of someone who's ridden so many k's. I ask 'the Buelligan', also known around the traps as 'Flossie', if she's had many spills. 'I broke my femur in three places riding my little Sportster. And there was this time I smashed my X1 into a cliff on the East Cape. There were about 10 of us on the way to a Buell rally at Tolaga Bay. It was stinking hot and we were stuck in road works. The road workers suggested we take this side-road they'd closed off, with a drop to the sea on one side and a cliff on the other. I'd gotten a bit ahead of myself, thinking the worst was over. I rode across a huge pothole, didn't want to get stuck, so gave it some herb and got out of it, but hit a massive rock and got a huge tank slap-on. It turned to custard and I smacked into the cliff face. I was trapped under the bike, the pipes and air cleaner were crushed, beautiful paint job ruined, and I'd taken a chunk of flesh out of my leg. Everyone gradually caught up, and, while they were standing around having a post-mortem, I started the bike up and headed for the rally. The others meanwhile had stashed my smashed air cleaner cover and bits and pieces and taped them all together to make a trophy, which was handed to me as a "hard luck" award at the rally.'

These day, Debbie works for Fairfax Media as an image re-toucher, and her enthusiasm for riding her Buells — *fast* — is undiminished. Twisty roads are her forte. 'I'm cautious if I don't know the road, but if I do, then I'm locked and loaded and I'll push the envelope. I find straight roads tedious; Beulls love corners!'

CRAFTSMAN — PAUL DOWNIE

Finding Paul's place is a piece of cake; just head for the city centre and ask directions. His workshop, which he and his partner live above in trendy Ponsonby, has one of those marvellous, cool and cluttered atmospheres that movie-makers try to create but just can't manage. Busy workbenches surrounded by a plethora of woodworking tools speak of a worker steeped in his craft.

After exchanging a warm handshake, I perch myself on a stool and ask Paul what exactly he does here. 'Well, basically, I'm building historic keyboard instruments. This one here is a copy of an 1825 Viennese grand piano which I'm building for Auckland University. I built a similar one for Canterbury University about nine years ago. It's wooden-framed, and so is much lighter than modern pianos by a long way. It's exactly the kind of instrument that Beethoven and Schubert and so on used in their lifetimes.' An instrument like the one taking centre stage in Paul's workshop would take him about a year to complete.

Incredibly, Paul built this beautiful piano entirely from scratch. The idea of creating something like this from raw materials just blows me away. He makes all of the components — the keys, tuning pins, pedals, pull-rods, absolutely everything — from the ground up. He shows me a little hammer shank he's been working on, made from locally-sourced pear wood. 'It pivots in this double-ended pin, which gives you essentially a frictionless bearing that will never wear out.' It's a very clever and elegant design. Paul prefers to work alone, which I suppose is understandable, as the standard of workmanship is quite remarkable. 'I just like to work at my own pace,' he says.

He reckons he's not a great player, but is skilled enough to know when an instrument is playing properly. You may wonder, as I did, how a person gets into making pianos and harpsichords from scratch. I put the question to Paul. 'Well, originally I was at university here in Auckland doing things that interested me, like Greek and German,' he begins, 'but I always had this idea to build a harpsichord.' (And I can't resist saying 'as you do'.) Paul is certainly unusual. Most people, I say to him, have always wanted to own a Harley or a sports car or trek in the Himalayas. 'I just wanted one for my own amusement,' he chuckles. 'As I had no money to buy one, I decided to make one.'

So Paul read all of the literature he could find on making harpsichords, and got stuck in. He had no woodworking experience, but was accustomed to using machines, as he'd help in the school holidays at his father's steel-manufacturing business. He was also a handy, self-taught car mechanic, and had used this skill to work on cars for a year to save enough money to buy the necessary machines and tools. That was way back in 1977. 'So this makes 40 years since I started,' he says.

After building his first harpsichord, Paul immediately started on another, having chopped up and burned the first one. 'It worked, but it took up a lot of space and I knew I could do better.' He also worked for a hire company, maintaining their machinery, while building his second one, which Paul says was quite therapeutic work. 'After I'd completed the second one, I contacted museums and started buying detailed plans that had been made when historic instruments had been pulled apart for restoration.'

I confess my ignorance to Paul, and tell him I don't even know what a harpsichord looks like, and he shows me pictures on his phone of a copy of a famous instrument built in Germany in 1728, which he built recently for a harpsichordist in Wellington who teaches at the university. 'See the two keyboards with the ebony and ivory stars?' says Paul. 'The keys are tortoiseshell and bone, with all this amazing marquetry around them. It uses a plucking action rather than the hammer action of a piano.'

Paul 'turned professional', so to speak, when he sold his third and fourth harpsichords. In the early days, he also continued his Greek and German studies at uni. He became accustomed to going from penury to suddenly having some cash in his pocket, and the sale of one instrument would not only cover his living expenses, but provide materials for the next project. 'But, of course, the cost of living back then was so much lower than it is today.'

He says he's never needed to advertise. 'It all started off with word-of-mouth, and basically it's been that way ever since. But my German studies led to some great contacts.' Another contact helped him land a job repairing instruments at a piano shop in Symonds Street, so that became another avenue for collecting revenue. 'It was very handy. I'd work in the workshop of the piano shop, then walk to uni for a lecture, before coming home to work on my own project.'

Around this time, Paul received a call out of the blue from a German lady who was visiting in Auckland. Apparently, her husband made and restored harpsichords in Germany, and, with Teutonic efficiency, had on file an article the *Herald* had published on Paul and had tracked him down. She kindly invited Paul to come and stay with them in Germany for a while, which in 1983 he did.

'My German studies were of course very useful. I met with makers of historic instruments in northern Germany, making many new contacts. My new friends then suggested that I build an instrument to show at a forthcoming exhibition in 1986. So I shot home, built a harpsichord very similar to the one I showed you on my phone, shipped it to the exhibition, and it was bought by a lady from Hamburg, who teaches harpsichord at the university there. It was funny,' he says, 'all she had on her was DM4000 (about $4,000) in cash, which she gave me as a deposit in four DM1000 notes, and it was another case of going from rags to riches. And that lady is still playing that harpsichord today.'

From then on Paul's reputation grew, his skills were in demand and work continued to come in, including restorations. As well as Europe, some restorations required Paul to travel and work in the Canary Islands, where many wealthy Spaniards and Germans reside. He started building a fortepiano on spec, which a university bought before it was completed, followed by another which was sold to a private customer. These days, Paul tends to stay put in New Zealand and work, and his diary is, not surprisingly, filled with restorations, maintenance work and new builds. He seems very laidback and relaxed, but does say that deadlines for projects can sometimes create a bit of stress.

My attention now turns to the two old motorcycles, half-buried in a corner of the workshop. Paul bought his first bike, a 500cc 1941 Army Indian, 50 years ago, when he was only 14. 'I was so obsessed with it, I simply had to have it,' he says. He kept the Indian for years, and used it for daily transport. 'It was very reliable, and I never had any trouble with it.'

Paul has owned many motorcycles over the years, including a 'great run of English bikes, a Ducati Darmah and a V50 Moto Guzzi. The Guzzi was like a Velocette,' he says. 'It was instinctive and would seemingly corner on its own.' He uncovers a beautiful 1950 600cc single Panther. 'I've also got a 1935 road-legal Panther down in my shed, and another one in pieces plus a war department 500 Norton in bits. But the Panthers have this big overhead-valve single-cylinder engine and aren't pulling a huge amount of weight, so they can actually go quite well. I'm a big fan of singles.' He then reveals a lovely 1956 Velocette Venom 500. 'They are a gorgeous machine. That bike will basically go all day at 80 miles an hour. Last week I had to go to South Auckland, and it sat comfortably in the outside lane on 75 miles an hour. And when you open the throttle, you know that there is plenty left.' The Velocette was supposed to do 101mph when new, and the handbook recommends that you not exceed 81mph in third gear — which says it all really. 'It's usually the fastenings, the old nuts and bolts, that go on these old bikes,' he says. When I foolishly ask where he gets new ones, he says, 'I just make them. Whitworth hexagons and Whitworth threads and things. Yeah, there's not much I can't do with the bikes.' I suggest that there's not much he can't do, period.

'It would be nice to have a holiday, though,' Paul confesses, 'as one project just seems to roll around into the next one. I quite fancy going on one of those motorcycle tours of India actually.'

Paul leads a very enviable life, working at his own pace in a great environment, doing something he's passionate about, and I'm quite reluctant to leave the bubble of calm and competence that surrounds him in his workshop. He comes outside to admire my modern Triumph before giving me directions on how to get out of Auckland.

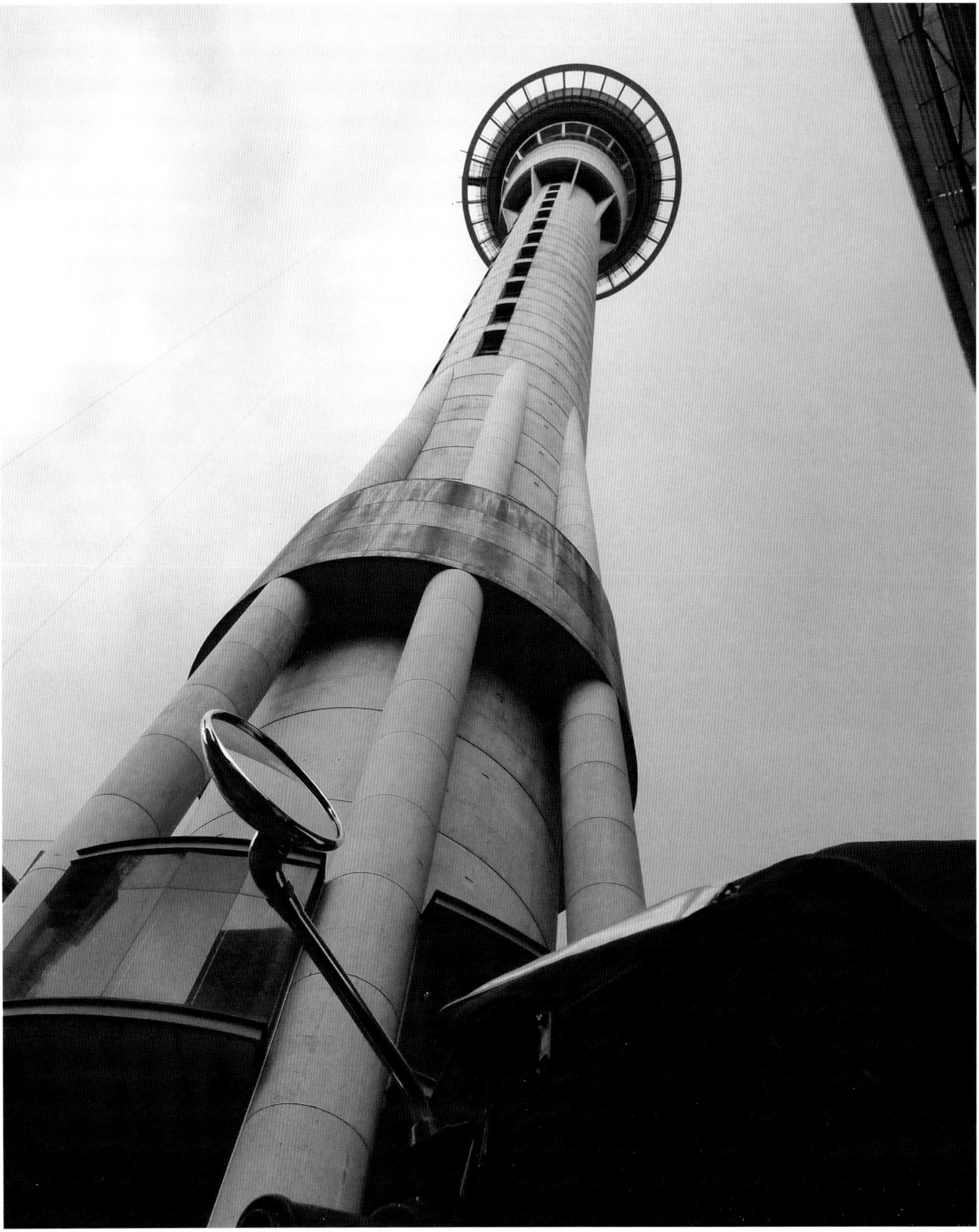

THE FAR NORTH: AN ARTIST, A JEWELLER AND A FIREFIGHTER

'Honkin' honkin' down the gosh darn highway.'
— The Beach Boys

Leaving Paul's place (and what a pleasure it was meeting him) I cruise through Ponsonby, where I feel right at home, having lived in Sydney's similarly trendy Newtown for 14 years. I then park-up on the pavement beneath the Sky Tower, causing a coach driver to toot and become quite irate, even though I'm about 20 metres away from his turning circle. Our discussion provides some entertainment for clicking tourists. I gaze up at to the tower, remembering the last time I was here, and shudder at the memory. God, it was brutal. In full firefighting gear and breathing from a cylinder on my back, I, along with 430 others, had laboured up the 1103 grey and unforgiving concrete steps to the top as part of the Auckland Firefighter Sky Tower Challenge. And to think I'd climbed it the previous year, and vowed never again!

With a cheery wave to my new friend the coach driver, I head across another iconic structure, the eight-lane Auckland Harbour Bridge. Just over a kilometre long, the original four-lane bridge was completed in 1959, making it the same age as me and the first Triumph Bonneville. Upon completion, 106,000 people walked across. Before that, they would have had to drive on a detour of 50 kilometres or use the ferry. In 1969, a further two lanes were added to each side of the harbour bridge — and are fondly known as 'the Nippon clip-ons'.

There follows more high-speed jostling on an excellent surface, on to the Northern Gateway bypass where I pass an electronic toll camera (for which I'll no doubt be fined for not paying). I head north through a mixture of pine, ponga and puriri trees to Warkworth, still in bright sunshine. I marvel at how Auckland's commuter belt keeps expanding, and how much Warkworth has grown since last I was here about eight years ago. Its population of almost 5000 (which has just about doubled since I was here last) enjoys a great little spot that was once connected to Auckland by steamship. I wander around the town on the picturesque banks of the Mahurangi River estuary, surrounded by orchards and fertile farmland. I succumb to a spot of lunch at a café surrounded by galleries, happy to be in the shade for a bit.

On the road, I'm in traffic again, and reflect on how spoilt we are living on the Mainland. It's not bumper-to-bumper here, but you're always conscious of the vehicle 20 metres in front and ready for their brake lights to come on, and so are less aware of the surroundings. But the twisties and the beauty of the Brynderwyn Hills placate me somewhat. The hills are part of a ridge extending east to west across Northland. By the roadside is a memorial to the worst road accident in New Zealand's history, when in 1963 a bus's brakes failed, causing it to leave the road and plunge down a sheer cliff face, killing 15 and injuring 21.

I bypass Whangarei (no offence to the town, it's just not in my Goldilocks Zone), and instead pull off the highway to ride the kilometre to sleepy little Hikurangi. To the west, the 1.2 million-year-old volcanic dome, Mount Hikurangi, rises to 365 metres. I'm soon sipping a fine flat white at an outside table and watching the world go by. The houses across the road are in dire need of painting, and the parked cars are mostly old clunkers. I drink my coffee outside as a gaggle of kids fresh out of school walk past my table and say 'hi'. Across the road, three girls let their horses graze by the swings in the park.

The first Maori to travel to England hailed from these parts. Mahanga was, understandably, amazed by early nineteenth-century London, and so astounding were his tales that upon returning home he was ridiculed and accused of telling porkies. When he visited King George III in the early 1800s, he expected to meet a mighty warrior, but was disappointed to discover a weakling who couldn't even throw a spear!

Not far up the highway, I nip into thriving and touristy Kawakawa. First stop is the train station, home to the Bay of Islands Vintage Railway, which operates steam and diesel trains on the former Opua track. A kindly old gentleman, whom I swear resembles the Fat Controller from *Thomas the Tank Engine*, asks me and an English family of five if we'd like a quick tour of the station. The father, in a thick Yorkshire brogue, tells us that stuff like this is all over the place 'back 'ome', and is not too impressed, although he's very polite about it. His kids look bored.

Nature is calling, and it's convenient that I've pulled up outside the world-famous Kawakawa public toilets in the middle of the high street. This amazing building, finished in 1999, was the last work of Austrian-born artist Friedensreich Hundertwasser, whose name is a work of art in itself. Kawakawa locals contributed to this hodge-podge with old bottles, recycled windows and hand-made tiles. It's so refreshing to see something a bit different, as we are, I think, all being drowned in a sea of corporate sameness. A throng of tourists wander in and out taking photos, and I'm surprised there's not a ticket-booth here, as I'm sure there would be in Australia!

There's a definite holiday vibe in the air that I can't quite put my finger on. Like a childhood memory of smelling coconut suntan oil on the beach or hot dogs at a fun fair. Winding down to Opua, I'm the last vehicle onto the ferry across to Russell. The lady driving the boat tells me she'll be 50 next week and plans to celebrate by walking up to Cape Reinga and back, and I wish her all the best. I'm soon booked into the Orongo Bay Holiday Park, where a much-needed shower awaits. In the morning it's a five-minute ride to Russell and Helen's place.

RUSSELL ARTIST — HELEN PICK

Helen's artistic roots go back generations. 'From the Farquharsons back in Scotland, to both of my grandmothers, and now my birth son and daughter are painters,' she begins. 'Though my son Rua has branched out quite a bit since the Christchurch earthquakes, when he lost all his materials. He's now into making Maori musical instruments down in Glentunnel in Canterbury. He uses all kinds of materials, including pounamu and recycled native timber from the local area.'

We're sitting in the small kitchen in Helen's cottage, sipping coffee and eating scones, hot out of the oven. She hands me a *nguru*, a small wind instrument Rua made from Oamaru stone, 'I'm still learning how to play it.' She laughs. 'You use your mouth, not your nose. Most days I can get a good loud whistle out of it.'

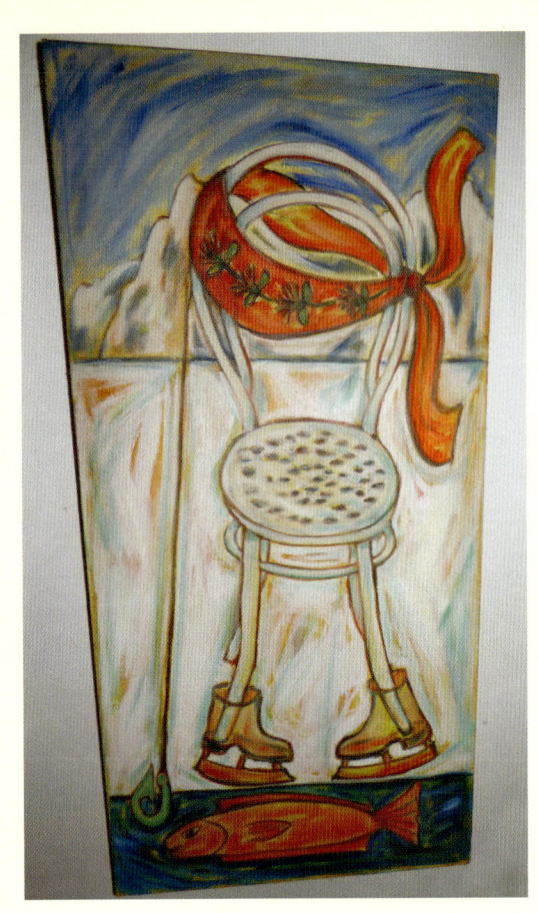

Both of Helen's birth children are full-time artists, and have been so all their working lives. Her daughter Séraphine lives in Wellington, and is well-known in the art world. 'Her art is studied as a symbol of female empowerment in a lot of schools. She's just gotten on and done stuff, despite the fact that she is deaf. It's so good that she's got this talent and extra vision. She's a really bright girl.' Her children's art, along with her own distinctive pieces, cover every wall in her cosy little cottage, creating a warm and welcoming ambience.

Helen was born and grew up in Invercargill, and at 15 had to move from Southland Girls' High School to technical college to take the exam to enter art school. 'And that was interesting for me,' she says, 'because the girls snubbed me and wouldn't talk to me, and it wasn't until years later that I realised it was because they thought I was somehow beneath them. And I just couldn't get over that snobbery.'

From that moment, Helen was determined never to judge or discriminate, and to try to be all-inclusive in her dealings with people. 'I also struck it with my first husband's family, who owned land in the Fens in the UK. Father Pick and his people were brought up in the culture of fox hunts and manor houses.'

The next stop on the train that is her life's journey was art school at Canterbury University in Christchurch. 'All five of us kids were put on a train from Invercargill and sent off north to "do something". I was given all my belongings, new sheets and blankets, my bike and clothes.' Helen thinks that serving in World War I at a young age had a profound influence on her father, who knew there was more to life than Invercargill could offer, and wanted his kids to grab it with both hands. 'I was the youngest at the university hostel,' she says, 'and I remember the boys coming over on my seventeenth birthday, lifting me up and carrying me around. And it's funny, because Séraphine has been doing a lot of crowd paintings recently, at concerts and Rugby Sevens and anywhere crowds get ecstatic, exploring the phenomenon of spirituality, and she painted a piece where a woman is being held up by a crowd, and it reminded me of that occasion when I turned 17!'

Helen spent two years at art school, before marrying her first husband, who was offered a job as art teacher in the Bay of Islands, which she says she and his mother arranged for him. 'So that's how I ended up here at 18,' says Helen. 'And we lived here in a home up the hill for 20 years. But Beresford never really wanted to be a teacher.' Beresford taught for three years before he and Helen landed a caretaking job for the Goodfellow family on the island of Moturua, off Russell, where they lived for the next two years.

'The Goodfellows had inherited money, were quite low-key and didn't live in a grand house, like some of the millionaires on the island,' she says. 'They were very old-fashioned. Lady Goodfellow would wear a sack apron, and Sir William would wear old cardigans like my dad used to wear. Rua was conceived on the island, but not born there as we had to get off.' Helen says that the old people on the island were having nightmares about her having her baby there. 'It's a very powerful place. Deeply spiritual. It got me fascinated, and I started to delve deeper into all things Maori and the *other* level.'

It wasn't until later, while doing environmental work and site inspections, that a kaumatua (an elder) enlightened her. Apparently, her son Rua, who was named after the island, was conceived on the site of a massacre.

'At the time, I *felt* it and I *saw* it, but I didn't *know* it!' Helen says. 'When Rua went south, they heard his name and discovered where he was conceived and wanted to know if he was worthy to carry the weight of that name. They went through it all and decided he was, and that's why he now works for Waitaha.'

Helen always wanted a large family, so found it hard to accept when her husband wanted to stop at two. 'He was a teacher,' she says, 'so didn't want to come home to a house full of kids.' Even so, Helen and Beresford started a foster family, and over the years provided a loving home to 11 foster children. 'And a lot of them married into the family, so my grandchildren and great-grandchildren came out of that line, too.'

In the end, though, such a large family was too much for her husband. 'That,' says Helen, 'is why I left their father, because he wouldn't allow me to be who *I* was.' Helen has always encouraged her children to be their own person, too: to be who they were and not settle for a stereotypical life.

After divorcing Beresford, Helen bought this place. 'As a single woman,' she says, 'this hundred-year-old cottage was the only thing I could afford. It was the last "doer-upper" in town, with grass up to the windows and every window broken.' Her ex-fisherman husband, Andrew, was originally the boarder and helped with repairs, and is now busy on the next round of repairs.

The Bay of Islands is one of the oldest inhabited areas in Aotearoa, and Helen reckons you can feel those who have been here before us. 'This is just a very powerful place. When you walk this land, you can feel them. What I love about this place is that their descendants still live here. And we're all slightly related, too, through my two great-granddaughters.' Helen really doesn't look old enough to be a great-grandmother, and when she tells me she's in her seventies I nearly fall off my chair. I tell her she must have found the elixir of youth up here in Russell!

Helen has been involved in environmental issues for years, and planner Andrew helps her out. 'Because I was familiar with planning speak, the local marae organisation got me in to help with their environmental resource consents,' she says. She also campaigned tirelessly for the building of the first marae to be in Russell for generations. Located on the waterfront, the marae was named Haratu, after the chief Rewa's whare, which stood close to the new site in the 1830s. It finally opened in 2009, after a 20-year struggle marked by considerable opposition.

'So, I've kind of lived a dual Pakeha and Maori life,' says Helen. 'And my wonderful whanau — my foster family — consists of Maori, Cook Islander, Indonesian, Samoan and Chinese.' I tell her I bet the family get-togethers are memorable, and she laughs. 'But since the whalers first came here, we've had all nationalities settling in Russell and marrying into Maori families. It's a microcosm of the whole world up here. This is the place I feel empty for when I'm away. This is the place I ache for. Invercargill is my birthplace, but this is my home place. I'm going to be buried here. I sold a painting and managed to buy a bit of dirt at Long Beach Cemetery, and once I'm buried there I'll really be a local.'

We then go for a walk through her wonderful garden — which is her pride and joy — to the studio, where she shows me some of her artwork, which is colourful and vibrant. One depicts Helen and Andrew getting married in the garden, and was part of an exhibition in Auckland and Whangarei in 1990. Most of Helen's work was shown at her own gallery here in Russell, along with five other artists. 'Another reason I love this place is because you have tides, which are magnetic and push and pull and have this tremendous energy, and I try to put that into my paintings.' She says she has two series of oil paintings she'd like to complete, then she will go back to doing some sculpture.

Before I leave, Helen shows me her swamp at the front of the property, which she says must be the last bit of swamp in Russell, and that even in times of drought she can grow things here. As I put my gear on, ready to leave, she says, 'When you contacted me to appear in your book, George, I told you that I wasn't really a character, but I am someone with strong opinions, who feels things. I appreciate the land where I live and I try to walk lightly on it. A lot of old people have told me that if you don't respect it, it will kick back at you.'

A stone's throw down the road it's a busy Saturday morning in Russell and pastel-clad tourists abound. Russell is another one of those picture-postcard towns that take tourists' breath away and we become somewhat blasé about. Surrounded by golden, sandy beaches, it sits snugly in its sheltered anchorage.

In the early 1800s this anchorage was perfect for visiting whalers. They were often away from their homes in the Northern Hemisphere for an incredible two or three years! Adventurous Maoris would sign on as crew, getting a taste of the wider world. It soon grew in popularity, and Kororareka, as it was known, became the first European settlement in New Zealand.

Kororareka also became a regular den of iniquity, and was known as the 'hellhole of the Pacific' because of its population of whalers, deserters, ex-convicts and general riff-raff. I've no doubt that Friday night on the town back then would have been a bit more eventful than the one I had last night at Orongo Bay Holiday Park, where I fell asleep with my book on my face.

Hone Heke, the famous Ngapuhi warrior chief, and his people owned much of the land in the Bay of Islands, although the concept of ownership was very different to that of the Pakeha settlers. Maori philosophy says that you can't own the land if you can't take it with you. Guardianship, or kaitiaki, would be more accurate. Hone Heke initially endured the loutish behaviour and insults from Kororareka Pakeha. As long as the supply of muskets, powder and ball, which made Ngapuhi feared throughout the land, kept coming, he said 'Hei aha?' ('What does it matter?'). He also became very wealthy from a toll he levied on all ships passing through the heads. He once sailed up and down the bay in his war canoe flying the Stars and Stripes, as he'd been persuaded to do by the American Consul. The Consul was promptly ordered to haul it down by the local British magistrate and admonished for 'encouraging native naughtiness'. Later, Hone Heke, strongly influenced by tales of the American War of Independence, cut down the British flag pole in Kororareka, instigating what became known as the Flagstaff War.

On previous visits with family, I'd mentioned to my wife that this was one of the few places I'd consider retiring to if we ever left Governors Bay. It, as Helen mentioned, has an ambience and community spirit that is quite rare in a place. It puts me in mind of a small fishing/tourist town in Massachusetts or Maine.

Unfortunately, the museum doesn't open until later, so I take a stroll along the waterfront. And of course the lure of eggs on toast and good coffee is irresistible, and I breakfast at an outside table gazing out across the calm Veronica Channel. A short ferry ride will take you across to Paihia, which in the 1800s started life as a mission station and hive of pious industry, in sharp contrast to Kororareka. And just down the road you'll find Waitangi, where, as all Kiwi schoolkids should know, the Treaty of Waitangi was signed in 1840 between the Crown and Maori chiefs (Hone Heke among them). It really is a must to visit, with guided tours and free entry to Kiwi residents, although I'm afraid it's the nature of my ride, which is essentially around the characters I'm visiting, that I can't see everything and Waitangi misses out.

The image of Maine or somewhere on the US east coast is complete, as the two neighbouring tables are full of Americans. I know they're yachties, because I can hear every word of their nautical conversation, as can everyone else along the waterfront.

Taking the little ferry back to Opua, it's not long before I backtrack through Kawakawa, where another coach-load is clicking away at the toilets, and find Pakaraka on SH1. Back in Auckland, Paul Downie had suggested that his sister Kate would make a great addition to my book, and has kindly phoned ahead to organise my visit. And it's her voice that surprises me as she calls my name from her front gate while I'm taking a photograph of a herd of cows that I know I'll delete later on.

ARTIST/JEWELLER — KATE DU PLOOY

Kate's involvement in art started 40 years ago. She reckons she was an obsessive artist through school and was all set to go to Elam Art School in Auckland where she grew up. 'Then,' she says, 'I was given a sterling-silver bangle for Christmas, and I remember spending the whole holidays just staring at that metal. Just staring at the solder joints and the warmth of the silver. I was simply captivated.' Most of us would admire the bangle and carry on with their lives, but Kate reasoned that if other people could create something like this, then so could she. Like many others

I've interviewed, Kate's eyes shine with enthusiasm for her craft. 'It was 1976 and I was 17, and everyone expected me to start my fine arts degree but I said, "No, I want to be a jeweller!"'

Her father accused her of being a juvenile delinquent, while all her schoolteachers could envisage was her sitting on Queen Street leaning against a shopfront with a velvet board with beads and feathers stuck into it. Kate couldn't get across to them that what she saw was art transferred into precious metal. Little did Kate know, the struggles and travails she'd have to endure to fulfil her dream of becoming a jeweller.

'I soon discovered that there was no art school or technical institution that taught jewellery-making. If I wanted to pursue it, then I would have to become an apprentice manufacturing jeweller.'

In 1976, being a 17-year-old girl didn't fit the mould of the usual 15-year-old male apprentice. So Kate dropped out of school and went to work in a shop on Queen Street selling cool T-shirts. 'I promptly got fired because I was such a useless shop assistant,' she says. 'Over the next year, I phoned absolutely everyone in the Yellow Pages. One guy gave me a couple of days' work experience in his workshop in Parnell, but told me the job was dirty and not nice for a girl and that I might break my fingernails. He didn't realise that I'd have been happy to scrub the ground with a toothbrush — I just wanted to do this!' By the time Kate had picked her jaw up from the ground, he'd shown her the door.

She finally got a break when Brian, a goldsmith in the Canterbury Arcade, grudgingly, and after much badgering, took her on for a year, but then sacked her so he could take on a boy apprentice. 'Because girls weren't supposed to be apprenticed, they were supposed to get married or be secretaries,' she laughs. 'I remember crusty old men coming into the workshop and asking how many rings the girl had melted today.' I shake my head. 'Yeah, in the '70s New Zealand was just crawling out of the Dark Ages.'

But that year was invaluable to Kate. Not only for the experience, but for the money she'd saved up. She then spent every cent buying the tools needed to set herself up, and at the ripe old age of 18 became self-employed. Over the next 10 years Kate got married, worked from home and taught her ex-husband to make jewellery. She'd often be found selling her wares in the Cook Street Market. 'But it has always been a hit-and-miss way to make a living,' she says. 'I'd walk around the duty-free shops and into the Auckland Museum shop, trying to sell stuff. It's a struggle, but you scratch by.'

Kate had her first exhibition in the early 1980s in the New Vision Gallery, which no longer exists. 'That gallery had been set up in the 1950s and was the first to pioneer crafters' art,' she says, 'but I had a few exhibitions in Auckland, which obviously helped spread the word.'

She then moved down to Gisborne with her husband and became involved in teaching. 'I saw this ad in the local rag,' says Kate, 'which advertised "Gisborne Silversmiths' Garage Sale". I cracked up laughing, imagining bent plates and teapots, so I went along to the fabulous Museum and Arts Centre and spoke to a very earnest older woman, who explained that they were raising money to buy tools for their Silversmiths' Group.' A jeweller had given a workshop to the group recently, and had filled them with enthusiasm. When Kate said that she was a jeweller, the lady cried, 'Everybody — we have a jeweller in our midst!' and everyone gathered around, beaming. And so Kate duly got talked into teaching a series of workshops for the group, and realised that she really enjoyed it. Not long after that, she landed a job teaching kids on a government-funded scheme. Kate taught jewellery-making to a class of six for 40 hours a week for the next nine months. 'It was great, but my own work had to take a back seat,' she says.

She did, however, find time to enter a piece in the first and only competition for contemporary jewellers, stone carvers and bone carvers. 'A guy called David La Plants, who was Professor of Art at Humboldt State University and over here running workshops on a Fulbright Scholarship, was judging the pieces. And I managed to get a Merit. I read his critique and thought, "Wow, this guy knows his stuff. Wouldn't it be great if I could study with him?"'

So Kate got to work and made it happen. She photographed her work and sent him the slides, along with a long letter explaining her philosophy on contemporary jewellery and asking him if she could possibly study with him. 'Thanks to David's efforts, and a QEII Arts Council grant, I was able to go and study with him in California. I had an incredible year. I always said I'd never call myself a silversmith until I could make a teapot. And I did.' Kate then gets up and unwraps the beautiful little teapot she made in the States.

Returning home, she started a year's work teaching at Waikato Polytechnic in Hamilton. 'But it was a bit of a messy year, because I inherited some very disillusioned students who had been getting a raw deal, and my marriage broke up at the same time. I also met my husband, Dirk, that year. But that full-time position really did me in so far as teaching goes. I found the politics at a tertiary institution unpalatable, to say the least. I really needed to put all the energy I'd gotten from America into an exhibition, so it was frustrating.'

So, Kate and Dirk, a Zimbabwean, moved to Auckland. She had lost her workshop in the divorce, and so had to start again from scratch. Then, in 1991, they went to live in Harare in Zimbabwe, where Kate taught a group of apprentices. 'Now that was a real challenge,' she says. 'Over there, the work of metalsmith was traditionally the job of the shaman. I only got the job because the older men refused to pass on their skills, fearing that they'd do themselves out of their jobs. And of course being a white woman teaching a man's job didn't go down well either.'

Dirk, who had fought with the SAS in the war of independence from Rhodesia, saw the writing on the wall in 1994, when President Mugabe started his terror tactics. He told Kate that he'd seen this before and that it was time to leave. 'So, we came back,' says Kate. 'I would have stayed there for the rest of my life, but it wasn't to be. Leaving the country absolutely crippled us financially. Back in Auckland we were living in a bedsit in Herne Bay with no furniture, and had to start from scratch once again.'

Kate started to ply her trade again, but was having trouble getting enough work, and then in 1998 Dirk experienced life-threatening intestinal health problems that meant he had to stop working. Things were looking grim, especially as Kate was having some difficulty getting paid for contract work. With Dirk sick and rent to be paid, she swallowed her pride, walked into the New World supermarket in downtown Victoria Park and said, 'Give me a job. I'll do anything.'

She worked in the delicatessen section for the next five years. 'I got over myself pretty quickly. Boy, do you find out about yourself and human nature when you have to do hard physical work for 50 hours a week on low wages. It was humbling, but I don't regret it.' In 2002 Kate applied for a jewellery job, and was left speechless at the interview when the guy, having read her extensive CV, said to her,

'You know jewellery is a very dirty job for a woman? What about your fingernails?' Kate once more cranked her jaw up off the ground and walked out the door.

A couple of years later she saw an advertisement for her dream job: a goldsmith/designer in the Bay of Islands. Tired of rejection and disappointment, she refused to think about it, but after a couple of weeks finally worked up the courage to apply, and got the job at Kerikeri Goldsmiths, and moved north.

'I loved working for them, but I was made redundant in 2006, says Kate. 'I still needed to pay the bills because Dirk couldn't work, so — you've guessed it — I started work in the deli at Kerikeri New World.'

I really wasn't expecting Kate to say that! 'Yep, I did another five years, but it was better than Auckland, because my workshop was set up at home and I had started to take some orders.' She damaged her hand at work and left in 2011, vowing never to return. So she took the plunge, started working from home, and since then orders have picked up and, with an exhibition pending, things are finally looking rosy.

Kate shows me her little workshop where she works on her tiny three-dimensional canvases. 'The worst day here at my bench,' she says, 'is always better than the best day at New World.'

Just down the road from Kate's I stop to take a photo of the Pakaraka Holy Trinity Church. The original church was built in 1850 by prominent missionary Henry Williams, who was ordained by the Bishop of London and played a part in persuading Maori to sign the Treaty of Waitangi, as well as translating the text. The current church was built on this site in 1873 by his wife and family as a memorial to him, for the princely sum of £1000. It's famous for deviating from the usual country church design, but, philistine that I am, the difference is not immediately apparent to me. Hone Heke was born in Pakaraka around 1808, and was buried here in 1850. In 2011, his remains were moved because of upcoming development.

I head north through a green and pleasant land, flashing through tiny and rather impoverished settlements like Okaihou, Umawera and Mangamuka. The green and pleasantness disguises one of the most deprived populations in New Zealand. Northland has the highest proportion of unsealed roads, and public transport is very limited. The only true urban area is Whangarei, containing a third of Northland's population. The use of methamphetamine or 'P' is widespread in the region, and a huge problem as a significant driver of crime.

I'm overtaking a semi-trailer carrying logs (and glancing down I note I'm just touching 100kph) when the dreaded blue-and-red flashing lights explode in my mirrors. 'Sorry,' the grey-haired, bespectacled officer of the law says when I've pulled over and taken my helmet off. (I always show my grey hairs as soon as possible in the hope of empathy or even leniency.) 'Just checking your warrant,' he says, and notes the tag behind my number plate. He then goes on to say how much he loves the new Triumphs, especially the mag wheels, and how he's wanted one for years but his wife would take some persuading. Poor bugger must have been having a slow day.

I speed up with the hope of riding up to Cape Reinga and then back to Kaitaia before day's end, but as the clock ticks I realise the folly of this idea. Although I'd visited the top of the country before, it would have been nice to do so again, just for form's sake. It's a good idea to slow down anyway, as some of the twisties riding through the 3000-hectare Mangamuka Scenic Reserve and Mangamuka Gorge are tight and deserve respect. The towai-forested hills and manuka scrubland of the reserve are a haven for the North Island brown kiwi, and the rare giant bullies and short-jawed kokopu are found in its streams. In no hurry now, I can pull over in a lay-by where tall, prehistoric-looking ferns, in sharp relief against the blue sky, grow down to the road.

Arriving in Kaitaia in the late afternoon, I book into the excellent Wayfarers Motel and fall asleep on the bed, while flicking between the news channels on Sky (a habit my wife and kids hate). Kaitaia on a Saturday night is a bit of a ghost town, so I return to my little sanctuary with fish 'n' chips and watch more television.

Checking out some old shows on UK TV makes me smile as I remember *The Professionals* in the late 1970s. Bodie, cynical ex-SAS, and Doyle, liberal ex-cop, were top CI5 agents and Britain's answer to *Starsky and Hutch*. Their boss, Cowley, portrayed by the excellent Gordon Jackson, battled to keep 'his boys' in check. I had short hair at the time, was in the Territorial Army and fancied myself as a bit of a Bodie lookalike. I remember one embarrassing Saturday night, posing down at a disco in Richmond, leaning on the bar. I'd been practising Bodie's steely-eyed, pouty look in the mirror at home, and reckoned I had it down pat. With practised nonchalance, I was hoping that Patsy had noticed me. She had noticed! For she was sashaying across the dancefloor now, making a beeline for me. 'I'm in!' I thought, visions of carnal delights dancing before me and mixing with the disco lights. She was now beside me, and I leant in to smell her perfume and peek at that tantalising cleavage. 'Is there something wrong with your mouth, George?' she asked. Pout and steely-eyed gaze now gone, I had a sudden need to find the toilet.

I check out in the morning, and I'm so close to my next interview I could almost wheel my bike across the street.

FIREFIGHTER — COLIN 'TOSS' KITCHEN

I'm sitting in the Kaitaia Fire Station with the Chief Fire Officer (CFO) of the Volunteer Brigade. I ask him about his nickname. 'I think it was from early in the brigade when we used to have those games where you line all the drinks up and toss them back,' he says dismissively, and then gets serious. 'We are the most northerly fire station in New Zealand. We cover the 120 k's north up to Cape Reinga, south to Mangamuka and all North Hokianga. I'd say we have the largest area to cover in the country.'

Most call-outs are to vegetation fires and motor vehicle accidents (MVAs). Up until a few years ago, the last section of road to Cape Reinga was gravel, which motorists — mostly tourists not being accustomed to unsealed roads — would regularly slide off. Most of the other call-outs are made up of structure fires and medicals. The brigade has two fire appliances, a PRT (pump rescue tender), a support van and a rural fire tanker.

Colin, Kaitaia-born and -bred, became a volunteer firefighter way back in 1968 as a 17-year-old apprentice electrician. 'Ken Murray,' he says, 'my primary-school teacher, was in the brigade, and when the siren would go, he'd shoot off and leave me in charge of the class.' I suggest he had experience being in charge from an early age!

'Back then, the culture in the brigade was a lot different,' Colin explains. 'In those times, you had to be middle-class, male and white, if you know what I mean.' I'm amazed at this. Things of course have changed from those unenlightened times, and today the modern Kaitaia Brigade reflects the 50 per cent Maori demographic of the region. Colin goes on: 'When I joined we had about 20 members and got about 36 call-outs for the year. Forty-nine years later, our multiracial brigade averages a call a day, and our busiest year was over 370 calls. We also have women in our brigade, which was unheard of back then.'

With call-outs predicted to rise to 400 per year, an enormous strain is placed on the employers of volunteers and on the self-employed members. Colin explains that the number of call-outs is not the problem; it's the duration of some calls. 'I've been to two calls in a day, and they've taken over eight hours out of my day.' If Kaitaia does get a decent-sized vegetation fire, they are on their own for at least 40 minutes until the nearest help from Mangonui, another volunteer brigade, arrives. Colin remembers a big blaze at the Juken Nissho Triboard Mill when he had to try to keep the fire at bay for three hours until help arrived from paid crews from Whangarei.

There is an auxiliary brigade at Ahipara, at the bottom of Ninety Mile Beach, about 15 kilometres away, which is very helpful for call-outs on the beach, equipped as they are with a four-wheel-drive Mercedes appliance and a 'smoke chaser' ute. 'We do take our appliance and rural tanker on the beach, too, via the forestry roads,' says Colin. 'And the tankers from the Kaitaia Rural Station and DOC also provide us with water.'

I ask Colin if there has been any talk of turning the Kaitaia Fire Brigade into a paid station. 'We think it will happen in time,' he says. 'We'll probably have what is called a Yellow Watch, where there is a paid crew on station during the daytime, and at night-time and weekends it reverts to the volunteer system we have now.' Colin runs a roster system for volunteers, and admits that sometimes he struggles to get a full crew in the daytime, but proudly boasts that there's never been a call-out where a truck hasn't left the station.

Next year the brigade will be 80 years old, Colin will have been CFO for 10 years, and will also be celebrating his 50 years of service. His full-time job for the past 21 years has been as a VSO or volunteer support officer with the New Zealand Fire Service, a position he recently retired from. But Colin is very active in his community, not just as a firefighter. He's in his fourth term as a Far North district councillor, and his fourth term on the Northern District Health Board. And if that's not enough, he's also on the board of Volunteering Northland, as well as being chairperson of Northland Civil Defence Management Group. 'So, I've got a bit to keep me busy,' says Colin, the master of understatement; 'I suppose you'd call it semi-retirement.'

Within the brigade, Colin has been very proactive, being involved in Fire Brigade rugby competitions, captaining the New Zealand rugby team in the early 1980s, and running firefighter competitions at provincial, sub-association and national levels.

'I'm a past president and life member of what we call the Northland Fire Brigade Sub-association, past president and life member of Auckland Provincial, which encompassed all brigades from Turangi north, and then I'm a past president and life member of the United Fire Brigades Association of New Zealand, and of course I'm a life member of this brigade, too.' In 1998 Colin was awarded the MNZM, or Member of the New Zealand Order of Merit.

Good grief, he's been busy! I can't imagine anyone more deserving of recognition. 'I bet you look like a South American general with all those medals,' I say. 'Yeah, well, they don't call me Jingle Bells for nothing,' he replies with a laugh. I congratulate him and say that he must be very proud.

'Well yes, I am, but something made me a lot prouder, George, and that was when my daughter, squash player Shelley Kitchen, got to number 6 in the world, won 25 national titles, 4 New Zealand titles, Commonwealth silver and bronze medals and was awarded the New Zealand Order of Merit.'

Colin has also competed in the World Firefighters Games, in Las Vegas, Perth, Auckland and Christchurch, where he won a silver medal with his mate in outdoor bowls. I tell him he really needs to write a book. 'I intend to write a book one day. The good, the bad and the ugly and the bastards I've met, or whatever,' he says.

Back in the 1960s when Colin joined the brigade, all of the training was done on station, with new members getting hands-on experience riding the trucks, getting stuck in, and learning in the field. 'We learned on the job,' says Colin nostalgically. 'Nowadays of course, what with the likes of OSH [occupational safety and health], things are a bit different. It's great the way we look after ourselves now, but I think things have become too bureaucratic. And with the upcoming merger of the Rural Fire Service and the Fire Service into Fire Emergency New Zealand, who knows? We'll just have to wait and see.'

In 1995 he left his job as manager of Smith and Brown, a furniture and home appliance store in Kaitaia, to take on the full-time role of volunteer support officer, a new role created in the Fire Service restructuring. This kind of role had traditionally gone to paid firefighters, and Colin was initially taken to task over it.

Colin says that for years he has had a problem with the way paid firefighters called themselves 'professionals'. He has always referred to them as 'career firefighters' or 'paid staff', and believes he may well have been instrumental in spreading this idea. 'We ride the same trucks, fight the same fires, and go to the same call-outs,' he says firmly, slapping the desk. 'We're all professionals, make no mistake about that. I've spoken to a lot of people on the subject.'

I tell him that he seems to be a good talker. 'Oh, I talk, don't you worry about that! I'll talk to the Lions Club or the prime minister; I'll talk to anyone. I'll tell them that the New Zealand Fire Service is a volunteer service that is complemented in the big urban centres, like Auckland and Wellington, by paid or career staff. To put it in a nutshell, George, there are about 1800 to 2000 paid staff, compared to urban and rural volunteers who number 13,000.'

Colin then gives me a tour of the plush and well-equipped station. In the bar, I get him to pose for a photo, pulling a pint. 'But don't get me wrong,' he says, continuing on a subject close to his heart, 'I'm not rubbishing anyone. We have a great working relationship, as other brigades do, with the career firefighters, and they give us great support.'

He says his leadership style is based on delegation. He has faith in his deputy and his officers and his crew. Most of the time they'll make a decision and he'll back them up. He believes that in a lot of brigades the chiefs try to become one-man-bands. 'I'm like the overseer, but if they stuff up, I'll let them know.'

Colin reckons he gets a lot of joy and pride from helping people out. He's been to some horrific MVAs with multiple fatalities, as well as fatalities involving structure fires, and some involving kids, which are particularly distressing. 'In the old days,' he says, 'there was no support. We'd see some horrific sights, come back to the station and have a beer or rum or something. But these days there is Critical Incident Stress Management available to anyone.'

I wind up by asking Colin what he plans to do when he *really* retires. 'Well, I love my fishing and I've got this electric torpedo with a timer that takes 25 baited hooks out. So my mate Ronny and myself are going to set up Toss and Ronny's Torpedo Tours.' And good luck to him! Colin also plans on writing his memoirs, warts and all, so watch this space.

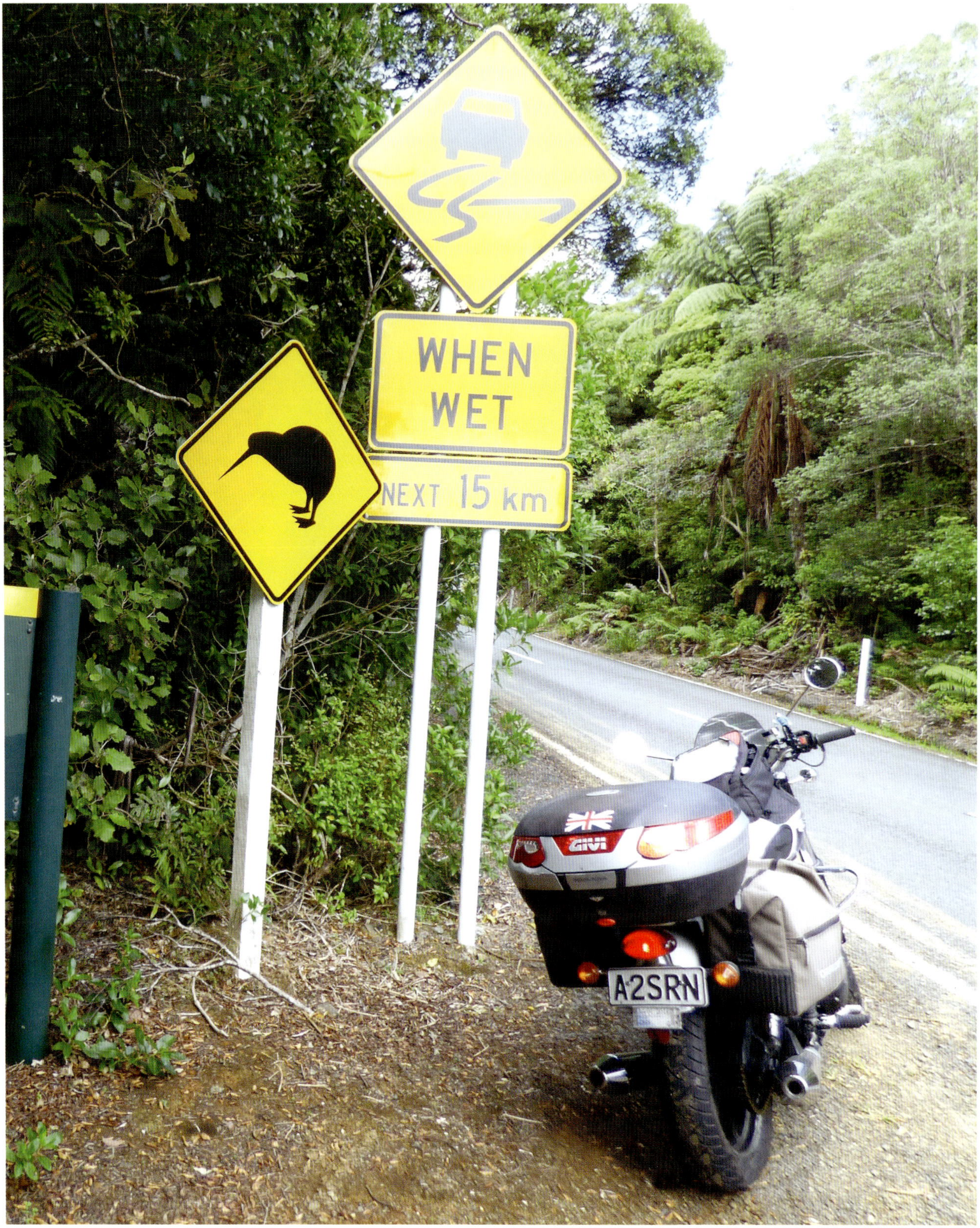
WHEN
WET
NEXT 15 km
GIVI
A2SRN

HEADING SOUTH: A COFFEE LADY, A TRIUMPH FAN AND A TRAINING COMMANDER

'The road leads into the quiet places of the shadows of your mind.'
— Tom T. Hall

I take SH10 out of town in the quiet Sunday morning stillness, with the road to myself. In no time, Doubtless Bay emerges on my left, a huge sweep of golden sand, fringed with pohutukawa trees and popular with holiday-makers. In the peak holiday month of January, the population around the bay increases tenfold.

Captain Cook named it in 1769. Although the wind was not favourable for venturing in for confirmation, he is reported to have said, 'It's doubtless a bay.' At Taipa there is a memorial marking the spot where, according to Maori legend, Polynesian explorer Kupe, discoverer of Aotearoa, landed in New Zealand. Coopers Beach, a bit further along, was so-named as it was here that the local cooper would mend broken storage barrels for visiting ships.

I climb off the bike in front of the historic Mangonui Hotel, which proudly boasts that it's the most northerly hotel in New Zealand. Across the street by the water is a line of mostly Harleys, whose owners I'm guessing are still sleeping off hangovers. According to an old guy with a limp and very bushy eyebrows who's walking his dog, there was some kind of rally here last night.

The fishing fleet forms the mainstay of the town's economy, and big-game fishing is also popular. Mangonui ('big shark') was originally a trading station and base for whalers, with as many as 30 whaling boats anchored here at any one time.

My Big Brekkie antenna is at it again, and leads me to the Little Kitchen café, where I'm soon in heaven, tucking into my calorific delight while gazing out to sea. Neil Sedaka plays softly from the café's radio inside, happy French tourists chat around me, and seagulls shriek overhead. It's an idyllic scene, but alas I can't linger as I've miles to go before I sleep. With the press of a button I'm away, and in less than an hour I find myself in Kerikeri, beholding Kemp House, the oldest surviving building in the country. Built as a missionary station in 1822 under the protection of Hone Heke, it sits in splendour on the banks of the Kerikeri inlet. Kerikeri ('to dig') is also famous for being the place where the first European agricultural plough broke the soil, in 1820.

From Kerikeri I head south and find SH12, a fantastic road that links the two coasts. Halfway across is Kaikohe, birthplace of another renowned Ngapuhi chief, Hongi Hika, uncle to Hone Heke and among the first Maori to travel to Old Blighty. He was invited so that potential colonisers and well-meaning missionaries could learn the Maori language. He was flattered by all the attention, especially when King George IV greeted him with, 'How do you do, King Honi?' He was showered with expensive gifts, which (apart from a suit of armour) he sold in Sydney on his way home, and bought muskets instead. Back in his pa, he armed his warriors and led them far and wide on a bloody rampage of destruction as far afield as Rotorua, in the first of the 'Musket Wars'.

SH12 must go down as one of the best rides of my trip, winding through the kind of sublime landscape that could be painted onto a chocolate box. The continuing dry weather and no traffic provide perfect riding, and brings me to the west coast and the sparkling Hokianga Harbour. I pull up in front of the dairy in Opononi, on the roof of which sits a statue of Opo the dolphin, who famously played and frolicked in the shallows with locals and tourists in the summer of 1955/56.

A group of teenagers sitting at the picnic table grunt 'hi' as their fingers alternate between eating chips and dancing over their cellphones. I wander along the beach and meet Mike, who's busy fishing. He's chatty and happy to stop and show me his catch. 'Some idiots call this "Maori tucker" and won't eat it,' he says, holding up his kahawai, 'but they're great eating. I'll smoke this one.' Mike came up here from Auckland with his wife 20 years ago, and he says they love it. 'It's taken off a bit in the past couple of years. I think people are realising how good the lifestyle is up here. I reckon it's the most beautiful harbour in the country,' he says, and it's hard to argue with that.

Hokianga Harbour is more laidback than the Bay of Islands, and is a little depressed economically, although it's hard for a traveller to share that depression, as the beautiful scenery and lack of tacky development does nothing but lift the spirits.

Not that long ago the land I'm riding through was covered in majestic kauri forest. Fortunately for early Europeans but *un*fortunately for the noble kauri, the tree was perfect for replacing masts and spars for ships, and later provided durable timber in house construction. Maori also used the mighty kauri for their waka, but treated the trees with respect, even engaging in ceremonies to appease the forest gods.

After the 1860s, when kauri on the surface became scarce, Europeans (mostly Dalmatians from the Croatian coast), followed by Maori, started to dig up the old forests. For 50 or so years, up to 1920, gum-digging was the primary source of income in Northland, providing high-quality varnishes for the English market, and what's more giving birth to the word 'gumboot'. One kauri stump which has been excavated with hand tools and back-breaking labour is said to be 150,000 years old!

The road (still SH12) narrows and snakes its way south through more forest, this time the Waipoua. Rounding another bend, a collection of parked vehicles and picnickers on a grassy bank tell me I've arrived at the Forest Sanctuary. If I can't pay homage to the departed spirits at Cape Reinga, then I can at least pay my respects to Tane Mahuta, the country's largest remaining kauri tree. This magnificent example stands over 50 metres tall and, although estimates vary, is thought to be about 1250 years old. After having my boots sprayed in a small booth (to prevent the introduction of kauri dieback disease), I join a mixed group of tourists on the short walk to pay homage to the God of the Forest, whose fragile roots are protected by boardwalks. I gaze up in awe, realising that this tree was alive before the first Polynesians arrived.

I'm pretty peckish now, and after a good run down to Dargaville I'm happy to spot a decent-looking café open on the high street that's doing a roaring trade with mostly young backpackers, all tapping away on cellphones and tablets.

It's no surprise that Dargaville was once a kauri timber and gum trading centre. Ships as large as 3000 tonnes would enter the Kaipara Harbour and travel up the Wairoa River to moor at the town's wharf. Huge log jams were common, often allowing people to walk from one side of the river to the other over the logs.

Replete with coffee, bread and dips, I ride over the wide brown Wairoa River and head south again, still on the wonderful SH12, following the river on my right as far as Ruawai, where I turn inland. It's a fast road east to join SH1 once more at Brynderwyn, and it's hard not to speed. I regretfully leave Northland, having completed a giant figure eight around it. My speedy progress south on this hot afternoon slows to a snail's pace on the outskirts of Warkworth as I hit the bottleneck of Aucklanders returning from their weekend or day away from the city. All week they sit in traffic for hours to commute to work, and then, after going away for a bit of stress relief, they have to endure it to get home. I take the piss a bit to be honest, with my lane-splitting, but once again motorists move over to afford me more room, gentlemanly behaviour that I acknowledge with a wave. It's then that an SUV decides to cut in from my right, for what reason I don't know, as there is a solid line of traffic on my left. I grab a handful of front brake and narrowly avoid rear-ending him.

Statistically there is probably an accident out there with your name on it. It may happen in 20 years, or today or never. All you can do is hone your skills, keep your bike well maintained, ride with your headlight on, wear visible clothes, assume all motorists are blind morons and wear clean underpants.

Over the harbour bridge the traffic thins out a bit, and it's not long before I'm south of the Manukau Harbour. The Awhitu Peninsula, just over an hour from downtown, is known in some circles as the Supercity's best kept secret, with its empty, sandy beaches and great fishing. I can smell the salt air and mudflats as I pull once more into Judy and Richard's driveway, ready again for a shower and cold beer.

COFFEE LADY — JUDY BOSWORTH

Weekday mornings from 5.30 to 11am, Judy can be found by the side of the road outside Glenbrook School, providing caffeine fixes to people commuting the 40 kilometres from Waiuku to Auckland, who often sit in traffic two hours each way. 'I feel I'm a kind of traffic control for yawning commuters, who often don't even know what day it is,' she says. 'But the main reason I'm doing it is so that I don't have to go up that road myself.'

We're sitting on the deck, eating fresh snapper that partner Richard caught in Manukau Harbour earlier, and venison he'd recently shot, along with salad from the garden. A couple of years ago, Judy had to take redundancy from the huge bureaucracy of Auckland Council, where she worked in GIS (Geographic Information System). After a bit of contract work for Waikato dried up, Judy looked for work locally. 'I didn't even get an interview,' she says. 'I think it was my age.' So, reasoning that if nobody would employ her, she'd employ herself, she saw a 'Coffee Guy' franchise and van for sale, and, being a big fan of coffee, took the plunge, if you'll excuse the pun.

'But it's bloody hard work and RSI can be a problem,' she says, chewing around a mouthful of avocado and fish. 'Most days I make about 110 coffees. And I've gotten used to people saying "But you're not a Coffee Guy", and me replying "You've got no idea what's under my T-shirt." But I get to know my regulars and what they drink, and I feel I'm providing a service.' Weekends find the Coffee Lady at various events and competitions around the traps.

While attending Balmacewen Intermediate, Dunedin-born Judy met her lifelong friend (and my wife) Karen, the pair of them then going on to Otago Girls' High. 'We had to take French, Latin and Embroidery. Check that out! I've got the most appalling pieces of embroidery, but my mother treasures them. I used to have a pet possum that peed on one of them.'

Judy ended up doing lab work for the University of Otago, and, along with Karen, went to polytech part-time to qualify as a lab technician, breeding mice on the side to sell to pet shops at 10 cents each. Eager to head off overseas, Judy went up to CIT in Wellington to finish her qualification on block release, and fractured her patella while dancing. 'That must have been a strenuous dance,' I say. 'People thought I'd drunk too much and fallen down,' she replies, laughing, 'but it just whipped out with such force that it broke.'

Judy and Karen then drove up to Hastings in Karen's little Mini to work and save money for their big OE. They were soon working quality control in the Birds Eye processing factory. 'We were kicked out of my friend's flat after two weeks, because her flatmate was an obsessive–compulsive guy called Owen who found us too messy. The last straw was when my brother and his mate came up on their motorbikes and slept a night on the floor in their sleeping bags and looked too untidy.'

First stop on the girls' OE was Australia, where they stayed in Sydney, Canberra and Brisbane. Their packs were so heavy that Karen would regularly topple over as she tried to wrestle it from the ground to her back. They gradually ditched things as they went, but finally Judy's straps broke under the strain.

In London, they moved into a squat in Stockwell, with Kiwi friends. 'I remember we had been travelling for 36 hours, and Karen had face-planted at Heathrow Airport,' laughs Judy. She worked in a variety of jobs, including hitting the lids onto plastic bottles of Gumption (Jif) with a piece of 4 by 2, followed by animal hormone testing in Welwyn Garden City. 'I was then asked to work at the company's HQ in Switzerland, which I thought was very exciting,' she says. 'I thought I was made. I soon had a Swiss bank account, and my mother liked to talk about "my daughter in Switzerland".' She had to board with a crabby old dressmaker while waiting for her documentation to be finalised. 'She would only let me have a bath once a week,' she says, and we all laugh when I tell her that when I was a kid in London I was *forced* to have a bath once a week! Asking to be moved, Judy then boarded with old widower Monsieur Briand, whose new Filipino wife had recently left. Judy's first inkling of Monsieur Briand's plan to have Judy take her place was when she saw a tall pair of high heels sitting by her bed! Keen to disabuse the old gentleman of this notion, Judy let him down gently and told him in less-than-fluent French that he was just like a grandfather to her.

Judy had started work in the lab HQ at this stage, and decided to fork out 1200 francs on a new 1981 Honda CB125 for commuting. She had struck up a friendship with an English girl called Jules, whom she'd met while having French lessons, and, with holidays due, asked her if she'd fancy riding to Italy on the back of her little Honda. 'So off we went,' says Judy. 'Jules carried all our gear in my old deer-stalker's pack. We had a ball, sleeping in fields, hiding from those Italian boys. Then, on the Italian Riviera, heading for Rome, we were run over by a truck. Jules was thrown clear and had her fall cushioned by my huge pack, but I knew I was in trouble. My foot got jammed up into the motor, and then was virtually torn off at the ankle. I remember telling the ambulance guys not to forget to bring my foot.'

Judy didn't feel any pain until after surgery, when she was relieved to awaken and see her foot still attached. She was something of a novelty at the hospital, with her pale skin and freckles, and, while there, received three proposals of marriage. Eventually, after being transferred to St Thomas's Hospital in London, she arrived back on crutches at the Stockwell squat.

She decided to return to New Zealand for a while, as she would be in plaster and on crutches for months. Having seen the computers in the Swiss labs, she realised that this was the future, and so studied data processing in Dunedin, where she was the top student for her intermediate year. For the whole of 1982 she was in and out of hospital because of cellulitis around the holes in her foot where the bolts and hot engine parts had met flesh.

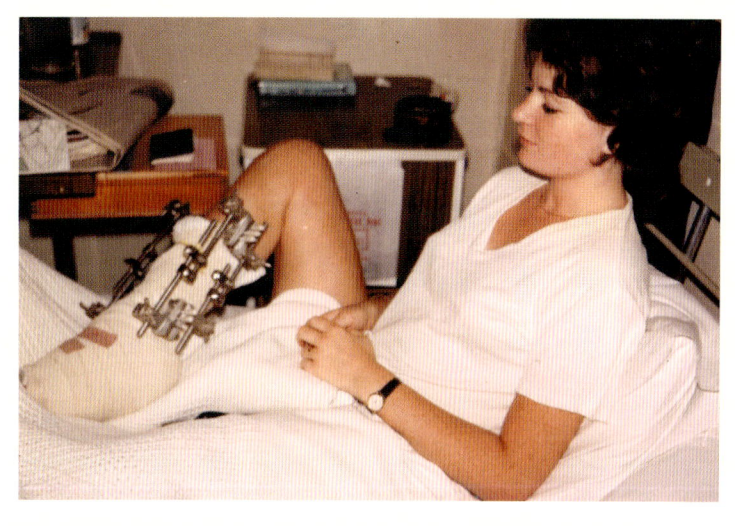

'I then moved to Auckland,' she says, 'and landed a job at the Auckland Medical School, mainly on the strength of my work experience in Switzerland. That's where I met Paul, a physicist, and moved in with him.'

Judy soon got itchy feet and wanted to travel again. Paul couldn't make up his mind, so she took off with Claire, a schoolfriend from Otago, to backpack around South East Asia for the next six months. 'In Rome, now on my own, I had an interesting experience with a priest who tried to seduce me in exchange for tickets to the Vatican,' she says, 'but that's another story ...'

Judy and Claire then worked on a farm in Norway ('we got incredibly fat because of all the dairy products we ate') and were joined by boyfriend Paul, who had changed his mind and flown out to meet her.

Back in London again, Judy and Paul stayed with old friend Karen, who had married a Londoner (me) while away in Africa. (Confused? I'm not surprised!) While staying at our flat in Ealing, Judy started work at the London Stock Exchange, which, she says, was gearing up for the 'big bang' (she was also there for 'the crash'). Judy and Paul came and went on many adventures, including motorcycling around Eastern Europe (she on a Honda CB250RS and Paul on an MZ ETZ 250), cycling from London to Morocco, and taking a yacht down to the Mediterranean via the French canals.

Eventually Judy and Paul made it back to New Zealand, and while riding her motorcycle (another CB250RS) into Auckland for a job interview, she was 'taken out' by a motorist on SH22. 'This time it was my other leg and both arms,' says Judy. 'I was devastated.' She spent the next three months in hospital, and that was the end of her riding motorcycles. 'I hadn't broken my neck, so thought I'd leave it at that.' Since then, Judy has been in and out of hospital, having bits replaced and tweaked, while remaining remarkably stoic throughout. 'It's been a bit of a nuisance' is as far as she will go.

After a messy break-up with Paul (and that's a whole other saga), Judy found herself here with partner Richard on the Awhitu Peninsula, south of the Manukau Harbour. She owns her barn/house and 16 acres, 8 of them planted in macadamia nuts, while Richard owns and manages his 700-acre cattle farm up the road. It seems to be a great arrangement, giving them both a certain degree of independence.

She still has the travel bug, and in 2009 she and Richard drove their Mitsubishi four-wheel-drive (without any punctures) from Peking to Paris via the Gobi Desert, Siberia and Finland. And next month she's off on the inaugural Flight 1980 from Dunedin to latitude 66 to see the Southern Lights!

But it's time for her to hit the sack now, as the Coffee Lady must get up at sparrow's fart, at 4.30am.

Before I hit the Southern Motorway, I pull into the lay-by at Glenbrook School and sit by the Coffee Lady's van, sipping a good flat white and watching her work. It's still blessedly dry and, looking back, I've only experienced a bit of drizzle twice on my way around the country! Judy chats away with regulars, mostly parents now dropping off their schoolkids with the commuter rush over. 'How's your old man's lumbago?' and 'Do you want a marshmallow with that?' she asks, as her hands fly like well-oiled machine parts between grind basket, hopper, tamper and knock box.

I'm back on the river of tarmac now, the Waikato Expressway, where riding skills go temporarily to autopilot and your mind can wander. I'm often accused of being stuck in the 1970s, and perhaps it's true, for that was my formative decade containing all my teenager-hood.

Among many others we said goodbye to in 2016 was a favourite of mine, Status Quo's Rick Parfitt. Not just three-chord wonders, Status Quo actually had more top 10 hits in the UK than The Beatles (admittedly, Quo's career lasted for well over 50 years). Francis Rossi was the virtuoso guitarist, leaning to pop, while the bassist Alan Lancaster, who it's rumoured was pushed out of the band in the 1980s, was more hard rock, which was my preference. Parfitt's rhythm guitar was like a thundering locomotive. I have an urge to play air guitar to 'Caroline', but must be content with some head banging. I soon desist as motorists are looking at me strangely. My mates ridiculed my love for Quo, all apart from my mate Richard 'Wilf' Willis, who I thought had terrible taste apart from that. We saw the Quo one memorable evening in 1976 at the Hammersmith Odeon. Clad in blue denim with long blond hair (before my military 'Bodie' phase), I fancied I looked a bit like Rick Parfitt, as did about 2000 other young geezers. There was something elemental about Parfitt's guitar as he stood in front of the amps, legs spread wide, head down, like a denim-clad Viking with an axe. When I saw them again in Sydney in 2002 it was as though time had stood still, and it took an age for the hairs on the back of my neck to stand down. Nostalgia is a dangerous thing, I'm told.

I slice through Hamilton, New Zealand's largest inland city and named after John Fane Charles Hamilton, commander of HMS *Esk*, four months after he had been killed in skirmishes with Maori at Gate Pa. Joining SH3, I move south through the rich, fertile farmland of the Waikato, to Te Awamutu, where I'm surprised by its hustle and bustle. Potatau Te Wherowhero, Maori warrior, leader of the Waikato iwi and first Maori King, was born here, and was buried in Huntly after his death in 1860.

The King Country, which I'm now riding through, is so-named because during the New Zealand Wars of the 1860s the Maori King Tawhiao was defeated at the Battle of Rangiriri, 50 kilometres north of Hamilton. Gathering his remaining warriors and fleeing south to the safety of the hills, tradition has it that Tawhiao threw his hat onto a map of the North Island and declared 'Here I rule!' of the area it landed on. Thus 'King Country' (or 'Rohe Potae', which means 'area of the hat') got its name, and for a short time afterwards it was a dangerous place for Pakeha to venture into.

It's lunchtime as I roll into Otorohanga, turn off the ignition, shed my jacket and helmet, and go for a wander down the pretty main street which the locals are obviously very proud of. Otorohanga proclaims itself as the Kiwiana capital of New Zealand, and colourful signs hang from lamp posts displaying pavlova, buzzy bees, kiwifruit, etc, to confirm it. This campaign looks to be successful, as tourists abound. I find refuge from the sun in the O Café, and enjoy a good sandwich and coffee while dipping into *Prosperity Without Growth* by Tim Jackson, in which he tries to redefine what prosperity really is, and suggests that the current model of 'a continually expanding material paradise has come unravelled'. He asks simple questions, like: Why does wealth not necessarily make a person happy? And:

Why, in a world more connected than ever, are so many people in the West lonely and suicidal? And he explains why higher gross domestic product, which is supposed to make normal people like you and me feel somehow good about life, is merely a smokescreen for corporate greed and more degradation of the environment.

As I climb on my bike and head out of town again, I ponder the truth of it — but not for too long, because that blasted Status Quo earworm of 'Caroline' is back! Te Kuiti is another town I've heard of but never visited, and is again prosperous and bustling, serving the rich farming district.

The road south from here is a motorcyclist's dream. Turning and twisting through the narrow Awakino Gorge (feeling sorry for the line of cars stuck behind a huge campervan), past abandoned coal mines and impressive limestone bluffs, we reach the North Taranaki Bight at Awakino. The beach here is black ironsand, and swimming is not advised due to some vicious rips. A little way down the coast I come to Mokau, meaning 'winding stream', and park in front of the little butcher's shop. My bum is sore and I could do with some shade. Crossing the road, I order a pot of tea (I have a feeling the coffee is not up to much, plus there's the fact that I'm dry), and realise that the only thing worse than loud commercial drivel on the radio is loud commercial drivel that's not tuned in correctly. Sulking, I drink my tea outside.

Where the beach road starts, painted red and mounted in concrete is a German mine that washed ashore in 1942. And it was here in Mokau that the last shots in the Maori Wars were fired. One of Colonel Whitmore's troopships, the *Sturt*, fired a couple of artillery shots at the kainga Te Kauri, but the marauding Maori party had already fled upstream.

It's another lovely ride along the Taranaki Coast into New Plymouth, where I park-up under the shade of a tree and wander along the seafront. I stop and stare up at a tall, thin sculpture that sways slightly in the wind. The Wind Wand was conceived by sculptor Len Lye, who died in 1980. His foundation had it made to celebrate the new millennium, and the red light on top was lit at midnight on 31 December 1999. Surfing is very popular here, with the famous Surf Highway heading around in a horseshoe to Hawera.

It's another road I'll leave for another trip, for I now have to cut inland and ride another 20 k's. Always travel as though you intend to return, I remember being told once, because if you treat your visit as your last, you'll try to cram in everything, get stressed and enjoy nothing. It's been another long day in the saddle, and I'm relieved to arrive in Inglewood and book into the White Eagle Motel, kick my boots off and have a nana nap, before my next interview.

'MATCHY' — ROBERT BULLOT

Robert's enthusiasm can best be described as 'full throttle'. Having phoned him 10 minutes earlier to tell him I was lost, I now see him waving from across the road. He motions me around the back, and, before I've even climbed off my Bonneville, he congratulates me on my choice of bike, because, as I soon discover, Robert is a big fan of Hinckley Triumphs.

Inside, Robert tells me his story. 'When I was kid,' he begins, 'my dad used to race scramblers. He and four other guys were founders of a scrambling track on Beach Road, in Omata, New Plymouth, where he raced his Velocette. He then raced a Matchless at the Waiwakaiho Speedway, which doesn't exist any more.' He stresses that that's why he acquired the nickname 'Matchy', and not because of being a firefighter for 25 years or because he's an arsonist!

'My first bike, which I bought as an apprentice mechanic, was a Honda 50, on which I thought I was the cat's pyjamas,' says Robert. 'I briefly rode an old James I rescued from a farmer's shed, followed by a G9 Matchless 500 twin, which leaked so much oil it seemed to make it. They were susceptible to cracked crankshafts, but I remember my dad's race bike had a nodule iron crankshaft in it.'

Robert has owned many motorcycles over the years, like a BSA Gold Flash and a BSA 650 twin. But he reckons he's the only person in the world to have owned a Ducatchless. 'The only Matchless parts were the motor and the frame,' he says. 'The front end was an '89 Ducati with a Scarab brake, with a pre-unit Triumph gearbox and Triumph rear end.' He had a lot of fun on that bike and rode it for many years, but remembers having what he thought was a major seize, with a guy on the back while motoring down a hill. 'It turned out to be a bolt that had come loose and jammed between the gears. I pulled the clutch in and left a big black mark on the road, not to mention a big mark on my mate's undies.'

In 1983, ex-plasterer and entrepreneur Sir John Bloor bought the Triumph Motorcycles marque when most thought they were dead and buried. When Robert heard a rumour in the late 1990s that Bloor was planning to re-launch the classic Bonneville, from the brand-new plant he was building in Hinckley, it would be fair to say that he was champing at the bit. 'I had a very serious health scare in 2001, when I discovered a big melanoma on my chest. The surgeon said he wanted me in surgery in January, so in December I bought myself one of the new Hinckley 790cc parallel-twin Bonnevilles and I rode it and rode it and I rode it. I said to the missus, "If I don't survive this operation, sell it and keep the money. I didn't want my sons to have that bike."'

The operation was a complete success (Robert shows me his scars), and he rode another 38,000 kilometres on that bike, before trading it in on a T100. That bike now belongs to a local lady who has put another 50,000 on the clock.

'I searched high and low for hot pipes that to me sounded like a real Bonneville,' he says. 'The factory pipes were just not noisy enough, and sounded like a sewing machine. So I talked to this guy doing dynos on Bonnies, and he told me what pipes to get. He said not to touch my jets, because the new pipes were made for the right back pressure, but I had to put in a new K-and-N filter. I got the pipes through a bloke in Australia who was very fussy and didn't like exporting, so I had to be cool. He told me not to open them up or sell them, and to take them off if I sold my bike.' When Robert put them on he says that he couldn't believe the difference, and he just powered along (noisily) with a happy grin on his face.

He then moved on to the new Triumph America, which was introduced into the Hinckley line-up in 2007. It was basically a more laidback cruiser version of the Bonneville, with the same 865cc twin-carburetted motor.

The beautiful 2014 fuel-injected beast, and Robert's pride and joy, is sitting outside as we speak, keeping my bike company. 'And those pipes are still on it,' he says, and promises to fire her up for me later. 'And after 12 years and 160,000 k's, they still resonate beautifully.'

He loves to customise his bikes and make them his own. Aside from his beloved pipes, he has small leather panniers from Holland, and many small touches that make his America unique. 'I get all my stuff from British Legends, in France. They deal in euros, and your merchandise never takes more than eight days to arrive.'

Robert's enthusiasm then ratchets up a notch as he tells me about his club. He and three mates would ride to Mokau every Saturday and every Sunday. They'd leave at 10.30 and have lunch at the Awakino Hotel. 'We don't drink, we just have a feed. But it's a lovely ride. Once you get to know those corners, you can have some fun,' he says, rubbing his hands, his eyes gleaming. One day, the lads were sitting, having a break at Mount Messenger, feeding bread to the roosters up there, as was their habit, when somebody said, 'Why don't we start a club?' Robert then points to his T-shirt and raises his eyebrows: 'The Old Cocks Motorcycle Club. Mount Messenger Chapter, that's us!' he says. 'Then we put it out there for riders to come along and join us.'

The Old Cocks Club, whose mantra is 'Any Bikes — No Attitude', started in

2012, and membership has grown steadily to 80 riders, until now they have their own table reserved for them at the Awakino Hotel.

Members give out cards to advertise themselves. 'We don't believe in clubrooms,' says Robert. 'Our clubrooms are the car park at Mount Messenger. We have air-conditioning and no power bills. But we are just a collection of decent people, George, who love to ride. We don't put up with any nonsense. Any nonsense and you're out. We have fast riders, slow riders, and women riders, and people who just want to be part of *us*.'

Anybody can meet up with them at 10.30 at various locations and go on a run with them. After a couple of runs they're given a T-shirt, and after half a dozen runs they can have a small patch if they want it. 'If they're the wrong sort, we'll tell them,' says Robert. 'We don't want a rider who stops and rolls up a joint of marijuana and starts smoking it. That's "attitude" to us. We keep it clean and have a great relationship with the police, although they do tell us to slow down now and then.'

We go outside, and he shows me the bits and pieces he's put on his Triumph. 'Listen to this,' he says as he fires her up. The pipes sound like a low-flying Hercules, and I have to cover my ears. Robert is grinning like a schoolboy. 'I'm called El Presidento,' he says still grinning, 'but it means nothing. I'm just the figurehead who does the talking. My mate Big Grey is second-in-charge and like a sergeant-at-arms, but there are no rules in our club. We even have members in Wellington and Christchurch!'

He's also a member of the Red Knights, the International Firefighters Motorcycle Club, and carries a little red knight on the Triumph as a lucky charm. Robert, or 'Matchy', gave up smoking 20 years ago, and recently gave up the demon drink. Now at almost 70, he says he just wants to keep riding.

'Look, George, I just love it!'

The great thing about motels is the element of luxury. Morning finds me lying in bed like a king, sipping tea and watching the news before the familiar ritual of packing the bike. I lubricate the chain, check my oil and I'm away on a road that's new to me, which in itself is always exciting. Down the road (still SH3) I manage to get a photo of Mount Taranaki, which is rare as it is often obscured by cloud. Rising to a height of 2518 metres, this domed volcano, dormant but not extinct, last erupted in 1636. The area's fertile soil is due to the volcanic ash — combined with the mini-weather system created by the mountain — radiating down from the rainforest of its lower slopes, run over 30 rivers and streams, further nourishing the pastureland around. Morning sun soon burns off the mist to reveal the lush Taranaki pasture.

Stratford, another Taranaki charmer, was named after Shakespeare's birthplace, and I read somewhere that at 10am the glockenspiel in the clock tower plays 'Romeo and Juliet'. As I head south once more, I wonder if it's the Dire Straits song.

There seems to be a disproportionate number of Americans in Taranaki, or perhaps they just make their presence felt. So far today I've spoken to three and passed four Stars and Stripes fluttering at the top of large poles. I come across one flying next to a warehouse with some antique petrol bowsers, and a sign on the door warning that trespassers at night will be shot.

A fast ride to Hawera brings me to the Arabica Coffee Bar in the main drag, and of course it would rude not to indulge in a spot of brekkie. As I tuck in, I realise that I may never sit in this street again, and that fact gives me a strange thrill.

I've never seen so many Fonterra trucks in one area before. At one time I overtake two, sandwiched between two double-trailer logging trucks, in one hit, like an Australian outback road train. In the little town of Patea on the South Taranaki

Bight, I stop to photograph a stunning monument of a group of Maori paddling a waka, mounted about 3 metres up on concrete columns. It was erected in 1933 as a token of remembrance from all the descendants throughout Aotearoa of Turi, legendary chief of the *Aotea* canoe, and his wife, Rongorongo.

The approach, and indeed all of Whanganui's main street, is lined with trees, providing welcome shade from another hot day, as well a nice, hometown ambience. My coffee antenna, however, isn't twitching, so I just stretch my legs. SH3 down to Bulls is straight and fast, and I pray there are no police or speed cameras, because there are times when I feel the need to get the Bonnie to lift up her skirt and fly. My bike is no speed demon, but the 68 British horses respond willingly, and not for the first time I marvel at modern technology.

I park-up in Bulls, for it's lunchtime. Bulls is roughly in the middle of the largest strip of grassland plains in the North Island, stretching from Whanganui down to Paraparaumu, and is the reason for the lengths of fast, straight roads. Bulls was founded in 1859, and was originally named Bull Town after James Bull, its first storekeeper.

A truck driver limps into the café and orders an all-day Big Breakfast, then regales those within earshot with tales of his past injuries. 'And me flamin' hip's been giving me gyp,' he complains. 'Oh, it's the weather,' says the young lady behind the counter, despite the fact that it's hot and sunny. 'I think that rugby tackle had something to do with it,' he mumbles out the side of his mouth as he passes my table.

I must now deviate north for a while to meet my next, and last, interesting character. I'm back on SH1 in the Manawatu, a district I've been riding in since just before Whanganui actually. About 60 k's up the road, at Mangaweka, I pause for a look at the strange sight of a DC-3 aircraft by the roadside, under which is a busy café. Mangaweka is home to many artists and has a fantastic old main street. There are also spectacular views down into the white-walled gorge to the Rangitikei River, popular with kayakers and white-water rafters. Through Taihape, where I've booked into a motel to stay tonight, I head on up to Waiouru with the sun still shining. Just past the Army Museum and through the small township, I turn right onto Ruapehu Road and present my bona fides to the security guy at the guard hut. With my visitor's pass in my tank bag, I'm given directions to Freyberg Place, although I've already been emailed a map of the base and know the way. Here, I'm met by the Training Commander's executive assistant, a very pleasant lady, who escorts me to Colonel Thompson's office. It's all very efficient, and I manage to stifle the urge to execute a snappy salute.

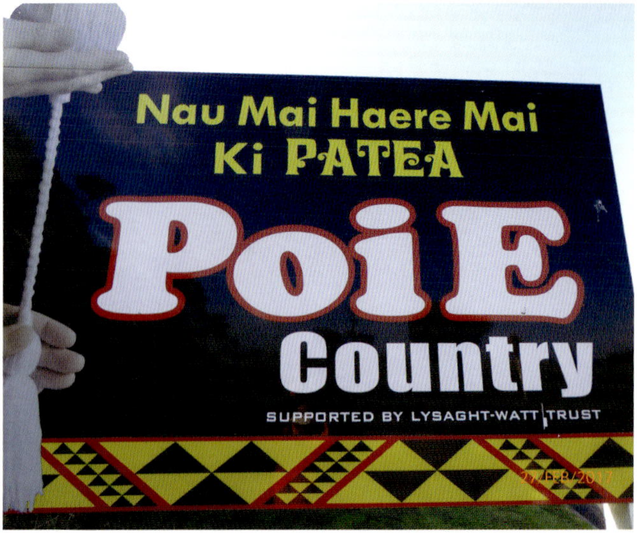
Nau Mai Haere Mai
Ki PATEA
PoiE
Country
SUPPORTED BY LYSAGHT-WATT TRUST

WARNING
IF FOUND HERE AT NIGHT YOU WILL BE FOUND HERE IN THE MORNING

WAIOURU welcomes you
To the Desert Oasis
Altitude 792 metres

TRAINING COMMANDER — COLONEL KARYN THOMPSON

Karyn is not from a military family. She was brought up on a high-country sheep station in the Manawatu and always loved the great outdoors, saving up her pocket money to put herself on various outdoor pursuit courses, tramping and hunting. 'We used to go and stay with my grandparents at Pleasant Point in Canterbury, and that felt like the "big city" to us,' she says. 'I remember the Army trucks used to drive through and the soldiers would stop for ice creams at the dairy, and I thought, "Wow, that would be good a job!"'

Colonel Thompson is pleasant and chatty and exudes a quiet confidence. She was head girl at Palmerston North Girls' High School, and had an interest in leadership from an early age. 'I thought the Army would be perfect for me. I could enjoy the outdoors, get extra skills, travel the world and develop my interest in leadership.'

Her initial plan was to join the Army, complete her one-year officer training course, leave after a few years, be a police officer for a while, and then go to university. 'My parents didn't want me to join the Army,' Karyn says, 'they wanted me to "do something with my life". They were a farming family and didn't realise what the Army had to offer.'

After joining the military from high school, Karyn hasn't looked back, and this year will be her twenty-ninth in uniform. 'I've travelled the world, completed a Bachelor of Arts degree and a Master's in Management,' she says. 'In fact, the military has allowed me to fulfil my life's dreams. And the people are amazing. We have some remarkable people in the New Zealand Army.'

There were 5 women out of the 55 in Karyn's officer training class at Waiouru in 1989, and out of the 33 graduates, 3 were women. Of the three women, Karyn was the only one straight from high school, as the others had worked their way up through the Army system. 'At the time, 7 per cent of Army personnel were women, so there were not many of us around.' Today that has risen to 13 per cent, a similar trend to the British, Australian and US armies. The Defence Force's aspirational goal is to increase that figure to 20 per cent women across the three branches by

2020. Currently the Air Force sits at 22 per cent, and the Navy is at 18 per cent.

After completing her officer training, and graduating from a communications and informations systems course in Australia, Karyn took command of signals units in Papakura, South Auckland, Linton and Palmerston North. Then, after further training, she spent three years as an intelligence officer. 'This basically involved gathering intelligence and analysing what's happening on the battlefield,' Karyn explains. 'At the same time I was the public relations officer for the units based at Linton, which was my first taste of dealing with the media, trying to get across to the public what the Army does. Now, of course, things like Facebook and Twitter have made it a lot easier to communicate with the public.'

As a captain, her first operational deployment in the mid-1990s was to the Sinai Peninsula in Egypt as an operations officer. 'I was responsible for the theatre of operations of a multinational force of observers,' she explains. 'Our role was to monitor the peace between Egypt and Israel, brokered in the Camp David Accords.' For a 24-year-old officer it was an amazing opportunity, and, being in an area so steeped in history, sparked Karyn's interest in the subject.

Her next overseas assignment, in 1998, was in Bosnia and Herzegovina, formerly part of Yugoslavia, four years after the end of the Bosnian conflict. She was attached to the British Army as an intelligence officer. 'Basically, we were travelling around the country interviewing people, looking for war criminals. It was quite an education. And a real eye-opener for me was studying the long and complex histories of countries like Bosnia.'

In 1999, Karyn was part of the first peacekeeping deployment to East Timor, initially under the auspices of INTERFET (International Force for East Timor), working closely with Australian troops. 'When we first arrived, the streets of Dili were empty, as people were hiding out in the hills, fearful of the militia who were still around,' she says. 'After six months, we swapped our berets for light-blue ones and transitioned to working under a UN mandate.'

Colonel Thompson's last overseas deployment to the Middle East involved her working for seven months alongside a coalition of 18 different nations, training the local forces. 'It was an amazing job in a very challenging environment,' she says, 'and was probably the biggest developmental deployment I've been involved in.' I suggest that it must have been very daunting. 'Well, it was. At first you wonder if you can do such a big job. But then all the resilience training comes to the fore. You tell yourself you know the theory. You can do this! And you think about what leader you want to be and you step up.'

Initially, it was difficult, as there were officers and soldiers working for her who were unaccustomed to taking commands from a woman. 'So I tried to be a collaborative leader,' Karyn says, 'I realised that the only way to make this work is if I empower my team, which I think I did, because at the end of my deployment seven months later I knew that I had the trust of everyone under my command and the team was running like clockwork.'

Karyn had two children while in command of a signals squadron. 'That was a very interesting time,' she says, 'being pregnant and becoming a mum while commanding a unit. One of my warrant officers summarised it for me one day. He came into my office and said, "Ma'am, the best thing that could have happened to you was to have children, because it's softened you and given you an understanding of what it's like for people with families in the military." And he was right. I was very focused and task-driven, but having children grounded me.'

Having children (two boys) at that time was indeed challenging, as Karyn's then husband was also in command of a unit. After 15 years of marriage, they divorced, and Karyn remarried an Army engineering officer. When their daughter was born, they were both posted to Waiouru, Karyn commanding the unit responsible for officer training. 'I think having a husband in the military has made life easier, as he is obviously more aware of the pressures involved,' she says.

Karyn likes the fact that the Army tries to move personnel on to new roles every two or three years. Regular postings to a new job or new location helps to keep things fresh and provide a new challenge. 'There are wonderful courses, so you are always learning, always developing,' says Karyn.

She became the Commander at Waiouru in September 2016, the first female to hold the post, and is responsible for training and doctrine (TRADOC). On camp there is the Army Command School and The Army Depot, both responsible for initial basic training, as well schools for training in the trades. Pre-deployment training for operational missions is also carried out here. 'I'm also in command of our three part-time infantry battalions,' Karyn says, 'based out of Auckland, Wellington and Christchurch.' I ask if they're the same thing as the Territorial Army in the UK. 'Same thing,' she replies, 'but we call them our Reserve Force.'

Karyn says that the Army still finds it difficult to attract women into combat roles, despite the fact that New Zealand was one of the first nations to allow women into the combat trades. There is now the More Military Women programme of work that Karyn established while working in HR. 'It's designed,' she says, 'for attracting, recruiting, retaining and progressing women through the Defence Force as a whole.'

In 2015, Karyn won a Women of Influence Award, and is proud of the fact that in such a male-dominated environment as the military she continues to help break down gender barriers. 'The main challenge for a mother in the Defence Force is being deployed overseas and leaving your husband and children behind,' Karyn says. 'My husband had been in South Sudan for six months, and shortly after his return I was deployed to the Middle East for seven months. Communications are so much better now, what with Skype and FaceTime, but it's still very tough.'

Karyn loves what she does and has no plans to stop. 'It's been a great career,' she says. 'There's still lots that I want to achieve. I'm fit and healthy enough to still pass my fitness test. I look on every job as a development opportunity.'

I tell her she's a great example for the empowerment of women. 'Well, it's all about showing women that they can do it. We had a saying going through school that "women can do anything", and that's a powerful message and one I firmly believe in these days.'

The role of TRADOC (NZ) Commander, like most positions at Karyn's level, rotates every couple of years, and at this stage she has no idea of her next posting. 'Fingers crossed, I'm heading overseas to do some high-level study,' she says. Whatever her new role, I feel sure that Colonel Thompson will handle it as the consummate professional that she obviously is.

Back in Taihape, I dump my gear in my room at the Coachman Motel and stroll around town. After a beer and a greasy burger in town, I catch up on some writing in my room. Taihape was originally a railway town, and there are still some old railway houses around. In 1881, peace was made with King Tawhiao, and Pakeha were free to drive a railway through the middle of the North Island into land previously closed to them. Settlers arrived from Canterbury in 1894 to work as roadmen and sawmillers. As well as being a service town for the surrounding farms and the Army Base, it's also famous for its annual Gumboot Festival.

The morning sun finds me setting off on the last leg of my North Island jaunt. I retrace yesterday's route back to Bulls, before stopping at the excellent Church Café in Sanson. Built with good old bricks in 1950, it now offers a more tangible spiritual balm in the form of bacon and eggs and coffee. On the wall behind the counter is a pearl of wisdom from Miss Piggy: 'Never eat more than you can lift.' I often muse on my idea of the perfect café. The priority is of course decent coffee, strong but not too bitter. I like bashed-up furniture with a bit of character, with little alcoves or snugs where you can get a bit of peace. I like eye-catching art on the walls, with maybe a 1942 Army Indian suspended from the rafters. Let's have Dylan or some old blues music softly drifting out from behind the counter, and shelves full of old books and magazines (but no *Woman's Day* or *New Idea*, thanks). And how about a globe on each table? And I'd like it to be busy, but not too noisy. A friend once told me that she thought I was an extroverted introvert (or was it an introverted extrovert?). I think I'll have to open my own coffee shop when I'm old!

A windmill catches my eye 30 k's down the road, and, intrigued, I pull off the main road, into Foxton on the mouth of the Manawatu River, to investigate. Foxton, named after Sir William Fox, has a long tradition of flax-stripping, which was used in the making of rope, matting and wool sacks. But the main focus of the town today is De Molen, a full-sized working replica of a seventeenth-century Dutch windmill, opened in 2003. The stone-ground flour it produces is for sale in the souvenir shop. Next to the windmill, the Te Awahou/Nieuwe Stroom, or community hub, is under construction, which will provide a cultural centre for the Dutch and Maori communities to learn one another's stories.

On the road again and through bustling Levin, it's another fast ride on the excellent new stretch of SH1 along the Kapiti Coast to Wellington. The ferry is well signposted and, as if on rails, I fetch up at the Interislander terminal. It's soon time to board the good ship *Kaiarahi*, meaning 'leadership' or 'to lead', and is a nod to the dolphin Pelorus Jack, who used to 'guide' ships through the Cook Strait and Marlborough Sounds, and is also part of the Interislander logo.

On the ferry heading for the Mainland and home, I recline in my seat and dreamily re-run some of the memorable roads it's been my pleasure to ride. The Lindis Pass, Buller Gorge, Rai Valley, the Waioeka Gorge and Northland's State Highway 12. Amazing vistas of alpine grandeur, ancient trees, empty beaches, windswept tussock and mighty rivers. Great little towns, some of which I doubt I'll ever see again. Great coffee shops, cafés and pubs. A kaleidoscope of images. But, most importantly, the wonderful, colourful characters I've met along the way. From the butcher, the baker and the candlestick-maker, to the rugby coach, the firefighter and the craft brewer. And as Morpheus takes me in his embrace, I realise, not for the first time, how fortunate we are to live on these islands in the South Pacific we call New Zealand/Aotearoa.

GREAT COAST ROAD
6 FOLLOW

LINDIS PASS ALPINE HIGHWAY

8

LINDIS PASS SUMMIT — 7 km

Tarras — 55 km

ALSO BY THE AUTHOR

LIVING THE DREAM

KIWI BIKERS

GEORGE LOCKYER

Expect Motorcycles All the time
ridetolive.co.nz

Roots bar — PLEASE BE AWESOME

Welcome To Little Kitchen! If your cup is half full, you probably need a different bra...... or another coffee! Come on in & have one.

NO BULL STEERS HERE

PLEASE DO NOT STAND ON TOILET SEAT — NO / YES

GO DEAD SLOW LIVE CHILDREN — 15